THE UNIVERSITY OF
WINCHESTER

Martial Rose Library
Tel: 01962 827306

2 5 OCT 2011

1 4 DEC 2012

- 5 APR 2013

To be returned on or before the day marked above, subject to recall.

A CULTURAL HISTORY OF ANIMALS

GENERAL EDITORS: LINDA KALOF AND BRIGITTE RESL

A CULTURAL HISTORY OF ANIMALS

IN THE RENAISSANCE

Edited by Bruce Boehrer

BERG

Oxford • New York

English edition
First published in 2007 by
Berg

Editorial offices:
First Floor, Angel Court, 81 St Clements Street, Oxford OX4 1AW, UK
175 Fifth Avenue, New York, NY 10010, USA

Paperback edition published in 2011
© Bruce Boehrer 2007, 2011

Berg is the imprint of Oxford International Publishers Ltd.

Library of Congress Cataloging-in-Publication Data

A cultural history of animals / edited by Linda Kalof and Brigitte Resl.
    p. cm.
  Includes bibliographical references and index.
  ISBN-13: 978-1-84520-496-9 (cloth)
  ISBN-10: 1-84520-496-4 (cloth)
  1. Animals and civilization. 2. Human-animal relationships—History. I. Kalof,
Linda. II. Pohl-Resl, Brigitte.

  QL85C85   2007
  590—dc22   2007031782

British Library Cataloguing-in-Publication Data

A catalogue record for this book is available from the British Library.

ISBN 978 1 84520 395 5 (volume 3, cloth)
    978 1 84788 819 8 (volume 3, paper)
    978 1 84520 496 9 (set, cloth)
    978 1 84788 823 5 (set, paper)

Typeset by Apex Publishing, LLC, Madison, WI

Printed in the United Kingdom by the MPG Books Group

www.bergpublishers.com

CONTENTS

ILLUSTRATIONS

CHAPTER 1

CHAPTER 4

CHAPTER 5

CHAPTER 7

SERIES PREFACE

A Cultural History of Animals is a six-volume series reviewing the changing roles of animals in society and culture throughout history. Each volume follows the same basic structure, and begins with an outline account of the main characteristics of the roles of animals in the period under consideration. Following from that, specialists closely examine major aspects of the subject under seven key headings: symbolism, hunting, domestication, entertainment, science, philosophy, and art. The reader, therefore, has the choice between synchronic and diachronic approaches: A single volume can be read to obtain a thorough knowledge of the subject in a given period from a variety of perspectives, or one of the seven main aspects can be followed through time by reading the relevant chapters of all six volumes, thus providing a thematic understanding of changes and developments over the long term.

The six volumes divide the topic as follows:

Volume 1: A Cultural History of Animals in Antiquity (2500 BCE–1000 CE)

Volume 2: A Cultural History of Animals in the Medieval Age (1000–1400)

Volume 3: A Cultural History of Animals in the Renaissance (1400–1600)

Volume 4: A Cultural History of Animals in the Age of Enlightenment (1600–1800)

Volume 5: A Cultural History of Animals in the Age of Empire (1800–1920)

Volume 6: A Cultural History of Animals in the Modern Age (1920–2000)

General Editors, Linda Kalof and Brigitte Resl

EDITOR'S ACKNOWLEDGMENTS

I am grateful to Linda Kalof and Brigitte Resl for supervising this complex, multivolume project and for giving me the opportunity to participate in its production. Likewise, I owe a great debt of thanks to the various contributors to this volume, who have worked hard, patiently, and cheerfully on its preparation. I have especially appreciated the support and assistance of Tristan Palmer, Hannah Shakespeare, and the entire editorial and production staff at Berg. I gratefully acknowledge the Florida State University English Department's Faculty Research Committee, which provided me with research funding during the work on this project. I am thankful to Susan Becker for her generous and accurate work translating Chapter 5 of this volume from the French. And I remain very personally indebted to my research assistant, Trish Thomas Henley, who has once again, here as before, proven herself a wondrous necessary woman.

The Animal Renaissance

BRUCE BOEHRER

By the end of the fourteenth century, medieval Europe had evolved a complex body of animal lore enshrined within the tradition of the bestiary and in related works on travel, geography, and medicine.[1] This material was largely *fabulous*—in the root sense of the word, story-centered—in character. It emphasized the exotic and miraculous; it presented the physical world as a "Book of Nature" correlative to scripture and offering similar insights into the character both of God and of creation; and it developed largely through a process of textual conflation that combined classical sources of varying genres with scriptural matter and works of more recent derivation. On the literary level, this tradition provided the basis for a broad range of moralizing sermons and animal-exempla, the miraculous tales of medieval romance and travelogue, and the genre of the medieval beast fable.[2] Following this tradition's emphasis upon the wondrous nature of the exotic, medieval princes and clergymen had done their best to amass and maintain private menageries of unusual beasts.[3]

But these collections—like the tales that purported to document their contents—represented a realm of activity largely divorced from the more general economic realities of the Middle Ages. From the standpoint of common, practical experience, the high medieval period was better characterized by feudal, agrarian modes of social organization in which a limited number of animals—the pig, the sheep, the cow, the goat, the ass, the hawk, the hen, the hart, the boar, the dog, the cat, and the horse—did a preponderance of the animal world's actual and symbolic work. Most of these animals, of course, were subject to domestication, training, and some measure of selective breeding, but with predictable exceptions among the great herds of manor houses, monasteries, colleges, and the like, the breeding was done from local stock.[4] While most domesticated animals were bred primarily for food, wool, or agricultural and commercial haulage, some were reserved for more exalted purposes. Dogs and horses were raised for the hunt in ways that left their imprint upon art and literature, and by the thirteenth century there had developed a highly visible cultural cathexis around the figure of the destrier or medieval warhorse.[5] On a humbler level, cocks, dogs, cats, and bulls were employed in a variety of popular blood sports and related pastimes such as the ritual torture of *Katzenmusik*.[6] A few animals—notably miniature dogs—were bred for companionship, and these proved especially popular with nobles and clergy.[7] (Two such lapdogs frolic on the Duc de Berry's supper table in the January miniature from the Limbourg brothers' *Trés Riches Heures;* likewise, Chaucer's Prioress owns a brace.)[8] But the Middle Ages saw no coherent effort to acknowledge what we might call the emotional integrity of animals. The ethical practice of vegetarianism, the legal protection of animals from cruelty, and the concept of animal rights were all alien to medieval social practice. These would emerge, centuries later, among the products of a process of social transformation that began in the fifteenth and sixteenth centuries.

Beyond such matters, the period from 1400 to 1600 set in motion a series of far-reaching changes in the role of animals within European culture. For the most part, these changes involved a steady broadening and deepening of human-animal relationships. The rigorous postmodern separation of nature from culture remained centuries in the offing; even in an early modern metropolis like London, "poulterers kept thousands of live birds in their cellars and attics, while one Jacobean starchmaker is known to have had two hundred pigs in his backyard."[9] Needless to say, horses, hounds, and oxen remained essential to the economy of early modern Europe and were visible more or less everywhere. And in general, more species and breeds of animal became available in Europe during the period from 1400 to 1600 than ever before; they became available in greater numbers, over a wider geographical range, than ever before; and they were put to a broader variety of uses than ever before. As a result, animals in the Renaissance begin to assume the status of mass commodities. The didactic and anecdotal idiom associated with them in the medieval literary tradition gradually proves inadequate to this shift in circumstances and is forced to coexist with an emergent discourse of empirical observation. And while the increasingly intimate connection between human beings and the natural world remains essentially exploitative—indeed, it grows more exploitative, in terms of its sheer breadth, than ever before— one can also detect, in the fifteenth and sixteenth centuries, the early stirrings of an ethical identification with and sympathy for the plight of at least some other animals.

EXPLORATION AND CONQUEST

By far the most visible feature of these changes is the period's growing program of overseas exploration and expansion. Driven by economic adventurism, political ambition, and geographical curiosity, one European kingdom after another invested in the proto-colonial enterprise. The earliest expressions of this impulse coincide with the start of the fifteenth century. In 1402, Gadifer de la Salle and Jean de Béthencourt began the Hispano-Gallic conquest of the Canary Islands. Thereafter, starting with the capture of Ceuta in 1415, the Portuguese steadily extended their investigation of the west African coast: João Gonçalves Zarco reached the island of Madeira early in 1420, Gil Eannes passed Cape Bojador in 1434, and Alvise da Cadamosto reached the Gambia River by 1455. These efforts culminated in the voyages of Bartolomeu Diaz and Vasco da Gama (1487–1488 and 1497–1499, respectively), which rounded the Cape of Good Hope and established a European sea route to south and east Asia. By then, of course, the expansion eastward had also spawned the westward exploratory voyages of Christopher Columbus, Amerigo Vespucci, Pedro Cabral, and their followers, which met with a wholly unexpected range of economic, and zoological, possibility. By 1600, these early navigational efforts had led to direct commerce between various European kingdoms and such far-flung regions as Peru, Japan, and the Philippines.

One immediate consequence of this contact was a rapid increase in what we might call the biodiversity of European civilization. European explorers quickly discovered that one of the best ways to confirm and promote their exploits was to import strange beasts. Columbus brought back parrots—probably Cuban Amazons—to Spain when he returned from his first voyage to the New World, and on subsequent voyages he brought back more.[10] (For better or worse, these stand as the first animals imported to the Old World from the New.) After Cabral discovered Brazil in 1501, he reappeared in Lisbon with "two parrots which are an arm [gomito] and a half long"—certainly some species of great macaw.[11] Also returning to Lisbon in 1501, the second Newfoundland expedition of Gaspar Corte Real brought with it "falcons," which the survivors of the expedition claimed to be as numerous in their homeland "as . . . are sparrows" in Portugal.[12] The daybook of King Henry VII of England records the receipt of "haukes from the newe founded Ilande" on November 24, 1503—these probably from the second Newfoundland expedition of João Fernandes—and, two years later, it registers two gifts of "Wylde Cattes & Popyngays of the newfound island."[13]

But these creatures were not the only living cargo brought home to Europe by the explorers of the Renaissance. Along with them came human beings as well: indigenous people separated from their homeland, more often than not, by dishonesty or brute force. In the same letter that describes the falcons brought home by Corte Real from Newfoundland, Alberto Cantino adds that Corte Real's men "forcibly kidnapped about fifty men and women of this country and have brought them back."[14] About the indigenous people he encounters on his first voyage to the New World, Columbus remarks that "If it pleases Our Lord, I will take six of them to Your Highnesses when I depart."[15] In 1509, Pietro Bembo relates that a French ship, recently returned from the North Atlantic, "took up a small boat constructed of a wicker frame covered with the stout bark of trees, in which were seven men, in height mediocre, in complexion darkish," whose "speech was incomprehensible." These Amerindian captives suffered the fate of most taken in such circumstances; "six of them died," Bembo concludes, while "a youth was carried alive to Normandy, where the king was."[16] By 1562, when Montaigne famously conversed with three Native Americans at Rouen, such stories were common enough for the great essayist to guess their phylogenetic sequel; these men he writes, must be "ignorant ... of the fact that of this intercourse will come their ruin."[17]

How does a cultural history of animals account for the presence of human cargo aboard the ships of Renaissance explorers? On one hand, of course, contemporary biology tells us that human beings are themselves a sort of animal—a notion also embedded in Hamlet's famous description of man as "the paragon of animals." Yet Hamlet's wording—man is not just an animal, but their paragon—also recalls the depth of culture's investment in differentiating humanity from other creatures. In the case of early modern exploration, it becomes quickly apparent that a given human being's status vis-à-vis the so-called lower animals is by no means absolute. Stephen Greenblatt has observed that the progressive European enslavement of New World populations is enabled by a fantasy in which the enslaved peoples gain their souls as recompense; for Greenblatt, this fantasy amounts to "a metamorphosis from inhumanity into humanity"—a move up the Great Chain of Being, purchased with a lifetime of servitude.[18] As for the people thus enslaved, their suffering doesn't necessarily implant in them a bond of heartfelt sympathy for brute creatures everywhere; as Keith Thomas has pointed out,

> nearly all the protests which were made on behalf of the poor and oppressed in the early modern period were couched in terms of the very same ideology of human domination that was used to justify their oppression. Slavery was attacked because it confused the categories of beast and man, while political tyranny was denounced on the grounds that it was wrong that human beings should be treated as if they were animals.[19]

An anthropocentric distinction between humanity and other animals seems to characterize the thinking of both the oppressor and the oppressed, although the latter would draw the line of distinction in a different place than would the former.[20]

In any case, European explorers of the early modern period brought home what living beings they could, and they wrote repeatedly about the rest. Within days of making his first Caribbean landfall, Columbus notes that

> Here the fishes are so unlike ours that it is amazing; there are some like dorados, of the brightest colors in the world—blue, yellow, red, multi-colored, colored in a thousand ways. ... Also, there are whales. I have seen no land animals of any sort, except parrots and lizards—although a boy told me that he saw a big snake.[21]

But this deficit of land animals was remedied soon enough. Writing in 1502 of his first trip to Brazil, Vespucci asks himself,

> What is there to say of the quantity of birds, and their plumes and colors and songs, and how many kinds and how beautiful they are? ... [W]ho could tell the infinite number of forest animals, the abundance of lions, jaguars, catamounts—not like those of Spain but in the Antipodes—so many lynxes, baboons, monkeys of many kinds and many large snakes as well? And we saw so many other animals that I think so many kinds could not have fit into Noah's ark, so many wild boars, roe deer, deer, does, hares and rabbits.[22]

Nor were such observations confined to the newly discovered Americas. In his narrative of Magellan's journey around the world, Antonio Pigafetta not only mentions such South American marvels as the penguin—"geese," he says, that "do not fly, and live on fish"[23]—but also Filipino bats "as large as eagles," Asian "sea snails, beautiful to the sight, ... which kill whales," and Old World parrots such as the cockatoo—"white ones called *cathara*"—and rosella—"entirely red."[24] Gomes Eannes de Azurara notes that when Affonso Gonçalvez Baldaya reached the Rio d'Ouro on the west coast of Africa, "he saw on a bank at the entrance of the river a great multitude of sea-wolves, the which by the estimate of some were about 5,000."[25] And so on, from land to land, from explorer to explorer.

As the exploration grows more extensive and systematic, so, of course, does the observation of exotic fauna. The scattered and confused remarks of travelers like Columbus and Pigafetta yield to more elaborate and exhaustive onsite investigations, sometimes conducted by scholars with a specific interest in natural history. The resulting works begin to redefine the medieval zoological world. The *Historia General y Natural de las Indias* and the briefer *Sumario* of Gonzalo Fernández de Oviedo (1535–1541 and 1526, respectively) catalog such New World beasts as the jaguar, tapir, and armadillo,[26] while also giving "the first scientific descriptions of rubber trees, the tobacco plant, and a multitude of medicinal extracts and edible plants."[27] In 1590 the Jesuit José de Acosta, who had visited Mexico and Peru, published his *Historia Natural y Moral de las Indias,* which includes, among its broader doctrinal concerns, some account of the New World's plant and animal life. Philip II of Spain dispatched his physician, Francisco Hernandez, to Mexico in 1572 to study the region's flora and fauna; the first version of his massive *Rerum Medicarum Novae Hispaniae Thesaurus*—which includes entries for such animals as the manatee ("a creature almost shapeless, like a bull-calf") and quetzalcoatl ("the queen of birds")[28]—appeared in Mexico in 1615, just beyond the strict chronological limits of the present study. The French monk André Thévet, cosmographer to King Charles IX, traveled to Brazil and apparently North America as well; his *Singularitez de la France Antarcticque* (1558) and *Cosmographie universelle* (1575) provide "the source for a number of first images of the New World flora and fauna,"[29] as well as accounts of such Old World creatures as the "Torterels" (sea turtles) of the Cape Verde Islands and the "Cocodrils" of Guinea.[30] Likewise, the Huguenot missionary Jean de Léry visited the short-lived French colony in Brazil between 1556 and 1558. His *Histoire d'un voyage faict en la terre du Bresil* (1578) includes "a veritable encyclopedia of flora and fauna,"[31] offered in part at least as a corrective to the work of the Catholic Thévet. Among the English, Sir Walter Raleigh's associate Thomas Harriot was named geographer to the Roanoke expedition of 1585 and published his *Brief and True Report of the New Found Land of Virginia* in 1588 as a summary of his findings, including in its few pages an account of animals like the "*Saquenukot* & *Maquowoc;* two kindes of small beastes greater than conies which are very good meat," and claiming to know of "eight & twenty severall sortes" of American beasts that remained to be described.[32] Such works gradually subject the discipline of natural history to a profusion of new material, material which, through its sheer volume and the methods whereby it is collected, occasions a gradual reorientation of the discipline itself.

THE SCIENTIFIC IMAGINATION

Of course, none of these works are zoological in the modern sense. In terms of genre and scope, these volumes all conform more or less to the standard set by the earliest and most influential digest of New World information, Peter Martyr's *Decades* (1511–1525). As for Martyr, his reports of New World exploration participate in an Herodotan model of historical narrative and a Plinian model of natural history, as these were preserved into the sixteenth century by subsequent generations. Thus on one hand the *Decades* supply an *annales*-style account of memorable events: Columbus's New World expeditions, Magellan's circumnavigation of the globe, Balboa's discovery of the Pacific, etc. Yet simultaneously, and in no particular order, they preserve a hodgepodge of information that is in turns geographical, ethnographical, botanical, mineralogical, meteorological, zoological, and more. In this context, the study of animal life figures as an integral part of larger structures of knowledge—either the diachronic structures associated with Herodotan narrative or the synchronic ones that characterize Pliny's *Natural History*. Animals do not figure here as a subject of independent disciplinary inquiry any more than they do in the later work of Acosta, or Léry, or Harriott.

In all of these writers we find ourselves to a greater or lesser extent confronting an alien taxonomic system, a system discussed most influentially in the past fifty years by Michel Foucault. Foucault's famous study of Western knowledge patterns in *The Order of Things* finds its starting point in Borges's ironic fiction of

> "a certain Chinese encyclopedia" in which it is written that "animals are divided into: (a) belonging to the Emperor, (b) embalmed, (c) tame, (d) sucking pigs, (e) sirens, (f) fabulous, (g) stray dogs, (h) included in the present classification, (i) frenzied, (j) innumerable, (k) drawn with a very fine camelhair brush, (l) *et cetera,* (m) having just broken the water pitcher, (n) that from a long way off look like flies."[33]

But one of the many pleasures of Foucault's text resides in its detection of a similarly bizarre structural sequence in the work of that preeminent sixteenth-century natural historian, known by contemporaries as the Pliny of his day, Ulisse Aldrovandi:

> [W]hen one goes back to take a look at the *Historia serpentum et draconum,* one finds the chapter "On the serpent in general" arranged under the following headings: equivocation (which means the various meanings of the word *serpent*), synonyms and etymologies, form and description, anatomy, nature and habits, temperament, coitus and generation, voice, movements, places, diet, physiognomy, antipathy, sympathy, modes of capture, death and wounds caused by the serpent, modes and signs of poisoning, remedies, epithets, denominations, prodigies and presages, monsters, mythology, gods to which it is dedicated, fables, allegories and mysteries, hieroglyphics, emblems and symbols, proverbs, coinage, miracles, riddles, devices, heraldic signs, historical facts, dreams, simulacra and statues, use in human diet, use in medicine, miscellaneous uses.[34]

Most of this material locates itself well beyond the space of modern biological or zoological inquiry—within the province of cultural studies, in fact—and in doing so it suggests how far sixteenth-century zoological procedure differs from that we know today. In fact, "the New World discoveries did not immediately transform all European habits of mind,"[35] and those related to the classification of animals provide a classic case in point. Aldrovandi's categories reflect the continuing influence of the bestiary tradition, with its emphasis upon the literary character of knowledge and its tendency to "view ... animals as a text to be read in order to reach a higher, allegorical, and usually Christological significance."[36] But even so, the great natural historians of sixteenth-century Europe fill their work not only with new material, but also, more gradually (and, one must admit, more on the level of practice than of precept), with new protocols for obtaining and organizing that material.

On perhaps the most banal level, the profusion of new species and new reports of exploration forces an increased level of specialization in the writing of natural history. In order to be thorough, the study of animals has to become at least nominally more definite, moving away from the all-inclusive surveys of Herodotus and Pliny and toward a more circumscribed field of inquiry. Moreover, the description of new species begins to force a practical reliance upon personal observation, and this, in turn, begins to call into question the reliability of the natural history purveyed by the medieval bestiaries and similar works. Pomponazzi's commentary on the *De Partibus Animalium* (1521–1524), for instance, "scrutinizes the text by various means, both *a priori* and *a posteriori*," in a way that "cannot help pointing out Aristotle's inconsistencies."[37] As Stefano Perfetti has recently remarked, this process could even involve a species of impromptu laboratory work, as when Pomponazzi disproves one of Albertus Magnus's claims about avian anatomy:

> Albertus seems to say that the chicken has both an eyelid and, behind it, another white protective membrane. But I have dissected a hen and not found this. I have wasted my hen without finding anything.[38]

Such appeals to practical experience begin to appear in the work of the sixteenth century's most influential natural historians. In producing his *Histoire de la nature des oyseaux* (1555), for instance, Pierre Belon "dissected as many of the birds he examined as was possible," while refusing "to include any illustrations of birds he had not examined himself."[39] Belon, Aldrovandi, and Conrad Gesner all corresponded with an extensive network of zoological informants who provided them with firsthand accounts of unusual species; they shared information with each other as well; they themselves traveled, when possible, in search of their subject matter; and while their compilations of natural history still retain many of the formal and material features of the bestiary tradition, they also point the way toward a mode of zoological inquiry that lends primary emphasis to "a particular and exact observation of the nature of every beast."[40] When in 1533 Pierre Gilles's edition of Aelian's *Natural History* appeared, containing among other editorial interpolations an early and important description of the turkey, Gilles compared the bird to a falcon; by the end of the century, Aldrovandi criticized this description as inaccurate and fanciful in its failure to note obvious physical features such as the male turkey's beard.[41] From here it is only a step to Sir Francis Bacon's complaint in *The Advancement of Learning* (1605) that

> in natural history we see there hath not been that choice and judgment used as ought to have been, as may appear in the writings of Plinius, Cardanus, Albertus, and divers of the Arabians, being fraught with much fabulous matter, a great part not only untried but notoriously untrue, to the great derogation of the credit of natural philosophy with the grave and sober kind of wits.[42]

While Aldrovandi, Gesner, and Belon would later be subject to a contemptuous association with the very sort of natural history Bacon assails (Buffon, for instance, sneers of Aldrovandi's *Historia serpentum et draconum,* "There is no description here, only legend"),[43] they anticipate Bacon's attitudes and methods in a variety of ways.

TRANSCULTURAL SPECIES

If the natural historians of sixteenth-century Europe begin to privilege personal observation in their descriptions of animal species, that is because personal observation became more feasible in the sixteenth century than ever before. Species moved from one part of the globe to another with unprecedented speed and in unprecedented numbers. By 1526, Oviedo could already declare of the parrot—the New World diagnostic species *par excellence*—"There are so many different species of parrots that it would be a long task to describe them. They are better subjects for the painter's brush than for words. Since so many different species have been carried to Spain, it is hardly worth while to take time to describe them here."[44] Seven years earlier, Diogo Velho da Chancellaria could say much the same thing of Portugal, with reference to a broader array of exotic species:

> Gold, pearls, stones,
> Gems and spices ...
> Tigers, lions, elephants,
> Monsters and talking birds, ...
> All now are quite common.[45]

Nor was the traffic in animals a one-way affair; as exotic species came to Europe, so indigenous species and breeds traveled elsewhere. By 1590, José de Acosta could divide the animals of the New World into three categories: "some that have been taken there by Spaniards; others that, although they have not been brought from Spain, are of the same species as in Europe, and others that are native to the Indies and are not found in Spain."[46] Some sixty-five years before Acosta, Peter Martyr could observe of Hispaniola that "[t]he number of pigs in this island is considerable. They all descend from some which were brought here."[47] And still earlier, when Hernán Cortés arrived off the coast of Yucatán with five hundred men and sixteen horses, he initiated one of the most portentous cross-cultural animal encounters in recorded history.

Horses, of course, were unknown to the indigenous peoples Cortés encountered in New Spain, and when such beasts appeared within Cortés's small private army, they served not only as a means of enhanced mobility but also as objects of wonder and terror. In their first encounters with the Spaniards, "[t]he Indians thought ... that the horse and rider were one creature."[48] Later, Cortés encouraged the Indians to believe that his horses were powerful, sentient beings whom only he could placate. Bernal Díaz relates how, during one tense negotiating session with the local tribespeople, Cortés had a rutting stallion brought before the tribal emissaries, at a place just occupied by a mare in foal. The results were predictable:

> [T]he horse began to paw the ground and neigh and create an uproar, looking all the time towards the Indians and the place from which the scent of the mare came. But the *Caciques* thought he was roaring at them and were terrified. ... When Cortés observed their terror he rose from his seat, went over to the horse, and told two orderlies to lead him away. He then informed the Indians that he had told the beast not to be angry, since they were friendly and had come to make peace.[49]

In presenting his horses this way, Cortés deliberately paired them with another crucial tactical resource: firearms. During the same parley in which he introduced his rutting stallion, he also caused his largest cannon to be loaded with a ball and powder, then, gesturing toward his artillery, he warned the native delegation that

> if they were not [well disposed], something would jump out of those *tepuzques*—*tepuzque* is their native name for iron—which would kill them, for some of those *tepuzques* were still angry with them for having attacked us. At this moment, he secretly gave the order for the loaded cannon to be fired, and it went off with the requisite thunderous report,

the ball whistling away over the hills. It was midday and very still; the
Caciques were thoroughly terrified.[50]

According to Peter Martyr, cannon and horses together made possible the conquest of the Aztec empire.[51] After five centuries in which guns have acquired
unimagined deadliness while horses have dropped into the dustbin of military
history, it is easy to overemphasize the importance of the former at the expense
of the latter. But this would be a mistake; European advantages in animal husbandry were a sine qua non of colonialism.

  This fact lends itself to various ironies. For one thing, Native American war-
riors quickly adopted the horse themselves, only to see this hard-won achieve-
ment neutralized by the increasing numbers and technological superiority of
European colonists. For another, the Europeans themselves were elsewhere
subject to their own deficiencies as horse breeders. In relating his travels on
the west coast of Africa during the 1450s, Alvise da Cadamosto pauses to describe the Portuguese outpost at Arguim, which carried on a steady trade with
the local Arab merchants. "These Arabs," he remarks, "have many Berber
horses, which they trade, and take to the Land of the Blacks, exchanging them
with the rulers for slaves. Ten or fifteen slaves are given for one of these horses,
according to their quality."[52] The Europeans, for their part, prized Arab, Turkish, and Persian horses as much as the Berber stock, and they set out with a
will to acquire and breed these beasts. In 1492, Francesco Gonzaga, Marquis
of Mantua, opened negotiations with the Turkish Sultan for purebred horses,
and thirty years later Francesco's son Federico II renewed the effort.[53] By 1514
the Portuguese had used their factory at Goa to corner the market for Arab
and Persian horses in India.[54] In England, matters progressed a bit more slowly.
Spanish and Italian horses had entered the realm during the Middle Ages, but
"these overseas trading links seem to have broken off in the mid-fourteenth
century," a fact which "inevitably had an adverse effect on the quality of the
stock."[55] According to Peter Edwards, it was only "in the reign of Henry VIII
that foreign horses once more started to come into the country in any number,"
and while Henry did receive some barbs from the Marquis of Mantua, his
principal imports were "draught horses from the Low Countries."[56] In 1587,
William Harrison lists the main "outlandish horses that are daily brought over
unto us" as being "the jennet of Spain, the courser of Naples, the hobby of
Ireland, the Flemish roil, and Scottish nag."[57] In England, the real popularity of
purebred Arab bloodstock—along with the development of high-quality native
breeds—would have to wait until the seventeenth century and beyond.

  When it came to sheep, on the other hand, the English largely had their
own way with things. Blessed with a wide range of native varieties, from the
mountain breeds of Wales and Cornwall to the Lintons of the north Midlands,
the Herdwicks of the Lake District, the Lustre Longwools of Lincolnshire, and

the prized short-wool Ryelands of Herefordshire, England had already earned a storied reputation for the production of fine wool in the Middle Ages.[58] In this market the English were the exporters of choice, and not only did they sell high-quality wool to an international market; they also traded their breeding stock. As Raphael Holinshed complains, "King Edward [IV] concluded an amity and league with Henry, King of Castile, and John, King of Aragon" in 1466,

> at the concluding whereof he granted license for certain Cotswold sheep to be transported into the country of Spain (as people report), which have there so multiplied and increased that it hath turned the commodity of England much to the Spanish profit.[59]

Harrison views this development with similar distaste: "What fools, then, are our countrymen, in that they seek to bereave themselves of this commodity by practicing daily how to transfer the same to other nations, in carrying over their rams and ewes to breed and increase among them?"[60]

But even Harrison has to admit that his protectionist sentiments are on the wane: "And it is so sure as God liveth that every trifle which cometh from beyond the sea, though it be not worth *3d.*, is more esteemed than a continual commodity at home with us which far exceedeth that value."[61] England, like Spain, Portugal, France, and Italy before it, was developing the beginnings of a global economy, one in which animals and animal products played a major role. Among the beasts brought to the New World by Europeans, Acosta numbers "sheep, cattle, goats, pigs, horses, asses, dogs, cats, and other such animals."[62] Moreover, yesterday's export could become tomorrow's import; "[t]he cattle of Hispaniola," Acosta continues, "are used for their hides," which "are imported into Spain and represent one of the chief products of the islands and New Spain."[63] In other cases, foreign species proved popular for a variety of purposes. The African trade in ivory, civet, rhinoceros horn, and skins was already well underway by the 1450s.[64] New World featherwork and furs also aroused interest.[65] European voyagers took careful stock of the beasts used for food in various foreign parts. Any number of travelers, from Léry to Francisco de Orellana to Sir John Hawkins and beyond, ate parrots and monkeys and turtles.[66] In West Africa, Cadamosto ate elephant—which was "not very good"—and ostrich eggs—which were.[67]

But the two exotic food-animals to achieve general popularity in Renaissance Europe were the guinea hen and the turkey. The former was in fact known to European diners in classical times.[68] The Portuguese became aware of it again in the mid-1400s, as they mapped the coast of Africa, and it was reestablished in Europe "by the 1530s."[69] As for the turkey, it came to the attention of New World explorers during their first visits to Central America. Distracted by the birds' semicircular tailfeather display and the iridescence of their neck-area, European observers initially thought of them as a sort of pea-cock.[70] They reached Spain by "at least 1511"; by 1538 they were clearly present in France, and had probably been there for some time already; Conrad von Heresbach, who is said to have kept them on his estate, claimed that they were in Germany by 1530.[71] Their introduction to England seems to have occurred in the mid-1520s, apparently through the New World voyages of Sebastian Cabot,[72] and once in England, they rapidly acquired aristocratic associations. In 1550, King Edward VI granted William Strickland of Boynton a coat of arms that featured a "turkey cock in his pride proper," this in apparent recognition of the fact that Strickland had accompanied Cabot to the New World and had taken a hand in importing the bird in question.[73] And these noble connections continued at table as well. Already in 1541, Archbishop Thomas Cranmer could insist that his clergy, when banqueting on "the greatest fyshes or fowles," should limit themselves to "but one in a dish, as Crane, Swan, Turkeycocke," etc.[74] By 1557 this example had reached Venice as well, whose magistrates "passed an ordinance repressing luxury, such as the eating of the rare turkey along with a second luxury such as the partridge."[75] In 1556, when King Charles IX passed through the city of Amiens, the local councilmen presented him with a gift of twelve turkeys.[76]

In case after case and nation after nation, the exotic animals of Africa, Asia, and the New World wrought profound changes in the material culture of fifteenth- and sixteenth-century Europe. From transportation to clothing to diet to the breeding of local stock and far beyond, these beasts made the Renaissance possible.

GENTLE AND UNGENTLE BEASTS

Perhaps the most outstanding feature of early modern European social organization, one regularly remarked upon by historians of the period, is its intense preoccupation with genealogically ascribed distinctions of rank. As it happens, the animal culture of the fifteenth and sixteenth centuries plays directly into this preoccupation on any number of levels. Animals themselves acquire various kinds of social significance, and in doing so they serve as social signifiers for the human beings with whom they are affiliated. They can attest, on one hand, to the hierarchical position of those who own them, thereby helping to consolidate and protect one's claim to gentility; on the other hand, procuring the right kinds of animals, in the right contexts, can facilitate social advancement as well.

William Strickland's turkey provides a classic case in point. To begin with, its acquisition endows Strickland with some of the prestige—and perhaps some of the income as well—necessary to pursue his heraldic claim. Then, once that claim has been granted, the turkey appears on the Strickland arms as a marker of rank assigned, rather than achieved. To this extent, it serves as a vehicle for the mystification of status—an instrument of social mobility that translates itself, after the fact, into a denial that mobility was ever necessary. Given their capacity for this sort of semiotic work, it makes sense that animals themselves should be subject to various kinds of social stratification, not only with respect to species, but with respect to breed as well. Nowhere is this fact better illustrated than by the two most versatile, and perhaps most essential, of Renaissance working animals: horses and dogs.

Among the former, one can trace a hierarchy of social relations rendered explicit by Harrison's "jennet of Spain, ... courser of Naples, ... hobby of Ireland, ... Flemish roil, and Scottish nag." The foreign breeds appear here, not by accident, in a roughly descending order of rank. As for this order, it is determined by variables that include a given breed's geographical proximity (the closer it gets to England, the less it is prized) and its work associations (jennets and Neapolitans were horses fit for warfare and the chase; hobbies were valued as "tractable, easy-paced riding animals"; Flemish horses were used for heavy haulage; Scottish galloways "could be employed for a wide range of tasks and were efficient and indefatigable workers").[77]

This hierarchical approach to the animal world is so common among early modern writers as to be second nature to them. It is as if they were unable to comprehend the order of nature except through the lens of their social preoccupations.

One consequence of this phenomenon is that Renaissance treatises on riding and hunting may be understood as a subgenre of the early modern courtesy manual. Castiglione points the way here when he has Count Lodovico da Canossa declare of the ideal courtier,

> Weapons are also often used in various sports during peacetime, and gentlemen often perform in public spectacles before the people and before ladies and great lords. So I wish our courtier to be an accomplished and versatile horseman and, as well as having a knowledge of horses and all the manners to do with riding, he should put every effort and diligence into surpassing the rest just a little in everything, so that he may always be recognized as superior.[78]

The prestige of horsemanship derives here from its relation to the military arts; in other words, the horses Canossa expects his ideal courtier to know about will be jennets and Neapolitans rather than Flemish roils and Scottish nags.

Likewise, hunting and hunting-related horsemanship gain social cachet from their affinity to warfare—the armigerous gentry's traditional raison d'être. As Canossa puts it again,

> There are also many other sports which, although they do not directly require the use of weapons, are closely related to arms and demand a great

deal of manly exertion. Among these it seems to me that hunting is the most important, since in many ways it resembles warfare.[79]

John Astley echoes these sentiments in 1584, declaring that the "Art of Riding and Horsemanship ... belongeth to the warre and feates of armes."[80] Twenty-four years earlier, Thomas Blundeville begins his *Arte of Ryding and Breakinge Greate Horses,* itself a loose translation of Federigo Grisone's *Ordini di cavalcare* of 1550, with a series of historical cases illustrating the martial excellence of his subject matter: the relationship of Alexander the Great and his horse Bucephalus, the battle hardiness of the French King Charles VIII's mount, etc.[81] In 1615, Gervase Markham can still declare that

> I thinke it not amisse to ...giue that recreation precedencie of place which in mine opinion ... doth manie degrees goe before, and precede all other, as being most royall for the statelines thereof, most artificial for the wisedom & cunning thereof and most manly and warlike for the vse and indurance thereof. And this I hould to be the hunting of wilde Beasts in generall.[82]

"Royall," "manly," and "warlike": this nexus of rank, masculinity, and military associations continued to lend prestige to hunting and horsemanship in the Renaissance, as it had done since ancient times. That is why the breeding of fine horses for warfare and the chase was associated with aristocratic privilege and obligation, as in England, where "three or four of the earliest authors on horsemanship emerged out of the circle of gentlemen-pensioners."[83] And that is also why the earliest English printed hunting manual (and one of the most influential early English works of its kind), *The Boke of Saint Albans* (1486), is divided into three parts, on hawking, hunting, and heraldry, respectively. The last of these three sections only fits with the preceding two if one takes it for granted that hawking and hunting function as signifiers of a sort, distinguishing "gentill men and honeste persones" as such, and thus, like heraldry, helping the reader to understand "how gentilmen shall be knowyn from ungentill men."[84]

And the social associations that hold true for horses apply equally to dogs. Like horses, dogs prove useful for a wide variety of purposes and are available in a wide range of breeds, some of which therefore emerge as attributes of rank and privilege. Where *The Boke of Saint Albans* presents itself as an exercise in social discrimination, John Caius's early and influential treatise *Of Englishe Dogges* (1576) goes further, elaborating a full canine taxonomy that conforms to the distinctions between peers, commons, and sturdy beggars. These three categories reemerge in Caius to differentiate dogs of "a gentle kynde" from those of more "homely" or "currish" disposition,[85] and again, as with Harrison's horses, one of the prime determinants of degree is the work for which a given breed is suited. While the nobler sort of dogs is distinguished primarily by its association with the hunt, those of "a course kinde" are employed for such varied chores as guard duty, "drawing water out of wells," and herding sheep; as for "Curres of the mungrell and rascall sort," they do some menial chores, such as operating kitchen rotisseries by running inside "a wheele which they turn ... rounde about with the waight of their bodies."[86] Otherwise, they are dismissed as "unprofitable implements, out of the boundes of [Caius's] book."[87]

In fact, things are a bit more complicated than this, for while concentrating upon dogs of the gentle sort (which predictably take up most of his attention), Caius subdivides these into three further categories: dogs employed for the chase; "Dogges seruing the hauke" (what we would now call retrievers); and then, perhaps unexpectedly, a "thirde gentle kinde" distinguished not by their hunting skills at all but rather by their ability to "satisfie the delicatenesse of daintie dames" by serving as "instrumentes of folly for them to play and dally withall."[88] These creatures complicate the hierarchy of rank by inflecting it in the direction of gender, and the result is a unique subgroup of canine society—a kind of inferior aristocracy, as it were—made in the image of a putative feminine frivolity.

To grasp the broad symbolic potential and appeal of such classifications, we need only turn to Shakespeare's early comedy *The Two Gentlemen of Verona* (ca. 1594). One of that play's most successful comic moments occurs when the lover Proteus tries to woo the disdainful Silvia with a gift—a "little jewel" of a lapdog like those described by Caius.[89] The token goes awry when Lance, the servant who conveys the dog to Silvia, loses it in the marketplace and in desperation substitutes his own dog, Crab, of a very different kind. Lance recounts the sequel:

> He [Crab] thrusts me himself into the company of three or four gentleman-like dogs under the Duke's table. He had not been there—bless the mark—a pissing-while but all the chamber smelled him. "Out with the dog," says one. "What cur is that?" says another. "Whip him out," says the third. "Hang him up," says the Duke.[90]

If hunting and horsemanship treatises constitute a subset of courtesy literature in the Renaissance, then it follows that horses and dogs themselves should grow subject to the dictates of courtesy theory, and Crab is a case in point. As a "cur," a dog from the lower end of Caius's taxonomy, he attempts to fraternize with dogs of the better sort only to demonstrate, through his comportment, his intrinsic and irredeemable baseness. Here Shakespeare views dog society through the lens of human behavior; in *The Merchant of Venice* (ca. 1596) he does the reverse. There Shylock complains that the Christians who have sought credit from him "foot me as you spurn a stranger cur/Over your threshold," thereby identifying himself with Caius's canine underclass.[91] In both cases, Shakespeare employs dog references in a complex and ambivalent way, creating a sort of social mise-en-abyme that defies full analysis in the present context.

The symbolic significance of Renaissance animals remains a vast, largely unexplored, subject, but the language of hunting, horses, and dogs provides a good indication of its potential for scholarship. To stay with that language—and its appearance in Shakespeare—a moment longer, not only did various animals and breeds have distinct social associations in Renaissance Europe; as with people, so too with animals, the associations in question were prone to slippage. By the late seventeenth century the Renaissance warhorses of choice—the jennet and the Neapolitan—could be dismissed as "Dull heavy Jades, fitter for a Brewers-Cart than the saddle."[92] And more portentously, the horse's martial associations were already beginning to decline in the late sixteenth century, in response to the gentry's incipient translation from a military class into a leisure class. Shakespeare registers this fact in his plays, which tend to depict chivalry as a "defunct ideology,"[93] while presenting its attributes in a correspondingly disparaging light. In the resulting dramatic environment, high-spirited coursers become the property either of knaves or of fools. The former include the French nobles of *Henry V* (ca. 1599), effete anti-Gallic caricatures who boast loudly about their horses ("I will not change my horse with any that treads but on four pasterns")[94] before their humiliation at Agincourt. The latter include Hotspur in *1 Henry IV*, an old-style warrior-baron who prefers his horse to his wife ("When I am a-horseback, I will swear/I love thee infinitely")[95] and proves pathetically unfit for the refinements of administrative intrigue.

And finally, to remain with Shakespeare and hunting still one more moment, there remains the subject of illicit hunting—that is, poaching—which acquires its own symbolic value in the fifteenth and sixteenth centuries. As Stephen Greenblatt has recently recalled, antiquarians of the seventeenth and eighteenth centuries liked to repeat a tradition that Shakespeare left Stratford-upon-Avon after being taken for poaching on the property of Sir Thomas Lucy. This tale has fallen out of favor with later biographers since it can only be traced to within fifty years or so of Shakespeare's own lifetime. But as Greenblatt notes, this same tradition proved popular with early biographers for good reason, because "in Shakespeare's time and well into the eighteenth century the idea of deer poaching had a special resonance; it was good to think with":

For Elizabethans deer poaching was not understood principally as having to do with hunger; it was a story not about desperation but about risk. ... It was, for a start, a daring game: it took impressive skill and cool nerves to trespass on a powerful person's land, kill a large animal, and drag it away, without getting caught by those who patrolled the area. "What, hast thou not full often struck a doe," someone asks in one of Shakespeare's early plays, "And borne her cleanly by the keeper's nose?" (*Titus Andronicus* 2.1.93–94). It was a skillful assault upon property, a symbolic violation of the social order, a coded challenge to authority.[96]

As Roger Manning has remarked, "unlawful hunting" could be "viewed as a game that men played or as an affirmation of prowess"; by the early 1600s it had also come to express "popular resentment of aristocratic hunting privileges."[97] Shakespeare's alleged poaching cannot be fully understood outside this network of reference. In such a case, animals account not only for a large share of the meaning of the poet's work; they also help to explain the terms in which his work and life have been understood.

THE RAGE FOR OWNERSHIP

Poaching, of course, is about ownership. It is a crime against property, with animals serving as the property in question. Their value as such derives not only from their material usefulness but also, as poaching demonstrates, from their concomitant power as symbols. As it happens, the fifteenth and sixteenth centuries witnessed an impressive expansion in the symbolic purposes for which animals could be held valuable, and as a result, European society in the Renaissance proved hospitable to a wide new range of unnecessary beasts.

Not all of them were alive. In December of 1521, some eight months after Magellan's death in the Philippines, his remaining followers found themselves on the Indonesian island of Batjan, whose aged sultan entertained them well and sent them home with various gifts for the King of Spain. Among these were two "extremely beautiful dead birds," which Antonio Pigafetta describes as follows:

> Those birds are as large as thrushes, and have a small head and a long beak. Their legs are a palmo in length and as thin as a reed, and they have no wings, but in their stead long feathers of various colors, like large plumes. Their tail resembles that of the thrush. ... The people told us that those birds came from the terrestrial paradise, and they called them *bolon diuata,* that is to say, "birds of God."[98]

The last part of this tale is nothing new; it is a traditional bit of medieval natural history usually associated with the parrot.[99] But the birds—they are still known in English as birds of paradise—*were* new, to European eyes at least, and so was the manner of their preservation. They were taxidermed, and when the remnants of Magellan's expedition returned home the next year, this technique of presentation proved almost as fascinating to naturalists as did the birds themselves. In 1555, Belon published the first European account of how to handle birdskins in this way; according to him, one should disembowel the bird through an anal incision, salt it thoroughly, hang it to cure, and then fill it with any of a variety of materials, ranging from pepper to tobacco.[100] Thus began the European fashion for stuffed animals.

In practice, Belon's method of taxidermy proved crude and unreliable. Salt-cured animals succumb easily to rot and insects. These drawbacks would only be overcome in the late eighteenth century, when Jean-Baptiste Becoeur developed an insect-proof preservative.[101] But in the meantime, moths and mildew did nothing to allay the growing popularity of taxidermy in the West, and this popularity, in turn, made it possible for stuffed and mounted animals to take their place in the private museums and collections, curiosity cabinets and *Wunderkammern*, that started to appear in Europe in the 1500s. Aldrovandi, Gesner, and Belon all developed such collections to further their research in natural history. Other cabinets, like the *Kunst- und Naturalienkammer* started by August Hermann Francke at Halle in 1598, "had a teaching purpose."[102] Still others (e.g., Elector August of Saxony's *Kunstkammer* in Dresden, founded in 1560) were the product of privileged connoisseurship and the private collector's mania. Many, like those of Ferrante Imperato in Naples and Francesco Calzolari in Verona, were developed by apothecaries with a professional interest in *naturalia*.

While these collections were the forerunners of the modern museum, they were organized in a manner—like that of Aldrovandi's and Gesner's natural histories—that "at first glance … appears incoherent," combining seashells and fossils, Roman coins and pressed plants, stuffed animals and statuary.[103] But underlying such chaos one can detect a rage for synthesis, channeled through the allegorical sensibility of the medieval bestiaries, through the common wonder elicited by all the objects of the collectors' passion, and perhaps most of all through "a restless desire to establish a continuity between art and nature."[104] In this spirit, the *naturalia* of the curiosity cabinet—pressed flowers, stuffed birds, animal skeletons, even minerals abstracted from their original setting—prove strangely denatured, whereas the cabinet's *artificialia*—elaborately wrought nautilus shells, richly fashioned drinking vessels made from ostrich eggs, ebony boxes inlaid with coral and ivory and *pietra dura*—can seem like carefully devised natural history displays. The objects of the *Wunderkammern* generate their own conceptual space, one in which automata aspire to the status of living beings, while birds and beasts are translated into inert matter.

But animals were collected alive as well as dead in the Renaissance. Just as curiosity cabinets were the precursors of the modern museum, the modern zoo found its antecedents in the menageries of Renaissance princes and prelates. These collections were not at all new to the fifteenth century, but they grew steadily in number and in splendor from the early 1400s on. As Jakob Burckhardt noted long ago, "By the end of the fifteenth century ... true menageries (*serragli*), now reckoned part of the suitable appointments of a Court, were kept by many of the princes [of Italy]."[105] Nor was Italy alone in this respect; such collections included the famous menageries of King Manuel I of Portugal and Duke René of Anjou, as well as those of King Ferrante of Naples, the Medici of Florence, and, by the early sixteenth century, the Medici Pope Leo X. The last of these assemblages, "one of the most advanced and professional installations in Europe at that time," existed in contact with other contemporary collections while also extending an already-established history of papal zookeeping.[106] Popes had maintained beasts of various kinds for many years prior to Leo X: Martin V kept a parrot, Pius II had a parrot and stags, Sixtus IV had an eagle and parakeet, and so forth. But according to recent scholarship, "it was not until the early sixteenth century, in the reign of Pope Leo X, that the true menagerie or *seraglio* evolved in Rome."[107] It developed in intimate connection with contemporary exploratory ventures. Catholic princes bent on overseas expansion imported wild beasts for their own private zoos, and they contributed gifts to the papal menagerie out of their own stock. In December 1515, for instance, a rhinoceros left Lisbon by ship, bound for Rome as a gift to the Pope from Manuel I; this was preceded, the year before, by the famous elephant Hanno, also a gift from Manuel I, which expired in the Vatican on June 8, 1516.[108] Other such donations included "spotted leopards, panthers, apes, and parrots ..., as well as several lions."[109]

Among the secular nobility such gifts circulated as well, staking out a space of diplomatic exchange marked by that exquisite blend of friendship and rivalry called "emulation." In 1406 the city of Florence sent King Wladislaw of Poland a pair of lions of either sex so that he might breed cubs from them.[110] The Mameluke Sultan Kaytbey presented Lorenzo the Magnificent with a giraffe.[111] Ferrante of Naples owned a giraffe and a zebra that had been sent him by the Sultan of Baghdad.[112] When Princess Margaret of Anjou (daughter of Duke René) wed Henry VI of England, "one of Henry's courtiers sought to curry favor with Margaret by bringing her a lion to Titchfield Abbey as a wedding present."[113] In 1552 King João III of Portugal presented an elephant to King Maximilian II of Bohemia and Hungary, and João's successor Dom Sebastião sent Maximilian a second elephant eleven years later.[114] And if such animal exchanges could mark the spirit of diplomatic commerce, the failure of diplomacy could be attended by the destruction of menageries. Entering Tenochtitlán in 1519, Hernán Cortés wrote at length about the extraordinary private zoo of Montezuma, which included "ten pools of water, in which were kept all the many and diverse breed of waterfowl," along with separate facilities for "birds of prey, lions, tigers, foxes, and every kind of cat in considerable numbers."[115] In his campaign to subjugate and demoralize the Aztec people, Cortés had this collection dismantled.

For most of the beasts residing in these great cultural facilities, life was solitary, poor, nasty, brutish, and short. Surviving at the Vatican for two years, Hanno the elephant did better than many. The rhinoceros sent to join him in 1515 didn't even make it to Rome alive. As for Margaret of Anjou's lion, it was presented to the new queen in part because nine years earlier, in 1436, all the lions in the Tower zoo had died within the space of a few months, leaving the kings of England "a glorious royal Menagerie with two hundred years of history and tradition behind it, and containing not one single animal."[116] Given the minimal expertise one could expect of fifteenth- and sixteenth-century zookeepers, this comes as no surprise. But if historians of zookeeping distinguish between "something commonly called a 'menagerie' and something else called a 'zoological garden,'" with the former defined as a collection of animals "kept 'simply' for purposes of display or for the aggrandizement of the owner" and the latter defined in terms "that privilege scientific endeavor and public education,"[117] it must be added that the failures of early menagerie keepers led the way to more rigorous "scientific endeavor" by demonstrating its necessity in the maintenance of exotic beasts.

While princes and prelates set the standard in collecting animals for pleasure during the Renaissance, less exalted individuals quickly followed suit. As Keith Thomas has observed of England,

> Pet-keeping had been fashionable among the well-to-do in the Middle Ages, and monks and nuns were repeatedly (and vainly) forbidden to keep them. Pet monkeys were imported in the thirteenth century. But it was in the sixteenth and seventeenth centuries that pets really seem to have established themselves as a normal feature of the middle-class household.[118]

Perhaps appropriately, the word *pet*, as applied to animals, is itself of sixteenth-century derivation. At first it seems to have been a northern usage; at any rate, the *Oxford English Dictionary*'s earliest recorded instance of the term, dated 1539, comes from the accounts of the Lord High Treasurer of Scotland. To begin with, the word appears to have referred primarily to lambs, specifically "cade" lambs, cast off by their ewe and therefore raised by hand. Introduced into the household for their own survival, these animals could become an object of particular attention, care, and affection, entering thereby into a special relation to the human beings on whom they depended. This special relation, in turn, could then provide the linguistic model for an entire category of animals conceived as participating in a kind of honorary humanity.[119]

Exempt from the need to do productive work, protected from the demands of the table, welcomed into the human household itself, where they performed the traditionally human function of providing entertainment and companionship, these privileged animals—whether lambs and kids, dogs and cats, or parrots and monkeys—existed in contrast to a parallel underclass of bestialized humanity: women and children; slaves, fools, and dwarfs; the poor and dispossessed; heretics and non-Christians; and the native peoples encountered by explorers in their travels and brought back to Europe, like exotic wildlife, under duress.[120] To this extent, the study of animals in the Renaissance proves inseparable from the study of social interaction, political oppression, and the growth of cultural hegemony.

NURTURE AND TORTURE

The increased popularity of pet keeping in fifteenth- and sixteenth-century Europe argues for an ongoing change in the way human beings and animals interact in the period, and among other things, this change raises questions about what we might call the emotional life of animals. One of the defining features of the owner-pet relationship, after all, is its affective component. So it becomes worth asking: what evidence survives of the emotional bond between human beings and other animals in Renaissance Europe, and how is that bond portrayed?

Already, toward the end of the fourteenth century, Chaucer's Prioress displays the indicia of the sentimental pet-owner. Her "smale houndes" enjoy an expensive diet of "rosted flessh, or milk, or wastel-breed," and any misfortune they suffer, whether sublime or ridiculous, occasions her sympathetic tears: "[S]oore wepte she if oon of hem were deed,/ Or if men smoot it with a yerde smerte."[121] Henri III of France lavished attention on his own lapdogs and was reputed to travel on progress with "over two hundred" of them, divided into groups of eight, each group with its own governess and packhorse.[122] By the first decade of the 1600s, King James I of England could affectionately refer to his principal secretary and lord treasurer, Robert Cecil, Earl of Salisbury, as "my little beagle"—an epithet of such frequent occurrence that the correspondence between the two men came to be known as the "Little Beagle Letters."[123] In 1599, Ben Jonson's *Every Man Out of His Humour* regaled audiences with the spectacle of the aspiring knight-errant Puntarvolo, a man so attached to his favorite dog that he brings it with him to the court at Whitehall and proposes to travel with it to "the *Turkes* court in *Constantinople*" and back.[124] At the dog's untimely death, his owner breaks down in "passionate ... funerall teares."[125]

In such cases, the Renaissance seems to have inherited and preserved something like the sentimental pet culture typical of twenty-first century Western societies. But this impression can be deceptive. Chaucer's Prioress, for instance, is clearly presented as an object of mild ridicule, and her fondness for dogs participates in a broad and fatuous delicacy of temperament: "She was so charitable and so pitous/ She wolde wepe, if that she saugh a mous/ Kaught in a trappe, if it were deed or bledde."[126] Henri III's dog fetish exposed him to ferocious condemnation from Huguenot critics who associated it with the king's extravagance, self-indulgence, and "divergent sexualit[y]."[127] Cecil's beagle persona was a flight of royal whimsy to be endured rather than celebrated, occasioning much mirth among rival courtiers.[128] As for Puntarvolo, Jonson subjects him to withering derision, which reaches its climax when another character poisons his dog and publicly mocks his tears of grief.

Such moments suggest that the emotional attachment to animals, while not alien to Renaissance social practice, was generally coded as an affectation of the privileged and idle.

Indeed, emotional engagement emerges from these records as itself a species of privilege, made available selectively, both to human beings and to other animals, on a rank-specific basis. Elsewhere, beasts were treated with a good deal less ceremony. Even as late as 1698—well past the terminus ad quem of this volume—a Dorset farmer could write matter-of-factly that "My old dog Quon was killed and baked for his grease, of which he yielded 11 lbs."[129] So much for sentiment.

Dogs like Quon often met their maker by hanging, a fact that the English language still registers in the adjective *hangdog*. In some cases, moreover, such treatment was even given judicial sanction. In both classical and Mosaic law, animals could be prosecuted, convicted, and punished, most often by death, for various legal offenses, most often manslaughter and bestiality, with the punishment in question often justified on the basis that the offending animal was an instrument of evil spirits. Roughly two hundred documented examples of such proceedings survive, both from the British Isles and from the Continent, with the earliest dating from the ninth century and the most recent deriving from the twentieth. Seventy-five percent of these surviving cases occur between 1400 and 1700, marking these three centuries as the heyday of the practice. In August of 1487, for instance, Jean Rohin, Cardinal Bishop of Autun, authorized a public anathema and sentence of exile to be pronounced upon the slugs that were afflicting farmers in his diocese; in 1516, the magistrates of Troyes pronounced a similar sentence upon the local weevils.[130] In 1474, the civic leaders of Bale "sentenced a cock to be burned at the stake 'for the heinous and unnatural crime of laying an egg.'"[131] In 1553, various swine were executed in Frankfurt for child murder; in 1578 a cow was similarly put to death in Ghent; and so on.[132]

In other cases, the execution of animals was attended by less legal fanfare; when Shakespeare's Duke in *The Two Gentlemen of Verona* commands that the

ill-mannered Crab be hanged, he is gesturing toward just such an unceremoni-
ous end.[133] But brutal and casual as such treatment could be, Shakespeare's reference to it suggests that it was not without its entertainment value. Just before
the Duke commands that Crab be hanged, one of his retainers calls for the dog
to be whipped—a punishment that recalls the regular whipping of bears and
jackanapes in the Bankside liberties of London, where animal entertainments
served as a kind of lowbrow *Doppelgänger* of the Elizabethan theater.

These entertainments could take many forms, from the benign to the sa-
distic, and they proved popular not only in London but throughout Europe.
Pope Leo X's elephant Hanno earned admiration in part because at its first
encounter with the pope, the elephant stopped in its tracks, dropped to its
knees and inclined its head devoutly, then arose, trumpeting three times in
salutation.[134] By 1614, on the other hand, Ben Jonson could refer to a "wel-
educated Ape"—apparently a common fairground attraction—that would
"come ouer the chaine, for the *King of England,* and backe againe for the
Prince, and sit still on his arse for the *Pope,* and the *King* of *Spaine.*"[135] In
the 1590s, a Scotsman named Banks captivated the citizens of London with
his performing horse Morocco, which danced, walked on its hind legs, and
counted with its hoof.[136] John Caius wrote of "dogges ... which are taught
and exercised to daunce in measure ... showing many pretty trickes. ... As to
stand bolte upright, to lye flat upon the grounde, to turne rounde as a ringe
holding their tailes in their teeth, to begge for theyr meate, and sundry such
properties."[137] These performing animals provided the inspiration, in turn, for
such theatrical beasts as Shakespeare's Crab and Puntarvolo's nameless dog in
Every Man Out of His Humour.

But the animal entertainments for which the Renaissance has proven justly
notorious could be far darker in nature, essentially a continuation of medieval
practices. These included various kinds of cat torture, such as the habit, alluded to by Benedick in *Much Ado about Nothing* (1598), of hanging cats in
bags and employing them as archery targets: "If I do [marry], hang me in a
bottle like a cat, and shoot at me."[138] Another such feline pastime is described
in Part 2 of *Don Quixote* (1615), where Cervantes' hero receives the following
reward for singing an atrocious love song:

> [O]n a sudden, from an open Gallery, ... came down a great Number of
> Cats, pour'd out of a huge Sack, all of 'em with ... Bells ty'd to their Tails.
> The Jangling of the Bells, and the Squawling of the Cats made such a dis-
> mal Noise, that the very Contrivers of the Jest were scar'd.[139]

Such play, in turn, evokes the spirit of the English theatrical jackanapes, the
monkey tied to a horse that would be chased around an enclosed space (such
as a theater or bull-baiting arena) either by dogs or with a whip. This was

already being done in 1544, when a Spanish visitor to the court of Henry VIII describes it as follows:

> Into the ... place they brought a pony with an ape fastened on its back, and to see the animal kicking amongst the dogs, with the screams of the ape, beholding the curs hanging from the ears and neck of the pony, is very laughable.[140]

Laughter, of course, is a notoriously subjective reflex, but Spanish guests and English hosts alike seem to have found much to enjoy in such spectacles. And the sheer diversity of related amusements bespeaks a lamentable richness of invention. The baiting of bears and bulls is so well known as to need little mention here; it was regarded as an English specialty. Cockfighting was widespread throughout Renaissance Europe. The whipping of blind bears also elicited mirth from the London theatergoing crowd. And then there were more rarified pastimes, made possible by the influx of exotic beasts into private menageries. When Pope Pius II and Galeazzo Maria Sforza visited Florence in 1459, they were regaled with a beast hunt in which lions were loosed on a collection of bulls, horses, boars, dogs, and a giraffe. The lions sensibly lay down and refused to play.[141] On June 3, 1515, Manuel I of Portugal arranged a confrontation between a rhinoceros and a young elephant, the latter of which panicked and burst free of the fighting enclosure.[142] By the early 1600s, King James I of England was baiting lions at the Tower of London.[143]

THE BIRTH OF COMPASSION

These amusements say a good deal about the emotional life of men and women in Renaissance Europe. If one believes, as I do, that the reactions we would take as evidence of an infant's capacity for fear and suffering should serve as evidence of a similar capacity in other animals, then the terror of Manuel's elephant also speaks to the emotional life of Renaissance beasts.

The resulting mental environment, like much else surveyed in this introduction, seems to extend and diversify medieval habits of mind and behavior. Like pet keeping, the maintenance of menageries, the culture of the hunt, the judicial punishment of animals, and the language of the bestiaries, blood sports appear to grow more widespread and variable in the fifteenth and sixteenth centuries. To this extent, the animal Renaissance may be viewed as an acceleration of tendencies already manifest in earlier European culture.

Yet at the same time one can detect unexpected pressures and opportunities that modify the older historical trends. After the battles of Agincourt and Crécy, the medieval cult of the warhorse begins a long, slow slide into archaism. Trade and exploration introduce new animal species to Europe, where they enrich breeding stock, enhance private zoos, embellish clothing, and enliven, as it were, the supper table. Under the pressure of new zoological discoveries, natural historians begin to invest their research with an unprecedented emphasis on verifiable observation. The discovery of taxidermy makes it possible to transform animals into inert and preservable matter.

Amidst these varying trends we may perhaps also recognize the emergence of a distinctive compassion for and emotional identification with animals. In its most basic form, this sympathy derives from the Middle Ages, as we have already noted. Yet where Chaucer's Prioress participates in a culture of effete privilege in which her humanitarian sentiments serve as a marker of preciosity, the Renaissance produces a sympathetic reaction to animal abuse that is largely bourgeois and sectarian in nature. In 1550 Robert Crowley could already describe the "terrible tearynge" of dogs and bears as "a full ouglye syght."[144] By 1597, Thomas Beard could warn his readers not to "delight themselues with the cruelty of beasts" rather than with "works of mercy & religion."[145] And in 1583, Philip Stubbes could exclaim,

> what christe[n] heart ca[n] take pleasure to see one poore beast to rent, teare and kill another[?] ... For notwithstanding that they be euill to us, & thirst after our blood, yet are thei good creatures in their own nature & kind. ... [S]hall we abuse ye creatures of God, yea take pleasure in abusing the[m], & yet think y^t the contumely don to the[m], redou[n]deth not to him who made them?[146]

These remarks attest to the growth of a widespread, organized body of belief that, among other things, encouraged sympathetic identification with the suffering of animals. This, like so much else involving the relations between human beings and animals, is a distinctive product of the Renaissance.

CHAPTER ONE

"Fowle Fowles"?

The Sacred Pelican and the Profane Cormorant
in Early Modern Culture

KEVIN DE ORNELLAS

INTRODUCTION

Geoffrey Whitney's 1586 *Choice of Emblemes and Other Devises* includes two pieces featuring the birds addressed in this chapter. One of the emblems—which wed moralizing verse to related visual images—shows the cormorant exhibiting what was popularly considered its primary habit—greedy, ruthless consumption of fish; another emblem demonstrates the pelican's supposed character of selfless bounty. In the former case, Whitney presents an emblem linking the routine perils of fish in the sea to the vulnerability of lower sorts who would seek to advance in early modern society (see Figure 1.1). The woodcut depicts a crudely rendered fish that has attracted the attention of two swooping birds. In the accompanying text, the birds are identified as either cormorants or seagulls—the illustrations, however, do not depict either species accurately. The accompanying lines of verse articulate a truism about life in the ocean—and in a hierarchical society.

> THE mightie fishe, deuowres the little frie,
> If in the deepe, they venture for to staie,
> If vp they swimme, newe foes with watching flie,
> The caruoraune [cormorant], and Seamewe [seagull], for theire praie:
> Betweene these two, the frie is still destroi'de,
> Ah feeble state, on euerie side anoi'de.[1]

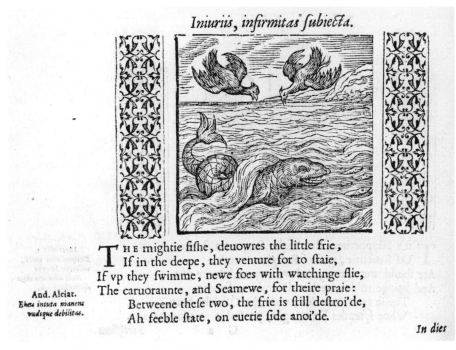

FIGURE 1.1: Woodcut, Geoffrey Whitney, *A Choice of Emblems and Other Devises* (Leiden, 1586), sig. G2v.

The "the little frie" is doomed if it seeks to move away from its ordained station. Larger fish will destroy it if it swims down into the underworld. And voracious seabirds will consume it if it swims too close to the water's surface. The Aesop-like moral for humans is clear: stick to your own station in life; those who seek inappropriate advancement will fail completely. The seagull ("Seamewe") has often been associated with an aggressive destructiveness, being depicted as aggressive even to humanity both in fictional and in ostensibly factual representations.[2] But the cormorant has had a more consistent and more damaging reputation as a purely vicious, opportunistic beast—as described in Whitney's emblem.

One species of the cormorant, *Phalacrocorax Carbo,* sometimes called the "Great Cormorant" is a large, familiar, but endangered bird in Britain, native to water habitats around the isles. For centuries, it has been proverbially viewed as depraved by gluttony. Indeed, many local, unofficial names for the cormorant in British regions—*gormer, goulimaw, gurmaw*—derive from a French root meaning "glutton."[3] Whitney exploits the bird's dark reputation to illuminate a moral point for his readers. His treatment of the species as a yardstick of human greed is typical of Renaissance—and post-Renaissance— investments in cormorant imagery. By complete contrast, the pelican is seen as a self-sacrificing, noble bird. In another of Whitney's emblems, a six-line poem

cites the pelican as a role model for us all (see Figure 1.2). The first two lines
of the verse describe the Pelican's feeding of its young in supposedly factual
terms:

> THE Pellican, for to reuiue her younge,
> Doth pierce her brest, and geue them of her blood.[4]

Gendered feminine, the pelican is maternal and giving, as gentle and consider-
ate as the cormorant is hostile and selfish. A perfect parent, careless of her own
well-being, the bird will injure herself to nourish her chicks. None of the several species of pelican are native to Britain.[5] In present-day England, pelicans
are seen only in collections of exotic wildfowl, while in early modern England,
actual pelicans were nowhere to be seen. Consequently, the popular belief that
the bird fed its young in such a manner was fanned by books and oral myths
that lacked fidelity to ornithological fact.

  Because no Englishman or woman could have seen a pelican in England during the period, the myth that the bird pricked its breast to feed its young was a
powerful one. The myth was exploited by Whitney, and many other artists and

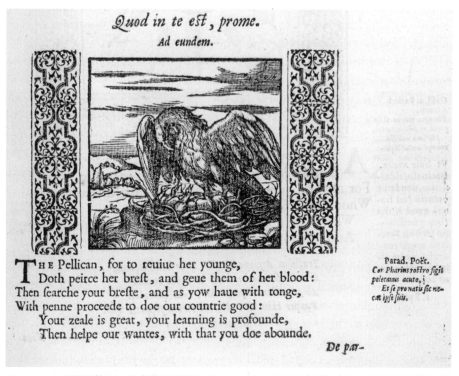

FIGURE 1.2: Woodcut, Geoffrey Whitney, *A Choice of Emblems and Other Devises*
(Leiden, 1586), sig. L4r.

writers, to make moral, socially relevant points. Whitney goes on to urge us to
behave like a mothering pelican:

> Then searche your breste, and as yow haue with tonge,
> With penne proceede to doe our countrie good:
> Your zeale is great, your learning is profounde,
> Then helpe our wantes, with that you doe abounde.[6]

It is not clear whom Whitney addresses as "yow," nor is it clear which "countrie" the person addressed should serve through writing. And the link between
writing and useful national service also remains vague. Moreover, the pelican
is not illustrated and accounted for in verse to satisfy some sort of curiosity about nonresident birds. Like the cormorant, it has a constructed identity
quite distinct from the material realities of its physical existence. The bird is
used to make a moral point: you should be as self-sacrificing as the pelican is.
In Renaissance English writing, many sermonizers, compilers of salient facts,
moralizing characters in plays, and didactic poets make similar points: humans
should behave more like the emblematic, generous pelican and less like the
emblematic, selfish cormorant.

In contemporary Britain, the nonnative pelican is regarded as an exotic
bird to be admired, an impressive, splendid creature. The presence of cherished
specimens in the managed environment of St. James's Park illustrates the appeal of these large, fish-eating birds: the pelicans have been a feature of the
park since their initial introduction in 1664.[7] By complete contrast, the native
cormorant is perceived as a monstrous beast that does nothing but prey on fish.
In the twenty-first century, the cormorant is still seen as greedy, selfish, voracious, and unnecessary. As I will show, the cormorant's bad reputation has led
to the angling-driven, government-sanctioned, mass slaughter of the animal.
I contend that this treatment of the hungry cormorant is the culmination of a
demonizing process that can be traced to the English Renaissance. In the sixteenth and seventeenth centuries, the cormorant was castigated as vermin and
mentioned only as a convenient parallel to the basest of human drives. It represented everything that benevolent Christian ethics denounced. The pelican,
however, was perceived to be sacred and Christ-like because of utterly spurious
assumptions about its self-sacrificing way of feeding its young. In this chapter,
I analyze some of the myriad Renaissance representations of these two birds,
popularly thought to be poles apart in terms of moral character.

Many birds in the period were associated with human characteristics. But
barring the ubiquitous allusions to the cuckoo—a symbol of marital infidelity,
of course—the cormorant and pelican appear to be the birds most inextricably
linked to their supposed traits: self-sacrifice on the part of the pelican, selfish greed on the part of the cormorant. It seems that every time a cormorant

appears in a printed early modern text, it is denigrated as appetitive and base; with an almost equal comprehensiveness, the pelican is linked to self-abnegating generosity. I write "almost" because while many sixteenth- and seventeenth-century writers rehearse the notion that the pelican is a totem of munificence, Shakespeare twists this proverbial association to create cynical overtones in a number of his plays. The first section of this chapter engages with Renaissance imaginings of the pelican, uncovering the variety of uses that its supposed generosity facilitated and culminating with Shakespeare's challenge to the bird's sacredness. This chapter's second section then pursues the supposed profanity of the Renaissance cormorant, accounting for the hatred that the animal inspired and outlining its use in sixteenth-century texts as a bestial analog to man's culpability. The third section pursues further the early modern investment in the construction of the devilish cormorant. Writers employ the Renaissance cormorant as a vehicle for satirical commentary on early modern commerce. With particular reference to a little-read pamphlet by John Taylor in which a "cormorant" speaks, I argue that fictional constructions of this bird constitute an all-too-piquant reflection of early modern readers. Anthropomorphized, the cormorant becomes too much like ourselves. The chapter's final section outlines some post-Renaissance engagements with both the material and the metaphorical cormorant. There is an alarming continuity between printed Renaissance depictions of the greedy cormorant and later depictions of this supposedly unwholesome species—a continuity outlined in this final section. Renaissance appearances of the profane cormorant in print lead us ultimately to conclude that Renaissance demonizations have somehow influenced present-day contempt for this now-endangered species. Unambiguously corrupt and evil, the Renaissance cormorant is the beast that must—still, in 2007—be driven away from the island of Britain.

THE PELICAN: WHOLLY PIOUS?

In Whitney's emblem, the pelican is cited as an exemplary being, one to be copied in the sense that it abnegates the self to promote the general good. Good servants of good countries sacrifice themselves like pelicans. A propagandist painting of Elizabeth I, dating from the mid-1570s, illustrates that the pelican-inspired connection between moral righteousness and patriotic devotion was valued by the Tudor establishment. This painting, attributed to Nicholas Hilliard and called "The Pelican Portrait" (see Figure 1.3), depicts a heavily jeweled, elaborately dressed Elizabeth in an attitude of poise and control.[8] A pendant in the shape of a pelican appears right in the center of Elizabeth's chest. Quite literally, the pelican is close to the monarch's heart; presented in graphic detail, the bright, shiny bird pricks its chest, causing a clear, substantial bleeding. The blood, bodied forth through a vivid redness, is as central to the identity of the idealized pelican as the idealized pelican is central to the idealized Elizabeth. The pelican appears, significantly, in a line directly below Elizabeth's facial features, with its head bent in the direction of Elizabeth's calm gaze. The pelican is often gendered feminine in representations of the period; for instance, the second, 1580 installment of John Lyly's prose romance *Euphues* relates moral conduct matter-of-factly to "the Pelicane, who striketh bloud out of hir owne body to doe others good."[9] The proverbial generosity of the pelican figures in George Wither's poetical epistle of 1615, *Fidelia,* which counsels a "comely" woman to be as "kinde or meeker than" a "Turtle Doue or Pelican."[10] A woman, then, should have the passivity of a dove, combined with the self-sacrificing bounty of the pelican. On top of its association with romanticized femininity, the pelican is also frequently bracketed with motherhood. In the "Pelican Portrait," Elizabeth functions as the romanticized mother of England, prepared to endure pain and loss to serve her subjects.

FIGURE 1.3: Nicholas Hilliard (attr.), *Queen Elizabeth I: The Pelican Portrait,* Liverpool, Walker Art Gallery.

The date of the painting is ironic. If we accept the conventional dating of ca. 1574, then Elizabeth was in her early fifties; hopes that the Queen could marry and procreate had already faded. The "Pelican Portrait," then, marks a crucial stage in the decline of the Tudor monarchy. Unable to nurture real children, Elizabeth can only cite the pelican as she is seen to nurture her country metaphorically.

The Tudor painting's investment in pelican imagery is clearly secular, contrived to project an image of a controlled, sensitive, generous leadership. This secular appropriation of the myth draws on representations of bountiful pelicans present in earlier texts. In Thomas Paynell's 1572 translation of the medieval European romance *Amadis of Fraunce,* Anaxartes vows to cause himself anguish to curry favor with the princess who has banished him,[11] even "doing more than the Pelicane for hir little ones."[12] This 1572 appearance of the medieval pelican myth not only illustrates how fictional characters strive to emulate the generosity of the pelican, but also demonstrates how an originally medieval text may preserve the pelican's reputation for ascetic conduct into the late sixteenth century. The Christian appropriation of the legend of the dutiful, suffering pelican derives from biblical imagery and didactic writings by early theologians.[13] In pious texts of the Middle Ages, the suggestion that humans should engage in pelican-like behavior becomes increasingly self-conscious. In a twelfth-century bestiary by the French moralist Hugh of Fouilloy, the pelican is reported to kill its chicks deliberately, so that they can be revived after three days in a clear parallel of Christ's resurrection.[14] According to the very unscientific natural history of the medieval writer, as God gives life, so does the pelican. The bird is said to be incapable of gluttony because of its small stomach capacity. Hugh of Fouilloy professes to envy the ascetic discipline of the idolized bird. "If only the life of the monk might become like this pelican, who eats little," he exclaims.[15] The pelican is not capable of any sort of hedonistic excess: the bird "does not live to eat, but eats to live."[16] It is revered because it cannot pursue any sort of meritless, worldly pleasure. The propaganda of Elizabeth's "Pelican Portrait," then, is secular in identity, but draws on long-established religious imagery to insist that the Queen lives to serve England, not to enjoy the benefits of high rank and status.

As mother of England, Elizabeth I will be like a pelican in that she serves others, recalling the humility of the self-denying Christ. More modest comparisons between human and pelican conduct abound in factual and fictional Renaissance texts. In a 1596 translation of an Italian prose narrative, *The Nature of a Woman,* an aging Duke employs the following comparison as he promises to give his sons good advice:

> It is reported of the Pelican, that with her owne blood she reuiued her
> dead yong, and so I though wanting blood to recall you from the dead

pleasures of yoong secure delights, yet shal my latest breath counsel you
to the careful desire of virtuous deedes.[17]

The Duke's remarks are evidently serious in their assertive comparison of the
exemplary pelican's behavior with the stern advice of a father who would steer
his children away from the seductive temptations of secular society. But the
allusion to the pelican could also be received in a negative way; the Duke uses
the striking aural imagery of his description of the blood-giving pelican to attract attention, to captivate his audience before rehearsing his rather dreary,
formulaic advice about the perils of gambling and sex.

   During the Renaissance, less cynical, demonstrably sincere allusions to the
pelican feature in devotional contexts. In William Drummond's *Flowres of Sion*
(1623), we are asked to gaze with wonder upon the legend of the mothering
pelican, because it will enhance our sense of wonder at the miracle of Christ's
resurrection. If we are amazed that

> The pelican poures from her brest her Blood,
> To bring to life her yonglings back againe?
> How should wee wonder of that soueraigne Good,
> Who from that Serpents sting (that had vs slaine)
> To saue our lifes, shed his Lifes purple flood,
> And turn'd in endless Ioy our endless Paine?[18]

Drummond's imagery insists not only upon a comparison between Christ and
the pelican, but upon the need for worshippers to retain a sense of awe. We
should be amazed, dazzled by Christ. Stories about natural wonders pale into
insignificance when contrasted with the world-changing generosity of the Sav-
ior. Drummond's highly regular, iambic verse may not appear fresh today, but
the call for a revivifying, wonder-struck devotion remains compelling. However, in another publication of 1623, Shakespeare's First Folio, the notion that
the pelican can be cited unproblematically as a yardstick for human goodness
is complicated because the myth is used cynically by self-interested male characters in times of crisis.

   The pelican is cited three times in Shakespeare's 1623 Folio.[19] In *Richard II*
(ca. 1595), John of Gaunt expresses his contempt for the decadent waste-
fulness of his young nephew, King Richard, by comparing Richard's father,
Edward the Black Prince, to a generous pelican:

> Oh spare me not, my brothers Edwards sonne,
> For that I was his father Edwards sonne:
> That blood already (like the Pellican)
> Thou hast tapt out, and drunkenly carows'd.[20]

In this speech, Gaunt retains the age-old discourse of the blood-donating, selfless parent, but the language used to describe Richard's acceptance of the blood ambiguates the concept of the pious bird. The unusual, clinical-sounding verb, *tapt*, depicts Richard as a greedy, ruthless consumer of parental bounty. In Gaunt's formulation, the Pelican can be an exemplary parent—but it can also be a voracious, self-interested child. In the previous representations of the pelican that I have addressed, agency always lies with the parent bird, who gives its blood through its own initiative. Richard, the greedy chick, demands to be fed, and fed well, metaphorically drinking "drunkenly" to excess. If the pelican young can be used figuratively to excoriate the conduct of one party, then the idealized concept of the giving, devoted pelican must be subject to complication.

In *Hamlet* (ca. 1600), another highly anxious, action-demanding character cites the pelican in equally ambiguous fashion. In Act Four, Laertes flies into a vengeance-seeking rage over the death of his father, Polonius. With hyperbole that recalls Anaxartes in *Amadis of Fraunce*, Laertes promises to reward anyone who will help him avenge the killing:

> To his [Polonius'] good Friends, thus wide Ile ope my Armes:
> And like the kinde Life-rend'ring Politician [*sic*],
> Repast them with my blood.[21]

A grateful Laertes will give as freely as the pelican gives life to its young. The Folio noun, *Politician,* is an error—the word appears correctly as *Pelican* in the 1604 Quarto of *Hamlet*.[22] It is tempting to suggest that the Folio misprint of *Pelican* as *Politician* is some sort of subconscious slip on behalf of the compositor. A generous, life-giving politician would be a rare thing indeed; still, it is possible—though impossible to prove—that the *Pelican* was not named properly in the 1623 text because the cliché of the self-sacrificing Pelican parent was not as inevitable as it may have been in the past.

Laertes, despite his bluster, cites the pelican in a calculated, cynical way, but the reference seems to refresh Claudius. During the previous fifty-odd lines of verse, Claudius has responded to Laertes' rage only in monosyllables: "Dead," "Let him demand his fill," and "Who shall stay you." Seizing on Laertes' pelican imagery, though, Claudius becomes articulate once more, denying (truthfully) any involvement in Polonius' death:

> Why now you speake
> Like a good Childe, and a true Gentleman.
> That I am guiltlesse of your fathers death,
> And am most sensible in greefe for it,
> It shall as luell [level] to your Iudgement pierce
> As day do's to your eye.[23]

Professing "greefe" as well as innocence, Claudius buys time to mollify and patronize the young Laertes, whose cynical use of the pelican image thus seems to inspire equal cynicism in the king. A pelican may well be pious, but its value as an exemplary beast is surely marred by the manner in which it is appropriated by self-concerned characters at moments of potential political disaster.

In Act Three of *King Lear,* written about six years after *Hamlet,* the pelican is cited in a bitter, hostile manner. Lear, observing the pitiful state of Edgar's alter ego, Poor Tom, aggressively tells Kent that only unsavory daughters could bring a man so low:

> Death Traitor, nothing could haue subdu'd Nature
> To such a lownesse, but his vnkind Daughters.
> Is it the fashion, that discarded Fathers,
> Should have thus little mercy on their flesh:
> Iudicious punishment, 'twas this flesh begot
> Those Pelicane Daughters.[24]

Here, the kindness of the parent pelican has been forgotten by disreputable children. Like Gaunt before him, Lear alludes to his enemies—his estranged daughters, Goneril and Regan—as pelican chicks. In the process, Lear does not even bother to mention the willing suffering of the parent pelican. It seems that in the bleak world of Shakespeare's tragedies, the pelican is a symbol not of piety but of antagonistic greed.

As it happens, scripture also casts doubt on the image of the unstained, spotless pelican, and early English biblical translators experience some confusion over this fact. At two points in the prophetic books of Isaiah (34.11) and Zephaniah (2.14), the pelican is described as an unclean animal, one fit only for a sinful, desolate landscape bereft of heavenly love. These references to morally unfit pelicans are retained in most Renaissance translations of the Bible in English; the Bishops' Bible, the Great Bible, and the Geneva Bible refer to an unholy pelican.[25] But in the Authorized, "King James" Bible of 1611, the unclean pelican has disappeared, replaced in both Isaiah and Zephaniah by an unclean cormorant.[26] The compilers expunged the unclean pelican from the main text with no apparent textual authority or precedent. In some circles, then, the binary of the opposition between the Christ-like pelican and the unsavory cormorant was not just maintained but perpetuated. In the three Shakespearean references to the pelican, its unsullied reputation is complicated by comparisons of its young with degenerate children. More recently, the pelican has not been lauded for its moral righteousness, although the species is admired for its spectacular appearance. The cormorant, however, is still often lambasted as a greedy, useless creature. Is it a coincidence that Shakespeare complicates the notion of a bountiful pelican just as myths about the bird began to lose their utility? And is it a coincidence that the cormorant has been continually demonized in a manner consistent with its treatment by Shakespeare?

THE CORMORANT: DEMONIZED UNAMBIGUOUSLY

The cormorant appears four times in Shakespeare's *oeuvre*. In all four references, the bird serves unambiguously as an exemplar of virulent greed. King Ferdinand of Navarre in *Love's Labour's Lost* decries the rapacity of a personified "cormorant deuouring Time."[27] Gaunt, employing a less complex metaphor than in his pelican allusion, attacks the irresponsible, resource-wasting greed of Richard II by calling him an "insatiate Cormorant."[28] Another weakened figure, King Priam in *Troilus and Cressida,* rails against "this comorant [*sic*] Warre" between Greeks and Trojans.[29] And in *Coriolanus,* an angry citizen of Rome complains about the alleged fixing of corn prices by "the Cormorant belly" of the state.[30] The concerns expressed by the Roman character reflect the cormorant's association with human financial skullduggery—an association that I will address in the next section of this chapter. The immediate thing to note about these four appearances of the cormorant is that they link the bird unproblematically to disastrous, death-causing trials: food shortages, war, and the ravages of time. Unambiguously, consistently, the Shakespearean cormorant illuminates the catastrophic, the disastrous. Notably the exact grammatical identity of the word *Cormorant* remains unclear in a number of these references. Does an actor playing Navarre think of the word *cormorant* in "cormorant deuouring Time" as an adjective or as a noun? And does the actor playing Priam intone his lines to suggest that "Warre" is like a *comorant,* or to suggest that *cormorant* is an adjective describing "Warre"? The lack of punctuation in the 1623 Folio leaves us wondering whether or not the word *cormorant* can be used as an adjective that describes nouns. Yet while the correct linguistic terminology for Shakespeare's citations of the cormorant remains elusive, it is clear that he draws upon a cultural stereotype of the cormorant as proverbially greedy and rapacious. There is no complication of this myth in Shakespeare: the four Shakespearean references to the cormorant reflect and indeed perpetuate the Renaissance demonization of this unhappy bird.

A brief survey of representations of the cormorant in sixteenth-century texts underlines the bird's reputation for greed. In an anonymous attack on Cardinal Wolsey dating from 1528—a mischief-making pamphlet called *Rede Me and Be Nott Wroth* that caused considerable perturbation for the Henrician establishment—Iaffraye (Jeffrey), one of two priests' servants who discuss the current state of religious orders, claims that monks will lavish attention on a rich man while poor men are lucky if

> They get a feue broken scrap /
> Of these cormorant levynge.[31]

The monks are greedy "cormorants"; they donate precious little to the poor. If a charity-seeking man is to be fed at all in an abbey, his meal will consist of scraps left over from the table of the selfish "cormorants." The cormorant's reputation for greed, then, is used as a weapon in an attack upon the perceived stinginess of Christian establishments. In a less politically sensitive but more sensationalist text published in English in 1569, *Certaine Secrete Wonders of Nature,* Pierre Boaistuau writes about the alleged greed of Alexander. The book combines amazing facts and stories from history with reflective morals that are relevant to the present. Boaistuau uses Alexander, whom he describes simply as "that great Cormorant," to illustrate an ever-present sin in human society: "that wicked and infortunate vice of glutonie."[32] Here, to be like a cormorant is to be focused primarily upon worldly matters, to eschew productive industry whether material or spiritual. Boaistuau's cormorant is a beast that can be emulated disastrously by humans; we will end up like the decadent, ineffective Alexander if we behave like the gluttonous cormorant.

In one of Thomas Churchyard's less-celebrated works, *Churchyards Challenge,* originally written in the 1560s, greedy men are denigrated as cormorant-like. Churchyard writes that

> Of cormorant kind some crammed Capons are,
> The more they eate, the more they may consume.[33]

Persons who eat too much are impotent fools, like cocks ("Capons") that have lost their sexual capacity through castration. The harsh, alliterative consonance—"cormorant," "kind," "crammed," "Capons," "consume"—rams home the message that excessive eating is beastly, a self-perpetuating downward spiral into physical and moral degeneracy. *Cormorant* is an adjective here— persons who eat like avaricious fools can be summed up if they are described as "cormorant"-like beasts. An even more striking image of cormorant-like sinning is called for in a dramatic text of the 1570s, Thomas Lupton's *All for Money.* There, Hell's inhabitants speak about the depravity that got them rejected from Heaven. At this point in the play, Judas and "Diues" (diverse persons) are onstage, so it is not quite clear whether or not it is Judas or one of the other damned souls who speaks the lines next quoted. It is clear, however, that the speaker must be dressed in a hellish black. This illustrates a connection that becomes more urgent during Shakespeare's period—the connection between the profane Cormorant and the conduct of satanic malefactors. A Hell-trapped soul laments his piteous state:

> Wo, wo, and wo againe to me for euermore,
> That consumed so much on my selfe and nothing on the poore:
> Poore Lazarus was at my doore, whose hunger was so great
> That he therewith soone died not hauing for to eate.
> When I with all fine fare lyke a glutton was serued
> And like a greedie cormorant with belly full forced.[34]

It is not easy being as gluttonous as a cormorant: excessive food has to be crammed ("full forced") into the stomach. This dramatic notion of the poor going hungry as the spoiled, cormorant-like middle sorts are served luxuriously recalls the attack on the allegedly stingy monks in *Rede Me and Be Nott Wrothe*. But in Lupton's play, we have an aural and visual dramatic assertion that to eat heartily while ignoring the undernourished poor is to be "like a greedie cormorant." In the period just before the time of Shakespeare, Englishmen and women could read about the cormorant's proverbial greed on the page, and they could see and hear about it on stage. By demonizing the cormorant, Shakespeare worked within a Renaissance tradition that castigated the bird almost unthinkingly. These sixteenth-century writers had no interest in the cormorant as a material beast. Rather, they used popular mythology about its supposed greed to make points about contemporary politics and to give advice about the inevitable destination for persons who behave like cormorants—Hell. The cultural exploitation of the Cormorant as a byword for gluttonous sin continued well into the seventeenth century and beyond, and became part of sophisticated attacks upon very particular social abuses.

THE CORMORANT: ITS ALIGNMENT WITH SOCIAL ILLS

In the pre-Shakespearean texts cited previously, the cormorant acquires proverbial associations with greed. Further, toward the end of the sixteenth century, the cormorant becomes a familiar emblem not only of greed but also of covetousness. In these later texts, men who are like cormorants experience not only their own insatiate lust for material excess but also the desire to deprive other men of their possessions. The cormorant becomes a symbol for cruel exploiters of the poor. In the 1528 satire *Rede Me and Be Nott Wrothe*, the monks are like greedy cormorants; Pierre Boaistuau's gluttonous, cormorant-like Alexander seems to destroy only himself. But in later sixteenth- and seventeenth-century texts, cormorant-like people seek energetically to cheat and swindle others. Angell Day's successful epistle-writing manual of 1586,

The English Secretorie, relates an anecdote about a cynical man who exploits a poor neighbor. It is worth quoting at length, because it typifies early modern horror stories about greedy landlords, and is typical in its castigation of exploitative businessmen as covetous cormorants:

> Hee [the poor man] had dealings with a neighbour … touching a farme whiche hee was for terme of yeares to take at his handes, and notwithstanding a promise and graunt thereof to this bearer made, in consideration whereof, hee payde him then in hand a good part of his mony[.] the iniurious cormorant glutting himselfe with extorting from the pouertie of this and many others, hath sithence that, not onely passed a demise as his act & deed in writing to an other, but goeth about to defraud the poore soule of his mony.[35]

The businessman is a cheat, one who pursues capital gain by breaking agreements and confidences. He does not honor his promise to rent the farm to the would-be tenant, and he keeps the money that the client has deposited with him. The poor man—"the poore soule"—is cheated by a devilish, cormorant-like scoundrel who causes harm to others. This is not just a one-off, hard-luck story about one hapless poor man, but an epitome of a widescale social evil—the maintenance of a discriminatory system that keeps the lower sorts dependent upon the elusive good faith of the middle sorts. To be like a cormorant is to be not just greedy but willfully contemptuous of other men's livelihoods.

Day's anecdote about a cormorant-like, extorting landlord is a cutting example of how early modern entrepreneurs were often accused of financial skullduggery. Although bitingly satirical, Day's anecdote appears within a morally neutral context; Day's wider project is to educate readers about the conventions of letter-writing. The tale of the racketeering landlord merely typifies the sort of prose that may be written in epistles. In a 1596 work by Thomas Bell, *The Speculation of Vsurie,* another alleged social evil receives a proverbial allusion to the covetous cormorant, and here, the intention is avowedly didactic and moralistic. Bell, a one-time Catholic priest turned propagandist for Burghley's Protestant regime, relates a professedly factual story about a moneylender who exploits the desperation of the poor. The anecdote's power derives from its simplicity:

> I heard of another poore man, who came to a rich cormorant to borrow money, but receiued this answere, I haue no money to lend (quoth the rich man) but thou hast a good mare, for which I will giue thee fiue nobles, and so thou shale haue money to doe thy needes: alas quoth the poore man I am not able to spare my mare, because shee is the greatest part of my poore liuing, wel saith the rich man, thou shalt presently haue her againe til a day, if thou wilt enter into bond, to giue me seuen nobles

for her: to which lamentable extortion, the poore man was inforced to yield.[36]

The gains of the "rich cormorant" may be minor—he may only gain two nobles if the poor man returns tomorrow with the seven nobles needed to buy back his crucial working animal. But the rich man may get to keep the horse, and if that happens, the impoverished, desperate man may lose his basic livelihood. The cormorant will destroy the most vulnerable, pitiful members of society for trivial financial gains; if he is "rich," he surely does not need two more gold coins. In this anecdote, we can see how far the metaphorical cormorant is from the material bird. The physical bird may well gulp down fish with what may be interpreted as an enthusiastic vigor, but the man who is like a cormorant will satisfy his own greed by wreaking havoc upon any person who is vulnerable to exploitation.

Bell's story of the cormorant-like usurer ends almost triumphantly, as he tells us that "this vsurer to the ensample of all others hath lately made a miserable ende."[37] The (unexplained) demise of the moneylender is exemplary: we too will suffer dreadful deaths if we behave like oppressive cormorants. I say "oppressive" because the cormorant became a synonym for human oppression of others as well as greed and covetousness. In the polemical sermonizing of the Anglican clergyman Thomas Adams, the cormorant is one of a number of birds that symbolize depravity and anti-Protestant conduct: in Adams's own words, "Sometimes we haue the wicked likened to fowles."[38] In *The Blacke Devil or the Apostate* (1615), Adams recounts the sins of those who behave like covetous cormorants in a deceptively vague manner:

> There is the Cormorant, the Corne-vo-rant; the Mire-drumble, the Covetous: that are euer rooting and rotting their hearts in the mire of this world.[39]

Here, the cormorant-like party is devilish because he is both gluttonous and slothful. This is as conventional as any of the cormorant allusions cited previously. However, Adams's cormorant allusion appears just after a comparison of the owl with militant Catholics:

> There is the Owle, the night-bird, the Iesuited Seminary; that sculkes all day in a hollow tree, in some Popish vault; and at euen howtes [hoots] his masses, and skreeks downefall and ruine to the King, Church, and Common-wealth.[40]

An owl is not a cormorant, of course, but Adams clearly represents both species of birds as parallel to evil people who threaten Protestant society's stability. In

Adams's sectarian discourse, the owl spreads evil at night as does the Mass-saying Jesuit and sleeps in holes in trees as Catholics sleep in priest-holes. Although each bird represents a particular sin, Adams makes a deliberate connection between them: some enemies of Protestant civility "haue in them the pernicious nature of all these foule fowles."[41] To be like an owl is also to be like a cormorant. In this sense, the cormorant represents all that is covetous and oppressive in the enemies of the monarchical Christian state. In a St. Paul's Cross sermon published a decade after *The Blacke Devil,* Adams returns to his theme of birds as parallels of vice. He tells us that in "the voice of the ... Cormorant" we hear "couetousnesse and oppression."[42] This seventeenth-century tendency to equate the Cormorant with oppression of the decent, Protestant poor was exploited to a huge degree in a populist work by John Taylor, the "Water Poet."

In 1622, Taylor published a verse satire entitled *The Water-Cormorant His Complaint.* It is prefaced with a crude portrait of a cormorant, of the type found typically in inexpensive books of the late Jacobean period (see Figure 1.4). This is no significant contribution to the history of avian illustration, but it does supply a pointed image of the species doing what it is axiomatically assumed to do without stop: eating fish. A sort of motto is placed just above the woodcut: this couplet acts almost as an alternative long title for the work:

> My Cormorant against these doth inuey,
> And proues himself much better for than they.[43]

"They" refers, in this context, to the various representatives of social evils whom Taylor's cormorant will castigate: a "Iesuite," a "Drunkard," a "Prodigall Gallant," and a "Cutpurse." In other words, the cormorant gives voice to Taylor's own prejudices, which include a hatred for Catholics, drinkers, unthrifty youngsters, and thieves.

Taylor—who very self-consciously wrote books to please a paying readership—seeks to satirize the aligned evils of Catholics and criminals by suggesting that the depraved cormorant is superior to both.[44] After another inelegant woodcut, this time depicting fourteen (barely recognizable) cormorants, and after a six-line summary of the book's purpose, which is to "tell these earthly Cormorants [sinning men] their faults," Taylor's prose address engages the reader directly.[45] The author acknowledges that his sustained use of the cormorant trope is novel and eye-opening:

> Svbiects may seeme scarce, or Printers lacke worke, when a Cormorant
> flies into the Presse, yet Cormorants oppresse and therefore [are] worthy
> to be prest.[46]

The concept of the oppressive cormorant recalls the moralizing of Adams and Bell in which exploitative humans are compared to covetous, oppressive

FIGURE 1.4: Frontispiece, John Taylor, *The Water-Cormorant His Complaint* (London, 1622).

cormorants. If a cormorant can oppress others through its greed—it is not clear here if Taylor refers to the actual bird or the human sinners who resemble it—then it can be "prest" by a printer who works as a functionary in the publishing of a text. But Taylor's avian conceit is developed still further, with the

worst habits of the birds compared favorably with the habits of the alleged
sinners that Taylor attacks:

> His [the Cormorant's] colour is blacke, I discouer deeds of darknesse. He
> grubs and spuddles for his prey in muddy holes and obscure cauerns, my
> muse ferrits base debauched wretches in their swinish dens ... The ods is,
> my Cormorants appetite is limited, but most of theirs is vnsatiable.[47]

The visual and moral blackness of the cormorant is shallow compared with the
bestial malevolence of the human cormorants that so exercise Taylor's ire. The
corporeal bird has a bottom to its pit of avaricious depravity, but the sins of
Catholics and criminals seem endless.

The main part of *The Water-Cormorant* presents a number of sinful characters. The first-person narrative of the cormorant, promised on the frontispiece,
does not materialize; instead, Taylor refers to the cormorant in the third person, citing its sins but dismissing them relative to the vices of those who oppress
English society. The first breed of sinner to be anatomized is the Jesuit, who is
compared superficially but powerfully to the comparatively innocent cormorant:

> First black's the coulour of the greedy fowle,
> And black's the Iesuits habite like his soule,
> The bird is leane though oft he be full craw'd,
> The Iesuit's hatchet fac'd, and wattle iaw'd,
> The Cormorant (as nature best befits)
> Still without chewing doth deuoure whole bits,
> So Iesuits swallow many a lordly liuing,
> All at a gulp without grace or thanksgiuing.
> The birds throat (gaping) without intermission,
> Resembles their most cruell inquisition.[48]

The comparison between the black fowl and the black-caped and black-hearted
Jesuit is evidently absurd and credible only rhetorically, but may find an appre-
ciative audience among those who see members of the Society of Jesus as exem-
plifying the wickedness of the unreformed Roman Church. Taylor's cormorant
is not as bad as a Jesuit, but it is still very bad, a negative image of a decent
Protestant. But Catholics are not the only religious tribe lambasted by Taylor
in *The Water-Cormorant His Complaint*. Independent sects are also attacked
for their supposed gluttony, avarice, and sexual perversion:

> That two of them like greedy Cormorants,
> Deuoures more then six honest Protestants.

When priuately a sister and a brother
Doe meet, ther's dainty doings with each other.[49]

Persons with more quotidian sins than those of Jesuits and sectaries are attacked
too. A "Trust-Breaker" is described as a greater thief than any cormorant—
"My Corm'rant is a piddler to him."[50] And a "Drunkard" is "a worse glutton
then my Cormorant."[51] In Taylor's work, the cormorant is compared favorably to the transgressing humans more than thirty times. The apotheosis of the
book's investment in Cormorant imagery perhaps comes near the end, when
a soothsayer—"a couzning cunning man"—is described consuming fools as
cormorants consume fish:

These [tricks] and a thousand more, as idley vaine
Fooles swallow, and he swallowes them againe,
And though the marke of truth he neuer hits,
Yet still the Cormorant doth liue by's wits,
And ne're will want a false deuouring tricke,
Till hels Archcormorant deuoure him quicke.[52]

The bluffing fortune teller who gulls susceptible people is irredeemable; he
will fool people for as long as he lives. But he will, at death, be swallowed up
by a greater cormorant—the devil. Long associated with hellish conduct, the
cormorant now is transmogrified into the devil himself. Over and above its sectarian rabble-rousing, Taylor's work urges us to reject any tendency toward the
oppression of others, because our souls will be swallowed up by the greatest
cormorant like the "little frie" consumed mercilessly by the vicious cormorants
in Whitney's epigram.

THE DEVILISH CORMORANT IN THE CIVIL
WARS AND BEYOND

Taylor's extended comparison between cormorants' supposed greed and human transgression is recalled in a more straightforwardly moralistic work of
1653 by Richard Younge—a Protestant preacher who, unlike the commerce-
minded Taylor, notoriously sought to give his books away. In *Philarguromastix, or The Arraignment of Covetousness*, Younge expands upon the Biblical
stricture that "there is an absolute contrariety ... between the love of God, and
the love of Money."[53] Persons who value money cannot value eternal life,
Younge insists. He provides numerous examples of human greed and compares
many of these evils to the alleged evil of the cormorant. For example, an en-
trepreneur who worries only about "the price of his Corn" and "the emptying

of other mens purses" is called, predictably, a cormorant.[54] This is formulaic, and fits in comfortably with the myriad previous references to the ill-
reputed bird of popular discourse. The difference is that Younge addresses the
exact contemporary moment by claiming that the unveiling of cormorant-like
scoundrels is "a subject very seasonable, for these Athiestical, and self-seeking
Times."[55] A scurrilous, lampooning pseudo-biography of 1652 also places cormorant imagery firmly, but subtly, within the context of civil conflict. George
Fidge's aggressive attack on William Marriott, *The Great Eater of Grayes
Inne, or The Life of Mr. Marriot the Cormorant,* contains a whole series of
extraordinary tales of the disgraceful greediness of Marriott, an alleged gour-
mand who "has more gutts then braines."[56] Many of the stories and linguistic
conceits are evidently contrived to amuse rather than inform—Fidge was not a
reliable biographer, as *The Great Eater* and other works indicate. In one tale,
we read of Marriott eating a dinner prepared for twenty men, with each plate
"cleanly licked" by the cormorant-like consumer of other men's food.[57] Still
more improbably, the drunken, insensate Marriott is dressed suggestively "like
a Bawd" and placed in his slumber upon the throne of the Archbishop of Canterbury.[58] The Archbishop is not named, but as he is amused by the incident,
we can be sure he is not William Laud—a figure who inspired few laughs for
any interested party in 1652. It is pure comedy for Fidge to assert jovially that
Marriott "makes but one meale a day, that is from morning to night."[59] But
there is a serious sense of melancholy when Fidge compares Marriott's stomach to a graveyard: his gut has "buryed more flesh in a week, then Stepney
Church-yard hath done Bodyes this dozen yeares."[60] Many victims of the Civil
Wars were buried in Stepney churchyard, and it is important that the decade
when the battles were fought provides the time scale for Fidge's narrative. The
satire against Marriott, then, has a nuanced edge to it: while the obese glutton
eats like an animal, his fellow countrymen are dying or suffering because of
conflict-caused shortages.

A hastily rendered, three-page publication that also appeared in 1652,
A Letter to Mr. Marriot from a Friend of His, attacks Fidge in turn for his attack
on Marriott. The pamphlet presents a woodcut of Fidge humiliating himself by
kissing the posterior of a triumphant (and not obese) Marriott. The woodcut's
caption serves as a first-person apology from Fidge: to symbolize my repentance
I place "my lips thus on your ar—."[61] The remainder of the short pamphlet is,
generally, much more serious, righteously accounting for the modesty, profes-
sionalism, and steadfastness of the "real" lawyer, Marriott. Unlike others who
have lost their way during the bleak years of philosophical and military conflict
within England, Marriott has "stood firm in these Nationall Huricanoes."[62]
The author of this spirited defense is unknown, but it is clear that the comparison of Marriott to a covetous cormorant had to be countered in print. In
these two pamphlets, imagery of the profane, evil cormorant is appropriated

first to denigrate a supposedly unpatriotic citizen and then to defend the same citizen. It is typical of post-Caroline satirical references to the cormorant that the pamphlets citing it address or at least allude to pressing difficulties contemporary to their publication.

The mid- to late 1680s was a period of pressing difficulty for a Britain busily dispensing with the ailing regime of James II. One R. W., however, attended to issues quite separate from the business of governing the nation: as many of his fellow countrymen sought to rid Britain of its Catholicism-tainted monarchy, R. W. was concerned with eliminating "vermin" from the countryside. The writer's 1688 publication, A Necessary Family-Book, presents itself as an essential guide to the subjugation of nonhuman creatures. The text deals with one so-called pest after another. Present-day readers may be distressed to see graphic woodcuts that depict foxes hanging from barbaric-looking, tree-fixed traps (although apologists for fox hunting would doubtless be amused by these accounts of the massed slaying of the mammal). Similarly, it is shocking to see that a magnificent bird such as the osprey is despised as a rival to humans, one that should simply be shot "with a Gun."[63] Naturally, the cormorant is one of the pests that R. W. discusses, and he calls for their virtual extermination:

> The Cormorant is a great destroyer of fish also, he useth the fresh Waters, and will dive under the water and take Fish of three or four Years growth. The only way to destroy them is by destroying their Nests in breeding-time; they breed in Islands and Rocks by the Sea. Some may be destroyed in Rivers and Pools with a Cross-bow or Handgun.[64]

Basically, a person driven to distraction by the fish-eating zeal of voracious cormorants should annihilate the birds by wrecking their nests. There is no ethical hesitation in the text: young and adult cormorants must be treated equally—as vermin to be destroyed. R. W. calls for an elimination of the material bird much as the many moral writers of the Renaissance call for cormorant-like sins to be eliminated from English society. Attitudes toward the osprey have changed dramatically in the 320 years since R. W. voiced a desire to eradicate them, but the cormorant remains a despised creature, one that still causes anglers to urge slaughter on a mass scale. These early modern representations of a demonic material cormorant and representations of it as an analog of human evil in avian typology fed each other, perpetuating the myth of the hellish bird. Even in the Victorian era, when the bird was hunted almost to extinction in Britain, it still provided a depraved image to enliven polemical, vituperative rants about social evils.

Two particular nineteenth-century polemics use the trope of the rapacious cormorant in ways that continue seamlessly from early modern attacks on human wrongdoing. One compares the Anglican Church to the cormorant; the other compares the Bank of England to the vilified bird. An anonymous pamphlet of 1831, *The Wonder of All Nations!! Or the English Cormorants Anatomized,* attacks the Church of England with withering contempt. The writer lambasts the state-supported Church for its refusal to sell its superfluous assets and for its exploitation of the poor. The writer goes on to poke fun at the alleged imbecility of Anglican clergymen—if a father has a son who is a "blockhead" or a "simpleton," he will send him off to be a rich Church of England clergyman.[65] More serious points are made about national prestige: other countries' elites do not discriminate against minorities in the way that the Anglican British discriminate against Catholics; in Catholic-dominated France, Protestants are tolerated in a way "that shames the persecution of the Catholics of Ireland to a degree at which even an Irishman might blush."[66] The French Revolution was a cleansing operation to be applauded because it abolished so many religious jobs; destroying so many comfortable positions means that the Revolution was "a National Blessing, and even Cheaply Purchased by all the Bloodshed."[67] Worse still for England, the Anglican Church is run so much for the convenience of its overpaid clergymen that concerns for social justice are greater "even in the papal tyranny of Rome."[68] The Anglican Church, then, is composed of Cormorants who feather their own nests—through state-sanctioned taxes and other means—while destroying others' nests. The pamphleteer climaxes with a rousing call for reform, and his pamphlet shows that the typological malignity of the cormorant was still a major tool in the hands of nineteenth-century writers.

An 1875 book, *The Cormorant of Threadneedle Street,* written by the obscure economist James Roberts, attacks another central pillar of the British establishment: the Bank of England. A link to the Renaissance is presented on the title page—an apparent Shakespearean misquote from *Timon of Athens* underlines the association that Roberts makes between greedy consumption of money and self-periling sin: "Let Molten Gold be thy Damnation." However, Roberts does not attack the general concept of financial dealing—he merely damns the unfair advantages held by members of the Bank. He seeks fairer trade, not an end to trade. The Bank of England is a state-served "monster" with "such power that it alters the rate of interest as and when it pleases ... for its own advantage."[69] In Roberts's formulation, the Bank becomes a living, organic entity, a voracious beast that can be compared to the gluttonous cormorant. Other than in his title, Roberts does not use the word *cormorant* until the last page, where he sums up his arguments with a flourish:

The foregoing statistical arguments all point to the fact that the Bank of the England is the CORMORANT of commerce that swallows all that arises within its range ... she is becoming firmly fixed in her position and is an object of fear and dread.[70]

Roberts genders the organic Bank as female, employing possibly misogynistic tropes to denigrate the monstrous, fear-inspiring institution. As the bird's name is rendered in upper-case letters, the comparison of Bank to cormorant effectively leaps off the page.

Metaphorical cormorants who ruin churches and banks may cause fear in nineteenth-century Britain, but the material cormorant caused little fear for Victorian hunters. They shot it almost out of existence in Britain and voiced little remorse while doing so. There is, however, one quite nuanced engagement with the bird in Victorian culture. Francis Henry Salvin wrote a section on Cormorants in an 1859 book that he produced jointly with Gage Earle Freeman, *Falconry: Its Claims, History, and Practice*. Salvin represents himself as what hunting practitioners would call a "sportsman"—in other words, he kills living creatures for pleasure. But he also sets limits. For example, he praises the trustees of Bamborough Castle in Northumberland because they "have the good taste to preserve the sea birds. How different from ... other places ... where they are disgustingly shot by the hundreds."[71] Still, Salvin believes that birds exist to give pleasure to humans. In particular, live, young cormorants can be taken from their nests for the express purpose of enlivening human leisure. Unlike the vermin-bashing pamphlet writer of 1688, Salvin does not see cormorants as merely pests to be exterminated, but as creatures that can be trained to serve and amuse. There is a centuries-old tradition of cormorant fishing in Asia: anglers tie up captive cormorants' throats, so that fish caught by the birds can be removed from their beaks.[72] Keeping and attempting to train cormorants became something of a craze for nineteenth-century English gentlemen, including Salvin. As the Shakespearean scholar and hunter James Edmund Harting puts it in his dated but seminal study of *The Ornithology of Shakespeare* (1871), "Ravenous as the cormorant is, it is easily tamed."[73] Harting and Salvin both view the cormorant as a rapacious consumer of food, but Salvin does not share Harting's belief that the birds are easily trained. Writing of his own captured bird—which he named "Isaac Walton"—Salvin declares that cormorants are "great eaters at all times"; "if a cormorant is unwell it is probably from digestion"; and "you must wear a fencing mask, otherwise the bird will take out your eye ... to a certainty, to say nothing of biting your face."[74] The cormorant can be "sulky"; they are "lazy birds"; and they will "eat meat greedily."[75] By controlling such a beast, Salvin insists that he is living up to his book's Old Testament motto: Man must exercise "Dominion over the Fowls of the air."[76] Yet in the materials surveyed previously, the cormorant refuses to stay conceptually subject to humanity. By using the cormorant so often as an analog for human behavior, Renaissance writers—and their successors—align the bird with humanity in unflattering ways. When writers demonize the cormorant, they demonize humanity.

CONCLUSION

The pelican lost its status as an emblem of self-sacrificing benevolence, possibly because the most canonical literary references to the bird—in Shakespeare's plays—undercut its virtuous associations. But the cormorant, demonized unambiguously by Shakespeare and other writers, has remained despised from the Renaissance into the twentieth century and beyond. Even the famed early twentieth-century naturalist, W. H. Hudson, who did much to raise the profile of wild birds in England, describes the British Cormorant as a "big, somber, ugly bird, heavy and awkward … disgusting in his habits."[77] The bird's long-standing association with all that is base, earthy, and filthy finds a fitting expression in its famed ability to produce mountains of feces. In the last century, the fictional cormorant has been represented in a consistently negative way. In Liam O'Flaherty's short story "The Wounded Cormorant," first published in 1925, an injured cormorant is attacked and destroyed mercilessly by other birds of the same species. Although terse in its relation, O'Flaherty's story seems to work as an allegory of malign humans' desire to vanquish the vulnerable, to exorcise suggestions of racial weakness. When not eliminating weak members of their own species, O'Flaherty's cormorants deal with the consequences of their excessive eating, "bobbing their long necks to draw the food from their swollen gullets."[78] The species' reputation for proverbial greed was as available to O'Flaherty as it was to Adams, Bell, Shakespeare, and Taylor more than three centuries earlier.

In a 1986 novel by Stephen Gregory, *The Cormorant,* a man adopts a specimen of the eponymous bird with great reluctance: he tells us in his first-person narrative of his contempt for a bird that does little except eat and defecate. The bird "spat out its guttural sounds. It splashed the walls and the books with its gouts of shit."[79] The harsh consonants in Gregory's prose convey vividly the aggressive, unpleasant physicality of the wild bird, which will eventually (and deliberately—the cormorant is given supernatural qualities in the novel) destroy the man's marriage. The bird represents the basest qualities of modern youths, youths dealt with by the bird's previous owner, a schoolteacher: "The cormorant was a lout, a glutton, an ignorant tyrant."[80] Ungrateful, unruly pupils metaphorically defecate on school books as the cormorant defecates on the narrator's books. Gregory's pointed comparison of the base cormorant with base humanity continues a centuries-old insistence that cormorants' outer blackness demonstrates the blackness of the species' collective soul. Even children's books sometimes depict the cormorant in antagonistic ways. In the Irish writer Eílís Ní Dhuibhne's children's story of 1990, *The Uncommon Cormorant,* a boy, Ragnar, is intimidated by talking cormorants. One of them, introducing his brother, tells Ragnar that the bird "probably won't eat you, unless he's exceptionally hungry."[81] An impressionable child could conceivably associate the beastly, abstracted cormorants in Ní Dhuibne's story with the actual birds that have returned to Britain and Ireland.

Cormorant numbers, ravaged during the 1800s, recovered during the twentieth century, but the species is again threatened. In September 2004, the British Parliament passed a bill allowing licensed gunmen to shoot up to 3,000 birds in a season— a move that has reignited fears that humans could effect the virtual elimination of the species from the British Isles.[82] Anglers have called for the destruction of the birds because they "steal" fish that should be caught only by humans. Anticormorant propaganda proliferates on the Internet. One Web site called *cormorantbusters*, run by two anglers, asks visitors to sign a petition calling for the decimation of the species in British waters, to save fish, other birds, and angling as a gentleman's pastime.[83] Many Web sites warn us in apocalyptic terms of the catastrophic impact of cormorant populations on humans and on nonhuman, noncormorant species of wildlife. But other Web sites plead for the species' preservation. The anti-angling group Pisces provides concerned readers with practical tips for protecting cormorants from "greedy anglers, not content with torturing fish."[84] Other Web sites showcase the suffering of cormorants because of oil spillages, although in these cases photographs of oil-covered cormorants are posted to address the dangers of pollution and/or war rather than the birds' own endangerment.[85] Careless attitudes toward cormorants have already caused the extinction of one species—*Phalacrocorax Perspicillatus*, the "Spectacled Cormorant," that thrived on the Bering Strait before it was hunted to extinction in the 1800s.[86] It is to be hoped that the species seen most often in the British Isles will not be rendered similarly extinct. Renaissance playwrights, poets, romance writers, and sermonizers demonized the bird, projecting base human characteristics onto it in ways that remain effective rhetorically but absurd scientifically.

In this chapter, I have argued for a continuity between representations of the profane cormorant in early printed books and in later representation. I have stressed that the demonized cormorant is a feature of Renaissance *printed* books, because there is one positive representation of the corporeal cormorant dating from the English Renaissance, but it was not published at the time. Edward Topsell, who compiled a number of substantial printed natural history folios, also worked for years on an ornithological survey, *The Fowles of Heauen*, but the work was not published until 1972. In Topsell's manuscript, he depicts a cormorant species that as well as eating, defecating, and procreating, enjoys simple pleasures. A relaxed, well-fed cormorant will enjoy sunshine: "they come to land & delight themselfes in the beames therof," he writes.[87] This is a cormorant that at least takes some respite from voracious consumption, unlike the avian and human cormorants so excoriated in other Renaissance accounts. Topsell regrets that the cormorant's "fleshe ... is not good for meate in the nature therof because the same is blacke & hard to bee disgested."[88] Yet while the species is inedible, it may still have a gift for humanity: "Their medicinall virtues are more acceptable for the vse of men." Topsell's cormorant is a useful species, one that can relax, enjoying basic, harmless activities, a species implicitly worth preserving because it may be useful to humans. No other early modern writer had anything positive to say about the species—its only known identity was as an emblem of human depravity. But few people could have read Topsell's nonaccusatory account of the cormorant. Manuscripts were passed around and read by interested parties during the early modern period, but it is still fair to state that a natural history manuscript cannot have had much influence on the public. Those who call for specimens of *Phalacrocorax Carbo* to be killed in their thousands exploit the centuries-old cliché of the disgusting, profane cormorant—a cliché problematized in Topsell's *Fowles of Heauen* work. Perhaps if Topsell's account had been published in the late sixteenth century when it was written, the Renaissance image of the unambiguously satanic cormorant would have been as unsustainable as the image of the idealized, Christ-like pelican.[89]

CHAPTER TWO

A Spectacle of Beasts

*Hunting Rituals and Animal Rights
in Early Modern England*

CHARLES BERGMAN

In a long letter to a friend, Robert Laneham described the extended visit of Queen Elizabeth I at Kenilworth in July 1575. During her stay, she hunted on four separate occasions, and Laneham describes one in enthusiastic detail. In the cool of the evening on Monday, July 11, the queen vigorously pursued a hart, or red deer. The hunters, including the queen, were on horseback, following a pack of hounds. According to Laneham, the beagles raised a constant cry, the deer ran swiftly, the footmen chased the deer breathlessly, and the hunters pursued them all on galloping horses. The sounds of blasting horns and "hallowing and hewing" added to the sense of wild abandon and transport, "the excellent echoz between whilez from the woods and waters in the valleiz resounding."[1]

In the end, the hart was driven into a pool of water. The deer swam for his life, while the hounds continued to pursue him in the water. Laneham wrote:

> Thear to beholld the swift fleeting of the deer afore, with the stately carriage of hiz head in his swimming, spred (for the quantitee) lyke the sail of a ship; the hounds harroing after, as had they bin a number of skiphs too the spoyle of a karvell; the ton no lesse eager to purchaz his pray, than wasz the other earnest in savegard of hiz life.

The spread of the stag's antlers reminded Laneham of the full sails of a large ship, or caravel. The dogs were like smaller boats or skiffs in full chase of the caravel. The image glances at England's growing naval prowess. In comparison to this image, the death of the deer was almost an afterthought. "Wel," Laneham concluded, as his language turned colloquial, "the hart waz kild, a goodly dear, but so ceast not the game yet."

Laneham wrote as a spectator, swept up in a "pastime delectabl in so hy a degree" that there could be none other in "ony wey comparable." His descriptions convey the enthusiasm and energy that made hunting one of the most popular sports of the early modern period, both as activity for nobility and as spectator sport. He bears witness to a defining spectacle of his time—a spectacle of running beasts.

As public spectacle, the symbolic and allegorical opportunities in the hunt were carefully exploited by the royal hunters. Queen Elizabeth used the pageantry of the hunt as a kind of theater in the woods, placing royal power and prerogative on display. Two days later, for example, the queen hunted again, on Wednesday, July 13. This time the stag ran quickly to water. At the queen's command, the hunter in the water cut off the ears of the stag, "for a raundsum." With this ransom, the stag "so had pardon of lyfe."[2] As queen, Elizabeth presided over life and death, power and pardon.

With its elaborate rituals and pageantry, its historical importance and its symbolic power, hunting from the Middle Ages through the Renaissance has been extensively studied by scholars. The scholarship can be understood to fall into four categories or stages, not strictly chronological and with considerable overlap among them. The first involves careful studies of the nature of the hunt, often conducted by hunters who are themselves students of the history of the chase.[3] Closely related are the works in which scholars have produced careful editions of medieval and Renaissance hunting manuals. Second are studies of the hunt from historical and cultural perspectives, from the perspective of its social and historical significance.[4] Third are studies that examine hunting as a richly symbolic activity, culturally influential in contemporary literature and art. Scholarship has focused on the hunt as a symbolic register for social status, manhood, gender relations, and "the love hunt."[5] Finally, a number of studies have begun to examine the hunt as a cultural phenomenon in its own right, about which a number of prohunting and antihunting arguments developed. In other words, they examine the ethical status of hunting during the period.[6]

This study is located in the interest in hunting as an ethical activity, and as a site of social contention. I will focus on hunting in the sixteenth century in England as an example of a broadly European activity, one that did not significantly change in its main outlines from the Middle Ages through the Renaissance. In this chapter, I will locate my interest in what Edward Berry calls the "culture of the hunt,"[7] or what Roger B. Manning calls "the deer-hunting culture."[8] The hunt for the hart or red deer was paradigmatic of the highest ideals and possibilities afforded by hunting in the Renaissance. A complex set of practices, symbols, and attitudes contributes to the making of the hunting culture of the time. I'm particularly interested in the way that hunting served as a cultural site for growing attention to, and disputes over, the nature and status of the animal. I will call this "the question of the animal." After a review of the hunt and its social context, I want to examine opposing attitudes toward hunting as the meaning of the word *beast* came increasingly to be questioned.

Both as a highly structured and heavily ritualized activity, and as the field of symbolic discourse about human society, hunting has received considerable attention. Yet hunting was also a complex set of discourses about the animals. Hunting was a way of talking about and knowing animals, both the animals that are pursued (the prey), and the animals that do the pursuing (the domestic allies of humans, hounds and hawks and horses). Hunting was also a discourse about humans as animals. The discourses about animals changed dramatically over the sixteenth century.

I will use the work of the twentieth-century Spanish philosopher José Ortega y Gasset to frame the way the hunt imagines nonhuman animals and their relations with humans. Written in 1942, *Meditations on Hunting* is notable for its forthright discussions of the elements of the hunt.[9] Ortega y Gasset identifies three elements of the hunt, as they emerged in the Middle Ages and through the Renaissance. The first is a relationship of hierarchy or superiority to the hunted animal. Such a relationship in the European hunt of the early modern period is so fundamental as to go almost unremarked by the hunters themselves. As Keith Thomas writes, "Man's authority over the natural world was ... virtually unlimited."[10] This is often implied in important hunting rituals, and is occasionally stated directly. The metaphysical assumptions about humans and animals helped to give the hunt its symbolic resonance as an ennobling human and social activity. As it was enacted in hunting, such supremacy was often criticized as tyranny, not nobility.

Second, the chase produced the potentially contradictory discourse of the hunt as an animalistic release of passion. This dimension of the hunt is most often articulated through the animals themselves, especially the crying of the hounds in the chase, along with the blowing of horns and hallowing of huntsmen. It was this intoxicating rush that contributed to the addictive quality of the hunt. This discourse could involve a dangerous swerve toward the Bacchic release of animal passions in human beings, and became a cultural trope for caustic attacks on hunting, in which human hunters were characterized as the true "beasts" in the chase.

Third, hunting is another kind of discourse of training domestic animals. This focuses on managing animals, training them, and taking care of them.

This discourse mediates the gulf that was assumed to exist between humans and animals. The training of the hounds and hawks and horses involved considerable attention in the hunting manuals, and is not frequently discussed in modern commentaries about hunting. Yet the hounds in hunting (and hawks as well) lead to a remarkable attentiveness to animals.

All three of these ways of conceptualizing animals in the hunt—through superiority, animal release, and training—define hunting as an activity that takes place at the boundary between humans and other animals. As the hunt became increasingly criticized, the nature of the animal as it was understood in the hunt itself became increasingly important. I will argue that hunting and antihunting discourses, taken together as a cultural site for contention over the nature of the animal, led by the end of the century to a new language for the beast. In George Gascoigne's remarkable hunting manual, *The Noble Arte of Venerie or Hunting* (1575),[11] the animals themselves assume an agency and a voice that move the question of the animal beyond hunting and ethics. Hunting rites and rituals give way to a proto-language of animal rights.

A SPORT FOR NOBLE PEERES, A SPORT FOR GENTLE BLOODS

As he was finishing his hunting treatise, George Gascoigne was invited to provide poetic entertainments for Queen Elizabeth during her royal progress through Kenilworth. It is easy to imagine him as one of the party with Robert Laneham, swept up in the festivity and courtly pageantry, with his book on hunting as a noble art still in his imagination. "It is a Noble sport," he concludes,

> To recreate the minds of Men, in good and godly sort.
> A sport for Noble Peeres, a sport for gentle bloods.
> The paine I leave for servants such, as beat the bushie woods,
> To make their masters sport. Then let the Lords reioyce,
> Let gentlemen behold the glee, and take thereof the choice.[12]

His enthusiasm is tinged with a hint of reservation for the pain of the servants, as they beat the bushes after game, and reflects the inescapable, social meaning of hunting at the time. His verses also reflect a sport that had reached a level of popularity, pervasiveness, and influence greater than at any time since the ancient world, and perhaps ever.

For the aristocracy and royalty, hunting for sport had become a consuming, often daily, obsession. A French invention, the practice spread through Europe and arrived in England with the Norman Conquest. According to

Keith Thomas, no nation was so addicted to hunting as the English. It was "an obsessive preoccupation of the English aristocracy."[13] According to Roger B. Manning, hunting "was the most esteemed pastime among peers and gentlemen, and for many of them it was the most time consuming."[14] Edward Berry describes hunting as "one of the most significant royal activities and manifestations of royal power."[15] By the time Gascoigne was writing in the sixteenth century, this sport for kings and queens and princes had become an important social marker for a rising bourgeois class. As Marcia Vale writes in *The Gentleman's Recreations,* "Sports of the kill represented a major portion of the gentleman's pleasure ... [and] the popularity of hunting among all sorts and degrees of gentlemen was prodigious."[16]

The social importance of the hunt is well known. It can be seen in the hunting habits of the Tudor monarchs of England. Henry VII took an active role in managing the royal forests to maintain a steady supply of game, and aggressively punished poachers in his forests.[17] Henry VIII was a passionate hunter, chasing animals from early morning until late at night, wearing out several horses in the process.[18] His poem, "Pastime with Good Company," insists on his right as monarch to the pleasures of hunting: "Hunt, sing, and dance, / My heart is set."[19]

Queen Elizabeth had a famous fondness for hunting. She always treated hunting as a show or ceremony. She hunted as a young woman and as an aging queen. In April 1557, "The Lady Elizabeth" engaged in a colorful hunt at Enfield Chase, near Hatfield, with a retinue of twelve ladies in white satin and fifty bowmen in scarlet boots. In a dramatic close to this theatrical hunt, the queen herself cut the throat of the buck.[20] In 1591, she was still hunting at Cowdrey Castle, where she killed "three or four" bucks by shooting into a paddock.[21]

The hunt was closely associated with royalty because European monarchs asserted their rights to the ownership of the forests of their countries, and the hunt was closely associated with the assertion of national control by European monarchs over their lands and peoples. Through their control of forests and their willingness to engage in public violence in the chase, the hunt became an expression of royal power and the creation of nations. The royal forests were maintained as private hunting reserves, and their prerogatives were enforced with complex laws and, when necessary, violent policing. The forest itself was defined as a privileged space, making hunting a privileged sport, highly artificial and rigidly formalized. As the Elizabethan John Manwood wrote in *The Lawes of the Forest,* "A forest is a certaine Territorie of wooddy grounds and fruitfull pastures, privileged for wild beasts and fouls of the Forest, Chase and Warren, to rest and abide in, in the protection of the King, for his princely delight."[22]

This intersection of geography and political privilege extended hierarchically to other spaces. Monarchs maintained the exclusive control over forests, but granted nobility the right to hunt in parks. Probably introduced by the Normans, parks were lands enclosed by ditch, bank, or pale, and served as private hunting grounds. They were immensely popular, typically attached to the grand estates and castles throughout England.[23] At the bottom of hunting's geography of privilege were warrens, also probably introduced by Normans for the rabbits they brought with them. Warrens came to be associated with the hunting of "lesser game."[24]

As much as one-quarter of all land in England was royal forest, and in 1300 there were as many as 3,200 private parks in England.[25] The legal administration of these lands, and their associated hunting rights, enforced royal and aristocratic authority. Hunting through the Middle Ages and Renaissance was inescapably associated with royal prerogative and political power. Hunting as a royal activity became, in many instances, indistinguishable from the act of governing. Hunting became a vehicle for political control and repression, and inevitably also for political protest and rebellion through poaching.[26]

The hunt at this time thus reflected a complicated world of legal privilege and prohibition, in which a political hierarchy was mapped onto physical spaces and the created world. The hunt was a central organizing principle for understanding the animals in these political spaces.

The prey were variously categorized, depending on the author. John Manwood lists three kinds of chase, and thus three kinds of beast:

Beasts of the Forest (or Venery): hart, hind, hare, boar, wolf.
Beasts of the Chase: buck, doe, fox, marten, roe.
Beasts of Free Warren: hare, coney, pheasant, partridge.[27]

Some texts, like *The Boke of St. Albans* (1486), list the hare as one of the "Bestys of venery."[28] It is important to note that these categories do not relate to the lives of the animals. By the time Manwood was writing at the end of the sixteenth century, wolves had been eradicated from England for a century.[29] Boars were also probably extinct.[30] Reflected in this hierarchy of beasts are the relative pleasures of the chase. As Richard Marienstras remarks, Manwood related the hierarchy of space to the hierarchy of animals by "set[ting] up a graded scale [for lands] similar to that for living creatures."[31]

Keith Thomas writes, "There was a social hierarchy among animals no less than men, the one reinforcing the other. The whole natural world was indeed conventionally assumed to be ordered on a hierarchical scale."[32] Hunting has to be understood at this high point in its history as a thoroughly cultural activity. It was the favored leisure activity of a warrior class without a war to fight. King James I of England, in 1599, advised his son to learn to hunt, "namely with running hounds; which is the most honorable and noblest thereof" as the "faire paterne, for the education of a yong king."[33]

Thus, the hunt functioned as a sign of social status. The natural world of the hunt reflected a highly stratified social structure, with a complex grading of power, privilege, and prohibition. In one sense, this was simply another expression of a fundamentally hierarchical view of nature itself. Yet the hunt went beyond signs to a symbolic control over nature and other humans that could be startling. In his 1577 work, *The Description of England*, William Harrison relates that Henry VII worried about the symbolic meaning that hunting could carry. The force and power of the mastiffs was prodigious. They could kill a bear or a lion. As a result, Henry VII ordered all mastiffs hanged, "because they durst presume to fight against the lion, who is their king and sovereign." He was said also to have ordered a falcon killed for attacking an eagle.[34]

As Roger B. Manning points out, the hunt functioned socially as a cultural site in which power was asserted, contested, and negotiated:

> Hunting was many things in Tudor and early Stuart England. Certainly it afforded sport and recreation for kings and aristocrats as it has always done and provided the opportunity to develop and display the skills and courage necessary for war. It was also a ritualized simulation of war involving calculated and controlled levels of violence carried on between rival factions of the gentry and peerage. ... Hunting was also more than a simulation of war. In a histrionic age when kings and aristocrats continued to feel the need to fashion an image, hunting was also political theatre and provided an occasion to display power. This was an age when both state and family were asserting themselves: the Tudor monarchs had attempted to suppress private warfare and punish rebellion very seriously; aristocratic families found the more overt forms of rebellion and civil war too dangerous and had to be more subtle and circumspect than their late-medieval predecessors in pursuing feuds or expressing political opposition. ... Hunting raids on deer parks and royal forests ... spoke a covert language which was clear enough to both courtiers and backwoods small gentry.[35]

Hunting was a political language in its own right.

The highly stratified and exclusive nature of this concept of hunting was incorporated into its techniques, its style, and its language. As aristocratic sport, the hunt distinguished itself carefully from utilitarian hunting, disdaining hunting "for the pot," as Thomas Elyot put it in 1531. Practical hunting "containeth therein no commendable solace or exercise, in comparison with other forms of hunting."[36] As a sport, aristocratic hunting was by its nature artificial, formalized, and structured by rules.

The artificial nature of this hunt as sport contributed to and underscored its vast symbolic power. The language of hunting, both as metaphor and as a figure of thought, pervades the literature of the time. It was a way of thinking, and could be employed in paradoxical ways. Thomas More offers a typical example of a writer who expresses the persistent association between hunting and manhood in a male-dominated society:

> Manhood I am: therefore I me delight
> To hunt and hawk, to nourish up and feed
> The greyhound to the course, the hawk to the flight …
> These things become a very man indeed.[37]

Yet at Nonsuch Palace in Surrey, Queen Elizabeth maintained a park full of deer and a grove to Diana, goddess of the hunt. The park included a fountain with a statue of Actaeon being turned into a stag by the angry goddess. It seems that class and power, even more than gender, dominated the symbolic import of the hunt. Nevertheless, hunting provided a powerful complex of images for gender relations, particularly love. At no time, I would argue, was hunting used so pervasively to examine the nature of love. Edward Berry notes that huntresses appear frequently in Shakespeare's plays, and argues that Shakespeare used erotic hunting to force characters to "confront some unsettling truths about themselves and about the nature of love."[38] Shakespeare could use the hunt to explore complex sexual relations, as between the huntress Venus and the young hunter Adonis; to describe Lavinia's rape in *Titus Andronicus*; or to express exquisite sexual longing, as in the hawking metaphors of Juliet's wedding night speech in *Romeo and Juliet*.

As a social and broadly cultural phenomenon, the hunt may have reached an apex in the early modern period. As a figure of thinking, it seems to have become part of the psychological as well as social make-up of the time.

HUNTING AND ITS ANIMALS

As a political activity and as a symbolic discourse, the hunt betrays a stunningly anthropocentric orientation, deriving from deeply held assumptions about "the special status of man," to use Keith Thomas's phrase.[39] Concern for animal suffering rarely figures in hunters' stories or manuals. Yet it is also true that the manuals lavish enormous attention on the animals in hunting—both the wild prey and the domestic creatures used to capture the prey. I would like in the remainder of this chapter to examine the ways in which hunters and antihunters talk about the animals in the hunt, and the way their talk contributes to a new understanding of animals themselves.

In this section, I will focus on three ways of talking about animals in hunting: through domination and conquest, release of animal energies, and training. It is customary to speak of hunting in terms of domination and control. These three categories complicate the usual notions of the hunt as a metaphor for domination of animals, particularly with regard to the presumed gulf between humans and other animals. Just as important, disputes about the nature of animals, and human sympathy for other animals, related directly to the language of animals in the hunt.

The right to use animals for human need and pleasure was a basic assumption of the hunt. In *Countrey Contentments,* Gervase Markham makes the assumption explicit: "It is intended that a man so good and vertuous as the true Husband-man, should not be deprived of any comfort, or felicity, which the earth, or the creatures of the earth, can afford him."[40] Hunting as a sport—deriving pleasure from the death of animals—is made possible by this presumption. Yet hunting does not make great effort in this period to justify its treatment of animals. Unlike modern works on hunting, the hunting manuals of the period do not justify the treatment of animals in the hunt. Nor do they try to use the hunt as a way of describing the grand scheme of things, the way twentieth-century hunting advocates use hunting as a descriptor of a predatory and violent world. Human superiority was taken more or less for granted in hunting discourses of the period. George Gascoigne refers to hunting as "ordained" for noblemen, suggesting that the subordination of other animals to humans in the divine scheme of creation is almost beyond question.

According to José Ortega y Gasset, hunting inevitably describes a hierarchical relationship between predator and prey. In *Meditations on Hunting,* he writes, "Hunting is what an animal does to take possession, dead or alive, of some other being that belongs to a species basically inferior to its own."[41] To put it another way, "Hunting is irremediably an activity from above to below."[42] The concept of hierarchical relationship underlies the military ethic of the hunt as a sport in the early modern period. Because this concept was reflected in the hierarchical presumptions of both creation and human society, it was almost invisible, and did not need justifying. Critics saw this domination as tyranny.

As a result hunting is used to describe the domination of civilization over nature more than it is of man himself over nature. The dominating of animals in hunting is taken to be a sign of analogous relations of dominance and submission in human society. It is, in other words, largely metaphoric. Thomas Elyot notes that dominating a fierce beast is useful, not in itself primarily, but as a demonstration of power to inferior men: "daunting a fierce and cruel beast" is central to the hunt because "it importeth a majesty and dread to other persons."[43]

One of the most important Elizabethan hunting stories thus emphasizes the political dimension to domination of the beast. John Selwyn, the Under Keeper of the Park at Oatlands Castle, in Surrey, is reputed to have leapt from his horse onto the back of a great stag, as both animals were running at top speed. Selwyn kept his balance, drew his sword, and stabbed the stag in the neck. He steered the terrified beast to the queen, where it dropped dead at her feet.[44] This allegory of domination and submission seems as much about human relations as it does about human and animal relations.

Nevertheless, the anxiety about maintaining the boundaries between humans and the other animals does reveal itself, indirectly, in the rhetoric of hunting. It seems to be an anxiety about civilization itself. Hunting was a jargon-filled enterprise. Hunting handbooks are often largely about vocabulary, and the linguistic rigors are considerable. For example, a one-year-old red deer was called a *calf*. At two years, it was a *brocket*. At three years, a *spayard*. At four years, *stag* or *staggard*. At five years, a *stag*. After six years, it is a *hart*. A similarly demanding and pedantic vocabulary applied to the *buck* of the fallow deer. As Edward Berry writes, "Hunting was thus not merely a physical but a verbal sport, and one in which the mastery of words implied both power over nature and society."[45]

The rituals of this style of hunting reveal the importance of the hunt as the triumph of civilization itself over nature. It was heavily ritualized, with the strict observance of several ceremonies. In the classic form of this hunt, in which hunters and hounds pursue a stag by scent (called hunting *par force*), rituals framed the key moments, and they are obsessively described in hunting manuals. The "Assembly" of hunters in the woods before the hunt, the presentation of dung to the lord of the hunt, the methods of rousing the deer, the protocols of the chase with the hounds, even the way the hart is killed—these all seem strange and artificial at a remove of centuries, yet were precisely described in the manuals. The defining ritual of this hunt, the breaking up of the deer after it is dead, suggests that one way these rituals can be understood is as an enactment of social and human control over the beast.

The ceremony of the hunt is important enough for George Gascoigne to describe it two times in *The Noble Arte of Venerie or Hunting*. First he gives the French manner of dismembering the dead deer. Then he gives "a special advertisement" of the English manner, because it differs in important details.[46] In general, it is sufficient to note that the breaking-up insists upon special knives, particular postures from the huntsman, offerings to the chief person in the hunt from the dead deer, and a particular order of cutting up the deer. Each member of the hunting party receives specifically designated cuts of the "dainty morsels" of the deer, according to rank. The hounds are also rewarded, to the hallowing of hunters and the blowing of horns.

These rituals are central to the spectacle of the hunt, and much of the meaning of these rituals is opaque to us. Marienstras believes that the break-up is a sacrificial ritual, distinguishing the violence of hunting from mere butchery.[47]

Edward Berry writes, "The ceremony as a whole represents the domination of man over nature, the imposition of a specifically human order upon the wildness of the animal."[48] I agree that this is a ritual of control exercised over the animal's body. Yet civilization itself is honored in the disarticulation, and subsequent rearticulation, of the animal. The body of the beast becomes a language of civilized order. It is possible that the quasi-religious observance of these ceremonies hints at doubt, on the part of the hunters, as to whether their use of animals for pleasure is fully justified. The ceremony provides the social sanction.

The second discourse of the hunt could be called "animalistic." It can appear to be the opposite of the discourse of the hunt as ennobling humans with respect to animals. The hunt seems to allow hunters to cross over the boundaries between humans and beasts.

The animalistic elements of the hunt center on the exhilarating release of energy it occasions. If hunting operates at the boundaries between human and animal, it can both police the boundary in a discourse of domination and blur the boundaries. In the Renaissance, hunting was loved paradoxically because it connected hunters to their own animality. They did not identify with the prey, except symbolically—a prince, for example, with the great stag. Rather, they experienced their own powerful sense of animal release through the energy of their domesticated animals, especially the hounds. Paradoxically, in a hierarchical and anthropocentric age, the hunt connected hunters to their dogs, in whom the hunters saw a release of their own animal passions. The dogs become the objective correlatives of a hunter's wildness.

Ortega y Gasset describes this dimension of the hunt through the sudden animation of dogs in the pursuit of the prey. The hunter

> feels himself a plant, a botanical entity, and he surrenders himself to that which in the animal is almost vegetal: breathing. But here they come, here comes the pack, and instantly the whole horizon is charged with a strange electricity. ... Suddenly the orgiastic element shoots forth, the dionysiac, which flows and boils in the depths of all hunting. Dionysios [sic] is the hunting god: "skilled cynegetic," Euripedes calls him in The Bacchantes. "Yes, yes," answers the chorus, "the god is a hunter!" There is a universal vibration. ... There it is, there's the pack! Thick saliva, panting, chorus of jaws, and the arcs of tails excitedly whipping the countryside! The dogs are hard to restrain; their desire to hunt consumes them, pouring from eyes, muzzle, and hide. Visions of swift beasts pass before their eyes, while, within, they are already in hot pursuit.[49]

This focus on the orgiastic release of animal energy in the hunt accounts for much of the pleasure of hunting. It explains why, as Markham put it, so many gentlemen were "addicted to the delight of hunting."[50]

This animal pleasure could be tame, or it could turn more carnivalesque, more elemental, more primal. The hounds are the central image of this release of energy. In full pursuit, they become images of uninhibited desire, as Ortega y Gasset suggests. It can border on the "dionysiac," and turn demonic as well. In *A Midsummer Night's Dream,* Hippolyta describes the pleasure of the hounds in full cry, as they bring a bear to bay in Sparta:

> Never did I hear
> Such gallant chiding; for besides the groves,
> The skies, the fountains, every region near
> Seemed all one mutual cry. I never heard
> So musical a discord, such sweet thunder.[51]

The element of Bacchic release is also associated with the blood of the prey. James I would personally cut his prey's throat and daub blood on the faces of his courtiers.[52]

The swerve toward the "bestial" in the hunt intoxicated hunters, but it was a principal theme of hunting's early critics. Hunters lost their reason and their humanity, degraded into beasts. A myth like that of Actaeon expresses the animality of the hunt as it turned demonic. The hunter becomes a deer, and is destroyed by his own hounds.

Finally the hunt contains a discourse of training animals, which helps to explain the central function of the hounds and hawks as allies of the hunter in the chase. The hounds were essential to the aristocratic conception of hunting. For nonhunters, the relationship between hunters and dogs is rarely mentioned, and not well understood. Gervase Markham begins *Countrey Contentments* with a definition of hunting:

> Hunting is then a curious search or conquest of one beast by another, pursued by a natural instinct of enmitie, accomplished by the diversities and distinctions of smells onelie, wherein Nature equallie dividing her cunning giveth both to the offender, and offended strange knowledge both of offence and safety. In this recreation is to be seen the wonderfull power of God, in his creatures, and how far rage and pollicie can prevaile against innocence and wisedom.[53]

The hunt is defined as the pursuit of one animal by another. The domestic animal is central in this artificial and contrived contest between two animals. As a sport, however, hunting reveals to hunters "the wonderfull power of God, in his creatures."

George Gascoigne begins *The Noble Arte of Venerie or Hunting* with an extended treatment of the antiquity of hounds, their several natures, their breeding

and training. The care and training of dogs cover fourteen chapters. Hounds
must be trained to understand horn blasts in the hunt, telling them if they have
missed a scent, overrun a scent, or should run counter to a scent: "their keepers
and huntsmen must teach them to know the Hallow as well by the horn, as by the
mouth, in this wise."[54] The hounds are carefully rewarded with morsels. Loving
care is lavished on the creatures. Gascoigne concludes his treatment on hounds
by observing that, in the kennel, "herewith shall you rub every night the feet and
folds between the clawes of your hounds with a linen cloute."[55] It is easy to see
why noble hunters were accused of caring more for their dogs than their people.

Hunters developed an intimate knowledge of their dogs' abilities and strengths.
According to D. H. Madden, this is an important feature of the hunt, then and
now.[56] Shakespeare's Induction to *The Taming of the Shrew* is an example of this
intimate type of talk about animals:

> Lord. Huntsman, I charge thee tender well my hounds
> (Brach Merriam, the poor cur, is emboss'd),
> And couple Clowder with the deep-throated brach.
> Saw'st thou not, boy, how Silver made it good
> At the hedge corner, in the coldest fault?
> I would not lose the dog for twenty pound.[57]

For Ortega y Gasset, as for the hunters of the early modern period, hounds
were an essential element of the hunt. As Ortega y Gasset puts it, "Man and
dog have articulated in each other their own styles of hunting."[58] In working
together, the two species create a space between them in which each is in some
measure recreated, human and animal. The domesticated dog, for example, "is
an intermediate reality between the pure animal and man, which, in turn, is to
say that something like reason operates in the domestic animal."[59] One need
not accept the fundamental otherness of the wild and the domestic to understand that Ortega y Gasset sees new potentials for thought and feeling in this
relationship with dogs in the hunt. The attention to dogs as human companions in the hunt applies as well to hawks and horses.

In the intimacies of care and understanding, hunters become students of
their companion animals. As Vicki Hearne remarks about the training of animals in *Adam's Task*, trainers have to look beyond the "Outsiderness, or Otherness" of animals.[60]

These three discourses suggest that hunting carries a double valence with
regard to the boundaries between humans and nonhuman animals. On the one
hand, it assumes a hierarchy of creation and reinforces the sense of human
dignity, superiority, and nobility. On the other hand, it blurs the boundaries
that God has seemed to ordain, in animalistic release of the hunt, and in the
intimacies of training.

THE ENIGMA OF THE ANIMAL

Over the sixteenth century, antihunting sentiment helped to generate a new feeling for animals. Critics attacked hunting at first, not because they felt great sympathy for animals, but because they loathed the effect of hunting on hunters. Critics deconstructed the hunt and its central claims, particularly the supposed nobility of hunters and the slippery term *beast*. The animality of the hunt made its critics believe that, as Sir John Harrington put it, "the royal sports of hunting and hawking ... were such as made me devise the beasts were pursuing the sober creation."[61] Such questions about the nature of the hunt and its participants led to questions about the nature of animals in the hunt.

A number of historians and literary critics have traced the development of an antihunting tradition through the Renaissance. Claus Uhlig locates the origins of a principled attack on hunting in John of Salisbury's *Policraticus* (1159). He identifies the principal features, or stereotyped topoi, of the critique:[62] hunting is the origin of tyranny, it causes social irresponsibility, and it leads to the degeneration of hunters into beasts. Uhlig traces these topoi through Erasmus in *The Praise of Folly,* Thomas More in *Utopia,* and Cornelius Agrippa in *Of The Vanitie of The Artes and Sciences.* Matt Cartmill follows the same development, saying that the sixteenth century saw "the first condemnations of hunting heard in Europe in fourteen centuries."[63] Edward Berry identifies three strands in a growing antihunting feeling: the humanism of Thomas More, Erasmus, and Agrippa; the sentimental sympathies of Montaigne and the ethical opposition of the Puritans.[64]

I will examine the way boundaries between humans and animals are contested in the debate over hunting in this period, especially in George Gascoigne's *The Noble Arte of Venerie or Hunting.* This work's power as proanimal discourse has been largely overlooked. It is a startling example of the way hunting itself seemed paradoxically to help produce a new view of animals in Europe. It challenges the main premises of the hunt as ennobling, develops the theme of the transformation of men into beasts in the hunt, and asserts a growing dignity for animals. They achieve moments of agency and depth as creatures, and are given voices by which to talk back. They rewrite the hunting narrative and even tell their own versions of hunting narratives. They explicitly raise the question of the representation of animals by human beings. In the context of a hunting manual, one is left with the impression that animals have made a major and unprecedented statement about their rights as creatures. A text of hunting rituals and animal rights in direct confrontation, Gascoigne's treatise provides a case study of how hunting could deconstruct itself and its metaphysical premises.

Amazingly, this deconstruction takes place in a text dedicated to teaching men to become hunters. The animal emerges with such force and power in the course of the hunting manual that it threatens to overthrow the project of the manual itself. The terms *man* and *beast* become increasingly equivocal in the text, which challenges not only the ethics of hunting, but also its metaphysical underpinnings.

George Gascoigne wrote *The Noble Arte of Venerie or Hunting* as a translation of the French hunting manual by Jacques du Fouilloux, *La Vénerie*. It is in many ways faithful to the original, but it is also in many ways a free translation.[65] The author of *A Hundreth Sundrie Flowers,* Gascoigne was a successful Elizabethan poet. But he had suffered disillusionment, served time in prison, and was perhaps using this translation as a way of resurrecting his writing career. According to the Proutys, at the same time he was working on the translation of this hunting manual, he announced that he was a reformed man, now working in God's service. He was present at Kenilworth Castle, in 1575, when the queen was hunting.

There is little to prepare one for the shock of some of the passages in Gascoigne's hunting handbook. He may testify to hunting as a noble sport, and urge its princely delights. But at key moments something quite unexpected takes over. The animals step out of the shadows and threaten the whole social enterprise of the hunt. The climactic moment of the hunt is the kill. After some forty chapters in which Gascoigne explains the care of the hounds and the proper methods of chasing a hart, he brings the reader to the beast at bay. And the beast fights back.

Gascoigne tells the story of the Emperor Basil, who had overcome many enemies in battle and done "many deedes of prowesse among men." Yet as he tried to kill a great hart at bay, he was

> gored with the hornes of a brute beast: yea (that more is) by a fearfull beast, such a one as durst not many days nor houres before have beheld the countenance of the weakest man in his kingdome: A Beast that fledde from him, a beast whome he constrained (in his own defence) to do this detestable murder.[66]

This is the moment when the heroic hunter should display his prowess. Instead, an animal stands to his own defense. Though the hart was previously a coward, fleeing even the weakest man, it seems to step out of its assigned role as the creature known by flight, defeat, and submission. It assumes its own agency in the story. In fact, despite the "detestable murder," the hart almost takes over the narrative and its significance.

Gascoigne writes that the incident should be a "mirror for al Princes and Potentates." But it does not show them their reflected glory. It is a mirror for them to see that the hart's self-defense is a type of all those who suffer "undeserved

CHAPTER THREE

Domesticated Animals in Renaissance Europe

PETER EDWARDS

Renaissance society would not have survived without domesticated animals. People kept them for food: as livestock, cattle and sheep and goats supplied them with dairy products, while poultry laid eggs and bees made honey. With their wool and hair sheep and goats offered their owners the further benefit of a renewable source of material for clothing and other items. Slaughtered, the animals provided meat and additional products, including hide, tallow, and horn, from which craftsmen made a variety of ware. Even arable farmers had to maintain livestock: they supplied motive power on the farm and road and their manure kept the land fertile. Riders employed equids, mainly horses, to get from place to place. Horses also played an integral role in the recreational activities of the upper classes, whether hunting, hawking, jousting, or the *manège*. Dogs accompanied their masters out hunting or hawking but among the population at large they performed more utilitarian activities. Sheepdogs helped shepherds in the management of sheep, and mastiffs guarded homes from intruders. Cats caught vermin. Some cats and dogs were truly domesticated, in the sense that they lived indoors, where they fulfilled a more social role.

By the Quattrocento man had been exploiting domesticated animals for 10,000 years, that is, ever since he had settled down to farm and herd.[1] Over millennia, moreover, man had so increased his control over the natural world that many people in Renaissance Europe believed the Earth's resources were completely at their disposal. To buttress their claims they could parade long-established arguments. Aristotle, in the fourth century B.C.E., for instance, declared man qualitatively different from plants and all other living creatures. Whereas each had a soul, only humans possessed one capable of reason.[2] The Bible reinforced the notion of man's superiority. According to Genesis, God had created the Garden of Eden as a paradise for humans and had given Adam dominion over all living things. At first, humans and beasts cohabited peacefully; Adam and Eve did not eat meat and animals were tame. Unfortunately, this state of affairs ended with the Fall: beasts became wild and aggressive and might attack humans. In turn, humans hunted animals for food and clothing. To be sure, after the purging effect of the Flood, God did reaffirm man's ascendancy, but the world was now a far more dangerous and intimidating place. As is stated in Genesis, "The fear of you and the dread of you shall be upon every beast of the earth, and upon every fowl of the air, upon all that moveth upon the earth, and upon all the fishes of the sea: into your hand are they delivered. Every moving thing that liveth shall be meat for you."[3]

Man's alleged special position in the natural world ostensibly validated his exploitation of animals; as Thomas has remarked, it could be used "to justify hunting, domestication, meat-eating, vivisection ... and the wholesale extermination of vermin and predators."[4] It might also condone ill treatment of animals. Descartes, for instance, likened animals to automata, without souls, devoid of speech or reason, and by implication incapable of feeling pain.[5] Beasts of burden certainly suffered. While it made sense to look after an economic asset, sheer necessity forced many people to overtax their animals, beating them into action if need be. Moreover, riders broke in young horses by instilling fear in them. At Elizabeth I's stud at Tutbury, staff used force to train colts and fillies and tied recalcitrant mares to a post to receive the stallion.[6] Even less edifying, the public watched staged contests between animals in the name of sport. Specially trained cocks fought to the death, while the audience roared them on and bet on the outcome. Another popular pastime comprised baiting a tethered bear or bull with dogs, either in succession or in a pack. Not uncommonly, the attacking hounds died or received serious injury.[7]

Nonetheless, during the late sixteenth century critics of cruelty toward animals became more vocal. By 1600 writers on horse management had softened their tone, emphasizing the need to cherish their charges rather than chastise them.[8] Proanimal writers began to question the basis of man's superiority, namely, his rationality and distinctiveness. Montaigne posed the question, "When I play with my cat, who knows if I am not a pastime to her more than she is to me?"[9] Even those who adopted an openly anthropocentric stance did not necessarily condone arbitrary behavior toward animals. Calvin pointed out that as God's creatures, they deserved respect and humane treatment.[10] Admittedly, the impulse was not always theriophilic in inception, the point being that cruelty toward animals inevitably led down the slippery slope to the abuse of humans. In the debate, whether animals possessed a soul or not became an important question. If they did, they could obtain salvation and therefore warranted better treatment. More important, did this trend merely mark a shift in the views of theorists and intellectuals, or did it affect the practice of people actually in charge of animals? The evidence suggests that among the population at large habitual abuse of domesticated animals continued.

In the early fifteenth century the importance of domesticated animals to the rural economy was growing. This was a natural consequence of the demographic crisis of the late Middle Ages, brought on by recurring bouts of plague and exacerbated by the ravages of war.[11] Because of the massive decline in the population, demand for cereals shrank and prices fell. In central Europe, for example, the average price of a kilo of rye halved at Strasbourg between the years 1351–1375 and 1501–1525 (50.6%) and at Königsberg between 1359–1399 and 1468–1506 (46.5%). In the Moselle area it fell by more than 70 percent (71.0%) between 1351–1400 and 1476–1500. In France the cost of a kilo of wheat in the years 1451–1475 was a third of the price it had fetched a century earlier. Inevitably, land went out of cultivation. As early as 1369 in France vast areas were reverting to scrub, marsh, or woodland. In Italy, only Lombardy escaped relatively unscathed. In Holland the settling of the peat on the reclaimed polders, combined with a rise in the sea level, made it impossible to grow winter (bread) corn there.[12]

If the farmers in the Dutch polders had to turn to cattle farming to pay for their bread corn, only obtainable through the market, their counterparts elsewhere embraced livestock husbandry to solve the problem of surplus land, hitherto under cultivation. The comparatively modest fall in the price of animals and their products reinforced this decision. As a result, livestock numbers increased dramatically. In addition, livestock and animal products retained their value to a greater extent than did grain. At the same time a shortage of manpower led to a rise in wages and an increase in the purchasing power of laborers, peasants, and artisans. Now, they could afford to eat meat and animal products more regularly. In England harvest workers in the early fifteenth century were allowed a pound of meat for every two pounds of bread compared with the one or two ounces they had received 150 years earlier. Looking back from the mid-sixteenth century, commentators as far apart as Swabia and Brittany recalled the good old days when peasant tables groaned under the weight of food. As an old Breton peasant observed in 1548, perhaps through rose-tinted glasses, "How far away is the time ... when it was difficult for an ordinary feast day to pass by without someone from the village inviting all the rest to dinner, to eat his chicken, his gosling, his ham, his first lamb and his pig's heart."[13]

As population rose in the late fifteenth or early sixteenth century, according to region, many farmers found it more profitable to grow cereals once more and the ratio between crops and livestock changed again. In France numbers had reached preplague levels by about 1550 and the vast pastures of the mid-fifteenth century were giving way to cornfields. This was especially so in the Isle de France, where the demographic recovery had been swifter and the Parisian market had stimulated an early return to cereal production. Farmers in Lowland England also switched to mixed farming in the late sixteenth century. In Spain members of the *Mesta*, the Spanish sheep-owners organization, suffered a drop in their fortunes as farmers plowed up the traditional grazing grounds for their sheep on the Castilian Plateau in the later sixteenth century. In eastern Europe the inhabitants of the plains and gentle hills that stretched from central Germany to Russia responded to the growing international market in corn by cutting down the woodland and producing huge acreages of grain, especially rye.[14] Of course, where conditions did not suit the cultivation of crops the shift was less pronounced. In Mediterranean countries like Spain and Italy, upland farmers maintained their traditional way of life based on rearing cattle and sheep. Rearing cattle similarly characterized farming on the edge of the huge forests of northern Europe.[15]

Even in resurgent mixed farming areas, cultivators could not dispense with their animals completely. As Conrad Heresbach, writing in Germany in 1570, observed, "without the seruice of Horse and Oxen, we can neyther plow, nor doung our ground."[16] When fertilizing their land, some farmers made better provision than others. One intensive system, found in a band of country stretching from the eastern Netherlands to Mecklenburg, involved regular weeding and generous application of manure, thereby eliminating the need for a fallow.[17] In Flanders and Brabant the emergence of a genuine mixed farming economy in the late Middle Ages enabled farmers to obtain large quantities of dung, which they further augmented by stall-feeding their animals. In France farmers in Normandy, Brittany, and around Boulogne, Limoges, and Poitou similarly integrated cattle with crops and reduced the area of fallow.[18] In parts of the country that emphasized cereal production, sheep provided the main source of organic fertilizer. Farmers folded them on the fallow, hurdling them on a different plot of land each night. In England, their counterparts mainly deployed sheep on light soils, such as the loams and sands of East Anglia and chalk downs.[19] Where farmers had access to extensive tracts of common grazing, they might hope to maintain sufficient animals to manure their arable land, but they had problems in overwintering them. For other cereal growers the situation was worse.[20] One solution was to increase the acreage sown with fodder crops, which was done in some progressive regions like Flanders. Nonetheless, their use did not become general until the seventeenth century.[21]

Farmers also required draft animals to prepare the ground, carry off the crops, and take them to market. Mainly they employed horses or oxen, the choice being determined by such factors as terrain, soil, type of farming, capital, status, and even diet. Horses were quicker than oxen, and on stony ground their sure-footedness gave them an added edge. In late sixteenth-century France Charles Estienne and Jean Liébaut extolled the virtues of horses, claiming that a good horse from the Isle de France or the Beauce was better than three of the best oxen of the Bourbonnais or the Forez.[22] On the other hand, horses cost more to feed, were prone to injury, and because of the taboo against eating their meat were virtually valueless at the end of their working life.[23] Oxen, though slower, were more reliable on heavy land, where John Fitzherbert, writing of English conditions in the 1520s, noted "horses will stande styll."[24] They did not require a varied diet and worked well if kept on good grassland. When too old to work, they could still be fattened up and sold as beef.[25] A status-conscious farmer preferred the horse because contemporaries considered it a superior creature. Ironically, in some localities in late medieval England small peasant farmers kept only horses, whereas the more substantial tenants and their manorial lords employed both animals. The horse's flexibility appealed to the smallholders, for if they could acquire manorial cast-offs, these were not prohibitively expensive. Larger farmers and gentlemen, on the other hand, had the resources to use oxen and horses for specific tasks.[26]

In terms of general distribution over the period, more horses were being used in northern Europe and more oxen (and cows) in the south. Thus, horses were taking over as draft animals in northern France, the Low Countries, Denmark, and northwest Germany during the course of the fifteenth and sixteenth centuries. They first appeared in northeastern France and in the Low Countries in the high Middle Ages. In the Low Countries horse densities were high, in 1601–1602 amounting to up to one per acre on the poor soils of Overijessel. Among other tasks, the peasants there used them to carry clods of earth that they mixed with manure and spread on the fallow fields.[27] Oxen and cows predominated in Spain, Italy, central and southern France, and southern Germany.[28] Naturally, there were exceptions, as farmers made more specific choices based on local conditions. In the grain-growing districts of southern Sweden, for instance, late medieval cultivators employed oxen.[29] In early sixteenth-century England, mixed farmers tilling the heavy clays employed oxen for plowing and carting, while their counterparts on light soil land were likelier to use horses. By the end of the century substantial clayland farmers were turning to horses, sustaining them with the fodder crops they were incorporating into their rotation. This trend was also apparent on the heavier soils of Lorraine. Only the wealthier farmers in the region could afford an entire team, normally of six horses (occasionally more) but others combined their animals to make a working unit. The superior speed of the horses prompted the change.[30]

Around the Mediterranean, a single draft animal could plow the thin soils that covered much of the region and farmers there often used mules, asses, or donkeys.[31] In France Estienne and Liébault called the ass a contemptible beast but admitted that it carried out essential tasks: plowing light soils, grinding grain, carrying corn to the mill, taking farm produce to market, and pulling light wagons. In the Auvergne, Languedoc, and Provence mules were preferred to oxen or cows. Mules were particularly valuable in Provence; because of the scarcity of horses and oxen, they were in great demand for draft and carriage work and this drove up prices.[32] In Sicily the mule was the normal draft animal on the farm. Along with oxen, they also tilled the land in Spain. In 1513, Alonso de Herrera compared mules with oxen, concluding that although mules were faster, oxen plowed the soil more deeply and economically.[33] In England, they were little used on the farm, though contemporary writers rated them highly: Mascall thought them "good to travel with the burden and to labour the earth."[34]

Among domesticated animals, horses were most esteemed. Heresbach declared that "the Horse may worthiest challenge the chiefest place, as the noblest, the goodliest, the necessariest, and the trustiest beast that wee vse in our seruice."[35] Michael Baret concurred, claiming in 1618 that "of all the Creatures of God made at the creation, there is none (except man) more excellent, or so much to be respected as a Horse. For in disposition and qualities hee is but little inferior to Man." He compared it to an elephant for strength; a lion for boldness; a roe or hind for speed; a hound for smell; an ox for toughness; a spaniel for affection; a serpent for intelligence; and a black swan for beauty.[36] These qualities suggest that the horse's status rested on its appearance and its usefulness to man. Clearly, the horse's status transcended its economic value for, as Baret observed, "for the vse of man, not onely for pleasure, but also for necessity and profit, there is none to be compared to him."[37] To own such a noble creature was a sign of distinction, marking a real social divide in society: a rider literally as well as metaphorically looked down on people on foot. Moreover, good horsemanship constituted an essential attribute of a gentleman.

By nature, horses could carry out a variety of jobs, but upper-class interest in them for specific, often nonfunctional, activities ensured that differentiation between the breeds progressed further than it did among other species. Wealthy horse-breeders aided the process by importing foreign horses with the required qualities. In 1565 Thomas Blundeville noted the growing specialization of function:[38]

> For some man perchaunce woulde haue a brede of great trotting horses mete for the war, and to serue in the field. Some other againe would haue a brede of ambling horses of a meane stature for to Journey and to trauayle by the way. Some againe would haue perhaps a race of swift runners to runne for wagers, or to galloppe the bucke, or to serue for such lyke exercises of pleasure. But the plaine countriman would perchaunce haue a breede onely for draughte or burden.

Naturally, the elite maintained a range of horses in their stables, often with a particular function to perform. Local gentry might keep ten or twelve horses, but the nobility would count them in dozens. The Crown possessed hundreds. When Henry VIII died in 1547 he left well over 1,000 horses in stables and studs scattered around the country.[39] Many humble villagers, on the other hand, had to ride on their work horses, perhaps sitting on a pannell (a padded cloth) or swapping a cart saddle for a riding one.

Small, wiry ponies, often no more than thirteen hands high, roamed the moors, heaths, and uplands of Europe. Accustomed to fending for themselves, they were hardy, sure-footed, and economical to keep and thus made ideal pack animals. In Britain semiwild herds grazed the open commons of the Welsh and Scottish borders, the Pennines, and the Southwestern moors.[40] On the continent they could be found in the woodlands of northwestern Germany, the Swiss mountains, Alsace, and the Vosges. Writing in 1576, Daniel Spekle described the horses of Vosges forests as "reproducing themselves, feeding themselves in all seasons. In winter, they shelter beneath rocks … Extremely wild, they are very sure-footed on the narrow, slippery rocks."[41] Compared to ponies, asses and mules were even hardier and cheaper to feed. Estienne and Liébault praised asses for their toughness and economical diet. Edward Topsell observed in 1607 that they throve on mean fare: chaff, young thorns, acorns and mast, osier twigs, and bundles of boughs. As a bonus, their milk reputedly remedied various ailments of the blood.[42] The mule, a cross between an ass and a horse, combined the stoicism and sure-footedness of the former animal with the endurance and strength of the latter and greater tolerance for hard work and harsh climatic conditions than either of them. According to Clutton-Brock, they were a perfect example of hybrid vigor.[43] Mules were bred throughout southern Europe but some regions gained a reputation for the quality of their stock. In France, Poitou was an important center.[44] In Spain the Pyrenean fair of Barbastro specialized in mules and disposed of stock obtained from both sides of the border.[45]

Horses carried less on their back than they could by pulling a cart: in England a full pack weighed up to 256 lb, whereas a horse harnessed to a vehicle could move six cwt.[46] On the other hand, pack trains traveled more quickly and offered greater flexibility, with carriers adding or subtracting animals according to need. Over rough terrain, pack transport had the edge, especially in the winter months.[47] In terms of stock, ponies predominated in northern Europe and asses and mules were more common in the south. Indeed, on the rough mountainous tracks in countries bordering the Mediterranean, mules were essential. In April 1522 Thomas Hannibal wrote to Thomas Wolsey, the Lord Chancellor of England, from Vittoria (Spain) to inform him that the horses he had set out with from Bilbao had "miscarried" in the mountains and that he had to get mules. English horses, he ruefully declared, would not do for that country.[48] Mascall later pointed out that mules could travel farther and carry greater loads than a pack horse, though his statement that they reportedly moved weights of five to six cwt. seems mere hearsay.[49]

Some of the biggest and best ponies in Europe came from the Celtic regions of Britain and were used as saddle mounts as well as for pack carriage. In 1599, for instance, Peter Keen wrote that Montgomeryshire was "noted cheefelie for ye best nagges in Wales."[50] Galloways of the Scottish border region were not only ridden but also raced. Indeed, modern thoroughbreds have Galloway blood in the veins, acquired from the dam side.[51] Irish hobbies were primarily saddle horses; they had some Spanish blood in them and, although not large, were well proportioned with a finely shaped head. According to Blundeville, they were "tender mouthed, nimble, light, plesaunt & apte to be taught, and for the most part thei be amblers, and therfore very mete for the saddle, & to trauel by the way."[52] They made excellent light cavalry mounts and with their turn of speed were often raced. Italian princes, who valued their sprinting ability, ran them at palio meetings. Among those who did business with Henry VIII were Francesco Sforza of Milan, Ercole and Alfonso d'Este of Ferrara, and Francesco Gonzaga of Mantua. In return, they gave the English king large and imposing saddle horses.[53] Mules served as saddle mounts too. Surprisingly, given their small stature and less than perfect conformation, they were ridden by monarchs, nobles, and prelates. Among others, François I, king of France, and Thomas Wolsey rode on mules going to and at the Field of the Cloth of Gold in June 1520. On May 30, for instance, Wolsey, dressed completely in crimson satin, rode a mule covered with crimson velvet and with trappings of gold. In September 1542 Edmund Bonner, bishop of London, informed Henry VIII that Granvelle, the chief minister of the Emperor Charles V, was going to send a mule to Barbastro for him.[54] When he died Henry VIII possessed five mules probably for the saddle, as well as twenty-two carriage and six litter mulettes.[55]

The Low Countries specialized in breeding strong draft horses, a practice that seems to date from the later Middle Ages.[56] The best came from Flanders, with Friesland producing a lighter, more compact version. North German horses were second in strength only to those from Flanders, but were coarser in conformation.[57] So great was the international demand for these horses that a thriving export market developed during the sixteenth century. The English king, Henry VIII, imported brood mares from Flanders, having found, while campaigning on the continent, that they performed much better than did native stock. As Andrew Borde noted in 1542, "Great studmares we bring up in Flaunders, we sell them in England." Later, Blundeville claimed to have seen "twoo or three Mares to go lightly away with suche a burthen, as is almost vncredible."[58] These horses spread farther south too. Jewish dealers from Metz sold horses to the French—they were particularly sought after in the Languedoc—while German merchants traded them with the Milanese.[59]

During the course of the Renaissance the upper classes took up the fashion for riding in sprung coaches, which originated in Hungary in the fifteenth century, if not before. In 1457 the Hungarian king, Ladislas V, seeking the hand of the daughter of Charles VII of France, sent him a number of gifts including a carriage with a suspended body.[60] Coaches were functional in the sense that they carried people from one place to another, but they also provided a highly visible and mobile means of ostentatious display. A richly embellished coach, adorned with the family's coat of arms, drawn by a fine team of matching horses and staffed by coachmen and postilions in rich livery, was an impressive sight and proclaimed the wealth and status of the owner. Obviously, the horses that pulled these conveyances had to be powerful enough to do the job, but strength alone did not suffice. Prospective owners considered aesthetic criteria as well: color, action, and conformation.[61] The ideal aimed at was a matching set of elegantly proportioned horses of the same height and with coats of a modish color. Thus, the upper classes, through selective breeding, improved the quality and appearance of draft horses. In 1563 John XVI, count of Oldenburg, established a stud where he bred a particularly fine breed of coach and carriage horses, crossing imported Barbs, Turcomans, Danish, and especially Spanish and Neapolitan stock with readily available Friesian horses.[62] The population at large benefited too. Stallions might cover draft mares belonging to tenant farmers, while superannuated stock, disposed of privately or at fairs, carried out similar services for their new plebeian owners.

For riding, contemporaries particularly rated the Neapolitan courser, an imposing creature on account of its size and strength, its well-proportioned body, and its fashionable convex profile of the head. They made perfect cavalry mounts for they were strong enough to bear the weight of heavily armored men-at-arms in battle and their riders could rely on them to perform with spirit and courage. By the middle of the sixteenth century, however, they were being supplanted by lighter and more mobile horses as military tactics increasingly emphasized firepower at the expense of shock.[63] Even so, coursers retained their role as parade animals. Public appearances were stage-managed and there were few better ways of demonstrating one's power and authority than to be seen dressed in fine robes sitting astride a fiery courser, richly caparisoned. A retinue of similarly attired men riding mettlesome steeds heightened the impact. To impress the French on the Field of the Cloth of Gold in June 1520, Henry VIII of England had scoured Europe for the best horses but to no avail. His procession numbered an impressive 5,704 persons and 3,223 horses, but the French king, François I, outdid him in all respects.[64]

Of the horses that replaced the courser, the ginetes of Spain, the Arabs and Turcomans of the Near East, and the Barbs of north Africa were the most prized. Ginetes had originated in Andalusia but had acquired north African blood in the Middle Ages as a result of the Moorish conquest of Spain. When the Spanish acquired Naples in 1502 they took ginetes with them and the infusion of their blood had the effect of producing a lighter strain of courser.[65] Fine saddle horses were being bred elsewhere in the Italian peninsula too. Because of their trading and diplomatic links with the Levant and north Africa, Italian princelings were able to obtain high-quality stallions and brood mares in spite of a general ban on their exportation.[66] The Mantuan stud, which contained Arabs, Barbs, and ginetes and cross-breeds, was particularly renowned. In 1514 the marquis, Francesco Gonzaga, sent a consignment to Henry VIII, which so pleased the king that he declared that he had never ridden better-trained animals nor had ever received a more agreeable present.[67]

In his discussion of cattle husbandry Gervase Markham described the bull as "the breeders principal instrument of profit," emphasizing its role as sire. Bulls made good draft animals, too, though they had to be harnessed in single file like horses because, if yoked, they were difficult to match.[68] Mascall offered a further explanation when he told farmers not to yoke a bull with oxen since "he wilbe stubborne and sullen, and loues to be a maister ouer the rest, whereby he wil but trouble them." Rather, he recommended that the bull be kept "lustie and fat, to couer always your kine, so shal ye stil haue faire calues and large withall."[69] Topsell cautioned farmers against putting the bull to the cow before the age of two but thereafter he reckoned that it could serve ten cows a year.[70] Cows first received the bull at three years old. As dams, Markham advised breeders to select cows that provided the most milk, accounting them the best both for the dairy and for breeding purposes: "for she which goes long drie looseth halfe her profit, and is less fit for teeming."[71] When looking for a suitable ox, Markham claimed that large ones were the most profitable for the draft and for feeding, "for hee is the strongest to indure labor, and best able to containe both flesh and tallow." For the draft, he also recommended those with the gentlest nature and a familiarity with man.[72] To train a young ox, Mascall maintained, it should be yoked with an old ox, one that was tame, strong, and gentle, for it would restrain the novice if too quick or pull it along if too slow.[73]

According to Heresbach, the best cattle came from Hungary, Burgundy, Friesland, Denmark, and England.[74] England possessed three celebrated breeds of cattle, though there were a number of others of local importance. The longhorns of Yorkshire, Derbyshire, Lancashire, and Staffordshire had black coats, stocky build, and short legs. They were fine all-purpose beasts, strong in the draft, notable milkers and, when slaughtered, a good source of hide, horn, and tallow. The large shorthorns of the Lincolnshire fens, pied but mainly white in color, were even stronger and therefore the fittest for the draft. The red cattle of Somerset and Gloucester were akin to the Lincolnshires and carried out similar duties. They also made excellent milkers.[75] In Friesland the black-and-white cattle were specialist milkers.[76] Italy produced the best-known breeds of oxen. Mascall wrote that the white-coated oxen of the Campania, though small, proved "very good to labour in the plough and till the ground." The white or red oxen of Umbria, especially in the duchy of Urbino, were "mighty of body and of a great courage," while those of Tuscany and the area around Rome were "well set and thicke and strong made to labour." The strongest were bred in the uplands. Mascall described the oxen of the Alps and the hills of Burgundy as "strong and can well endure all labour, & fayre likewise withall." Topsell plumped for the oxen of the Apennines, though criticizing their appearance.[77]

By the end of the period some regions were developing a specialization in the management of their cattle. In 1597, for instance, a Shropshire M.P., speaking in the enclosure debate in the English Parliament, described the county as consisting "wholie of Woodland, bredd of Oxen & Dairies … and … hee hoped that as Herefordshire and the other Countries adioyning, were the Barnes for the Corne … this Shire might and would bee the Dayrie howse to the whole Realme." He could also have included nearby Cheshire, as well as other pastoral areas of the country such as the Forest of Arden, Wensleydale, and parts of Somerset and Suffolk.[78] On the European mainland dairy farming had progressed the furthest in the polder districts in the Low Countries, beginning in Flanders in the fourteenth century and spreading to Holland and Friesland in the fifteenth. Intensive farming methods, including the widespread use of fodder crops, raised yields to the highest in Europe. In the late sixteenth century the output per cow on Hemmema's farm in Friesland averaged an astonishing 42 kg of butter and 27.5 kg of cheese. In the polder areas of Flanders milk yields approached average figures only to be obtained elsewhere at the beginning of the twentieth century. As a result, farmers in the Low Countries were able to export nine-tenths of their cheese. Even Spanish colonists in the Americas purchased it (illegally).[79] Intensive dairy farming also spread along the coast eastward into Germany. Large consignments of cheese, produced by farmers in Ditmarsch at the mouth of the Elbe and in the Bay of Kiel, were sent to Hamburg and Bremen and further into Germany, as well as to Amsterdam and Groningen. In France, middlemen provisioned Paris with cheese from Normandy, Brie, and Picardy to the north and from Touraine and Auvergne to the south. They also supplied Auvergne cheese to Marseilles.[80] Growing international demand similarly stimulated the cheese trade in the Mediterranean. Italy had to import much of its dairy produce, for instance, because cows there were generally used for the draft. Boats loaded with Sardinian cheese sailed from Cagliari, bound for Naples, Rome, and Leghorn and to Marseilles and Barcelona as well. Farther east Venice obtained cheese from its subject territories, Dalmatia and Crete.[81] Dairy farmers weaned their calves early and disposed of all but replacement heifers. In the uplands of Auvergne, as in Shropshire and elsewhere, livestock farmers bought their corn by selling dairy produce and lean beasts.[82]

Cattle rearers acquired the surplus stock of dairy farmers, adding them to their own calves, which they allowed to run with their dam for up to a year.[83] At about the age of three, droves of cattle moved off, many to feeding grounds but some to mixed farming areas for training in the yoke and others to dairying districts as replacement heifers. The dealers assembled store cattle, in particular, into large herds and regularly transported them considerable distances, even crossing state frontiers. Inevitably, some attenuation of the herds occurred in transit either through theft, injury and death, or purchase by locals who needed them for their own purposes. In general, the pattern of movement was from the periphery to the center. In southern Europe merchants in the fifteenth century obtained cattle in Hungary, Wallachia, and the Black Sea coast and drove them to central Europe, especially to south Germany. After the Turks overran Hungary and the Balkans, supplies were obtained from Poland. In the sixteenth century, herds, often comprising 16,000 to 20,000 head of cattle, left Poland for the market at Buttstädt north of Weimar. Among those engaged in this long-distance trade were the Hirschvogel family of Nuremberg. From his base at Venice in the middle of the fifteenth century, Lienhart Hirschvogel controlled a complex commercial network that stretched from Hungary to the Baltic and that included the movement of cattle purchased in Hungary to Germany. At the other end of the continent drovers in Britain took large herds from Wales and Scotland down to southeastern England. Farther north Scandinavia sent stores to the rank (fettig) marshlands of north Germany and the Netherlands.[84]

The fattening of livestock tended to be dominated by large farmers because, as Everitt points out, the business required time, capital, and knowledge of marketing techniques, in all of which small men were deficient.[85] Many gentlemen engaged in fattening animals on their estates, both for domestic consumption and for the market. In Denmark fattening cattle for export was a noble privilege. In Oldenburg, during the course of the sixteenth century, the counts developed a very profitable cattle-fattening enterprise, using local beasts, augmented by stores from Denmark and the north German coast. Moreover, the business could only be conducted properly in areas where natural conditions favored it, as in fen- and marshlands or in the vicinity of large centers of consumption. By the end of the sixteenth century, however, the practice of fattening for the market had expanded, stimulated by growing urban demand and by the greater use of fodder crops.[86] Apart from stores the meat market comprised superannuated cattle (and sheep) fattened for slaughter at the end of their working life. These beasts were more likely to be fattened and sold locally, though dealers, graziers, and butchers touring markets and fairs for stock might buy them and take them farther afield. Clearly, their meat was tougher and less palatable than that obtained from younger stores, but it did provide an income for farmers for an otherwise redundant animal and a valuable addition to the diet for people of comparatively humble means. In Italy, where cattle were extensively deployed in the draft, there was a shortage of beef cattle, even near towns. In France and England, too, many of the animals were not reared primarily for meat. The evidence therefore suggests that veteran cows and oxen (and sheep) constituted a significant proportion of the meat market.[87]

Apart from upper-class demand, the burgeoning towns of Renaissance Europe provided the most clearly defined market for graziers. In England London was by far the most important center of meat consumption and its rapid growth in the late sixteenth century encouraged Home Counties large farmers with access to grazing grounds such as Romney Marsh to specialize in fattening stock. By 1600 the continuing increase in metropolitan demand widened the area from which the capital drew its supplies of meat. At the same time, provincial demand was growing and this prompted some cattle rearers to turn to fattening for the regional market, thereby threatening the flow of stores to London.[88] On the European mainland the extensive feeding grounds in the coastal marshes bordering the North and Baltic Seas supplied the towns of north Germany and the Netherlands with fatstock. In this respect, fattening ventures often complemented dairying enterprises because they thrived on rank marshland grass, unsuitable for milking herds.[89] Here too fattening was the preserve of the large farmer. Also, as in England, some of the suppliers of stores in Schleswig-Holstein, Jutland, the Danish Islands, and Skåne began to fatten their own animals. The cattle were subsequently driven to the Hanseatic towns of Lübeck, Hamburg, and Bremen and later to towns in Flanders, Brabant, and Holland.[90] Because fattened animals lost weight on long journeys (80 kg per 330 km) graziers had to bulk them up again on pastures close to their destination. For the counts of Oldenburg this was a particular problem because they sent most of their fatstock to Cologne, though they also sold cattle at Emden, Hamburg, and Amsterdam. The trip to Cologne took three weeks and to enable their beasts to compete with locally fattened animals, their agents had to graze their animals daily en route and finish them off on pastures near the city prior to the opening of the specialist cattle fairs there.[91]

Sheep and goats thrived on poorer soils than those that sustained cattle. Goats cost virtually nothing and earned an income in terrain unsuited to other animals, being kept, as Markham explained, in "wilde and barraine places, where Cattell of better profit can hardly be maintained." Because of their voracious appetite, however, they had to be kept away from gardens![92] Their hair was strong and possessed water-resistant properties, making it suitable as coarse packaging material or, if twisted, as rope for seafarers. Craftsmen made shoes and other items from their skin and goods as diverse as knife handles and lanterns from their horns.[93] While sheep could not compete with the omnivorous goat, they were still profitable and economical. Mascall declared that they were "one of the chiefest & fruitfullest for the vse of man." Not only did

farmers obtain a fleece from them each year but they could keep them with
"small trouble."[94] Even so, in upland regions shortage of pasture necessitated
the seasonal movement of flocks, often over long distances.[95] The sheep grazed
on the high pastures in spring and summer and in autumn moved down to the
lowlands.[96] In Castile millions of sheep belonging to the *Mesta* traveled along
the droveways (*cañadas*), leading from the northern highlands to the southern
valleys.[97] In France sheep migrated from Dauphiné to Provence or to Piedmont
in Italy. In the peninsula itself large composite herds and flocks left the western
Alps for the lowlands of Lombardy, Venezia, north Emilia, and even for Sicily.
Other routes led from the Tuscan Apennines and the Maremma and from the
Abruzzi to the coastal plains of Latium and Apulia.[98]

Sheep were primarily valued for their wool, the quality of which varied
by breed and environmental conditions: soil, herbage, and climate.[99] The fine,
short-stapled, curly fibered wool grew on the backs of small sheep grazing on
thinner soils on hills, moors, and downs, while the longer, coarser, straight-
fibered wool came from larger sheep kept on richer lowland pastures. As Heresbach observed, "The ritch & the champion countrey, breedeth a large, and
a great sheepe: the barraine and the clyffey, a reasonable stature: the wylde
and the mountaine grounde, a small and a weerysh sheepe." He rated English,
Rhineland, and French wool the highest.[100] At the opening of the fifteenth century England undoubtedly produced the finest wool in Europe, with the best
coming from the Leominster area of Herefordshire and from parts of Shropshire. It was much in demand abroad.[101] Two hundred years later the situation
was not as clear-cut. On the one hand, Markham could pronounce, "If you
desire to haue Sheepe of a curious fine Staple of Wooll ... you shall see such in
Herefordshire, about Lempster, and other speciall parts of the Countrie; in that
part of Worstershire ioining Shropshire and many such like places." He was
right for the Ryeland wool of Herefordshire and the March wool of Shropshire
remained without peer. On the other hand, in the Midlands and Lincolnshire,
traditionally areas of fine wool, enclosure and ranker grass had coarsened the
fleece of sheep grazing there.[102] At the same time the Spanish merino wool was
improving in quality, probably as a result of a program of cross-breeding native sheep with north African imports that had begun in the mid-fourteenth
century.[103] In an early sixteenth-century treatise Clement Armstrong thought
that "Spanysh woll is almost as good as English woll, which may well be soo,
by that Spayn hath housbonid ther wolle frome wurse to better, and England
from better to wurse." Armstrong, with his own point to make, undoubtedly
overstated the case and merino wool probably did not surpass the best English
product until the late sixteenth or early seventeenth centuries.[104] In contrast,
most of Italy's sheep produced coarse wool, probably on account of the hot climate. The best came from Apulia, Venetia, and possibly the Maremma.[105] As a
result of the poor quality of the native product, the traditional textile industry

in northern and central Italy had to obtain raw material from abroad. Como's supplies came from Germany, Provence, Spain, and England. The industry suffered from the dislocation caused by the Italian Wars and subsequently from Venetian competition. Nonetheless, by the end of the sixteenth century the old centers under Spanish control were making a comeback, using merino wool to manufacture cloth in the Venetian style.[106]

Many farmers kept sheep and goats for their milk. In England William Camden reported on the milking flocks of Essex in Elizabeth I's reign but the custom, widespread in the fourteenth century, was in decline by then. It disappeared from demesne manors in the fifteenth century.[107] Nonetheless, it remained a common practice in Mediterranean countries. According to the Italian Crescenzi, milk and cheese from sheep were preferable to dairy produce made from cows' milk.[108] Heresbach thought that, next to a woman's milk, goat's milk provided the best nourishment. Markham concurred, declaring that it was an "excellent restoratiue." Estienne and Liébault reckoned it to be better and healthier than ewe's milk.[109] They also agreed on the quality of kids' meat, which, Markham pronounced, made a "daintie Venison."[110] Ironically, he praised Welsh sheep as furnishing the "sweetest" mutton in Britain only to damn them for their small stature and the coarseness of their wool.[111]

No farmyard scene would have been complete without the chickens scratching around in the yard or the ducks and geese swimming in the pond. In the summer months the buzzing of the bees flying to and from their hives in the garden or orchard added to the "soundtrack." Farmers might also fatten pigs in a sty, though if they had access to commons, especially woodland, they turned them out to feed on whatever was available there: acorns, beech mast, hazelnuts, ash, crab apples, wild pears and plums, thorn and briar. Mascall advised farmers to collect plenty of acorns in the autumn so that they could feed them to the pigs throughout the year.[112] Swine and poultry bred prolifically and brought quick returns to their owners. Poultry, for instance, produced large clutches of young. Well-fed sows farrowed at the age of one and for a further six years produced three litters per annum, each comprising twelve to sixteen piglets.[113] Fitzherbert therefore recommended that pig keepers should rear boars and sows rather than hogs. Boars cost no more to feed, gave better meat, and sired numerous piglets.[114]

Some farmers reared these farmyard animals on a commercial scale. Dairy farmers fed pigs on dairy waste and their counterparts with extensive common rights in woodlands could maintain large herds. Most people kept them mainly for domestic consumption.[115] Moreover, because they required little expenditure they were popular with people of modest means. In the eastern part of Basse-Provence, a region characterized by small units of production, local farmers fed pigs on acorns in the oak woods of the area. Markham repeated contemporary opinion that swine were difficult to manage, accounting them "troublesome, noysome, vnruly and great ravenours," but thought that their utility and value more than compensated for this. As they thrived on kitchen and farm waste, he declared them to be "the Husbandmans best scauenger and the Huswifes most wholesome sinke."[116] Mascall recommended geese: "among all other the Goose is most profitable for the buier, and also the seller and to the husbandman, because they need not haue to great a charge and care for their meat as other must haue." He thought ducks cost a little more, being "great feeders." Markham disagreed, declaring that they "asketh no charge in keeping, but liueth of corne loft, or other things of lesse profit."[117] The two writers also differed over the cost of rearing turkeys, introduced into Europe from the Americas in the early sixteenth century. Mascall described them as "a right cofer for oates, and a sack for corne, a gulfe, a swallower of barns, a devourer of much meat" and regular strayers to boot. Markham denied these charges, claiming that they were cheaper and easier to maintain than any other domesticated fowl.[118] Bees provided the greatest incremental profit. Even cottagers benefited, for as Heresbach pointed out, "the poore soule of the countrey that hath no ground to occupy, may rayse hereof, and that without charges a great commoditie." He cited an occupier of a house in Spain with no more than an acre of ground, who made £80 a year in "ware and honey." According to Markham, no creature was more necessary, wholesome, or more profitable, nor less troublesome or chargeable.[119]

All but the poorest sectors of society profited from these farmyard animals. First, they obtained a comparatively cheap source of meat, primarily chicken with some duck and goose. Turkeys, as a more recent addition, divided opinion. Mascall described the meat as "delicate, but heauy and harde of digestion," while Markham declared them to be "most delicate, either in Paste, or from the Spit, and being fat, far exceeding any other house fowl."[120] Contemporaries had a particularly high opinion of pig meat. In an allusion to the Jewish prohibition against eating the meat, Heresbach observed that they could not have tasted French gammon. In his homeland of Germany the flitches of Westphalia, which came closest in quality, were not only esteemed throughout the country but also as far away as England and Rome. "Surely," he asked, "there is no beast besides, that makes more dainty dishes, there is in him neare 50 different tastes, where euery other beast hath but one."[121] In addition, poultry produced a renewable supply of eggs, an everyday food for Europeans. Their feathers provided a further income. Mascall in England and Estienne and Liébault in France emphasized the value to the housewife of geese feathers, collected once or twice a year.[122] Bees not only supplied honey but also a guide to humans on how to live their life! It seemed to Heresbach that God had specially created these insects, who "with the good example of theyr painfull diligence and trauaile, encorageth man to labour and take paines, according to his calling." He also pointed out that they obeyed their prince.[123]

Most people who kept dogs and cats did so for utilitarian purposes. Cats' traditional role was to keep down vermin and patrol the house and yard. Although some were allowed inside, mostly they fended for themselves and slept rough in out-buildings. Indeed, in order to encourage them to hunt many householders did not feed their cats properly.[124] The archetypal working dog in a largely rural Europe was the sheepdog, which Heresbach described as the most "necessary creature" on a farm. It helped herdsmen, shepherds, goatherds, swineherds, and drovers manage their herds and flocks and protected them from danger.[125] Working closely with their dogs, herdsmen were well aware of their intelligence: in England sheepdogs were left alone with the flock overnight and, according to Topsell, used their initiative to keep the sheep from straying. They needed no support because they were a match for any predator in the country. On the mainland of Europe, however, wolves presented a tougher challenge and for extra security, shepherds might employ a mastiff or a wolfhound.[126] Mastiffs (or bandogs) were used against fox and badgers, to drive wild animals and swine out of pastures, meadows, and orchards and also to bait a bull. In addition, they acted as guard dogs, especially at isolated farms and cottages or in remote places. Caius characterized them as "vast, huge, stubborn, ugly, and eager" so, even if they did not move very quickly, they were fierce and intimidating.[127] Householders also kept smaller dogs, called dog keepers or village dogs, which barked to warn of intruders. Incidentally, contemporary writers thought that geese and (for the gentry) peacocks provided as good an alarm service as dogs.[128]

Among the elite, hunting was extremely popular and aristocrats maintained a variety of dogs and hounds, each with their specific role. *Par force* hunting, that is, hunting on horseback with running hounds,[129] provided the best sport and the hart the noblest quarry. In particular, it offered the prospect of an exhilarating chase and the dramatic tension of an uncertain outcome. Its appeal lay, as Cummins notes, "in its complication and subtlety, its duration, the music of the horn, and above all the craft of working hounds."[130] In stature running hounds resembled the modern foxhound but squarer, with shorter legs and a flatter face. Some of the hounds were "sprinters," in that they started quickly but soon tired. As noted in Edward of Norwich's *The Master of Game,* a largely fifteenth-century copy of Gaston de Foix's *Livre de Chasse,* they were suited to hunting the wild boar and were therefore found in Spain and the Basque country. To chase the hart, slower but steadier hounds were preferred.[131] When the huntsmen wanted to find the quarry, they used a lymer, a hound with excellent sense of smell and trained to operate quietly. Somewhat larger than the main pack of running hounds, it nonetheless had a good turn of speed and as Caius noted, took its prey with a "jolly quickness." The lymer's lineal descendant is the bloodhound, emerging as a breed in the sixteenth century. In Scotland the latter was called a sluth hound and in

Germany a schlatthund.[132] A lymer or a brachet, another scenting hound, also led hunters toward wounded animals. In 1580 the Earl of Leicester gave a brachet to Lord Burghley, who thanked him for a gift which "maketh my hunting very certen; she hath never fayled me; and this last weeke she brought me to a stag which myself had strycken with my bow, being forced to ye soyle, wher with help of a gretar water spannyell yt forced hym out of ye water yr good brache helped pluck hym down."[133]

In bow and stable hunting the participants and onlookers were not on horseback and the outcome was preplanned and certain. Beaters drove the quarry toward the waiting party, who shot at the animals with crossbows. Conversely, keepers unleashed the hounds to pull down the moving animal as it was being driven past the spectators. These dogs were known as gazehounds because they hunted by sight. The most ferocious were the large, powerful alaunts and, as such, they had to be handled with care as they might attack the horses, huntsmen, or other hounds, as well as any domesticated animals that came within reach. From Topsell's description it seems as though the French imported them from Britain to kill their bears, wolves, and wild boars.[134] Alaunts often worked with the faster, though lighter, greyhound, which seized the animal first, before they arrived with their firmer grip. Edward of Norwich wrote that alaunts "by themselves … could never take a beast unless greyhounds were with them to make the beast tarry."[135] The best and most useful greyhounds were of medium size because they could hunt both large and small quarry. They were also very quick. According to Edward of Norwich, "A good greyhound should go so fast that if he be well slipped he should overtake any beast." When in 1544 Sir Henry Saville wrote to William Plumpton about his proposed visit to hunt, he described a bow and stable event with greyhounds, promising him that "Ye shall see your arrow fly and your greyhound run and all those that come with you." The gentry also enjoyed watching greyhounds course hares, even though Elyot, damning the sport with faint praise, defined it as pleasant for persons of a studious mind or timid disposition.[136] Greyhounds chased foxes as well. Of course, while beaters or dogs could start hares in the open, huntsmen had to use terriers to drive the fox from its den.[137] Harriers, as the name indicates, hunted the hare by scent and, according to size, foxes, wolves, deer, badgers, otters, polecats, lobsters, and rabbits too.[138]

Although hunting dogs were highly valued by their owners and well treated, they were not pets. Thomas defines a pet as an animal that was allowed into the house; that had a personal name; and that was never eaten.[139] Upper-class households in the Middle Ages regularly contained pets, mostly cats and dogs, but they only spread widely when the middling orders adopted the practice in the sixteenth and seventeenth centuries.[140] Pet dogs were the antithesis of hunting hounds because fashion dictated that they should be very small. As Caius wrote, "These puppies the smaller they be, the more pleasure they provoke, as

more meet playfellows for mincing mistresses to bear in their bosoms, to keep
company withal in their chambers, to succour with sleep in bed, and nourish
with meat at board, to lay in their laps and lick their lips as they ride in wag-
gons."[141] In the early sixteenth century the archetypial lapdog was a toy spaniel. Katherine, duchess of Suffolk, one of Queen Katherine Parr's maids of honor,
kept a pet dog called Gardiner, satirically named after the archconservative
bishop of Winchester.[142] Initially, fewer people owned cats but, even so, by the
end of the sixteenth century they had grown in popularity as pets. A cat shared
the third Earl of Southampton's cell in the Tower, when he was imprisoned there
after the failure of the Earl of Essex's rebellion in 1601.[143] Southampton subsequently commissioned a painting to commemorate his stay in prison, including
in it the cat that had accompanied him and that had been his sole companion.

One of the reasons why cats were slower than dogs to rise in public estima-
tion was the notion that because of their diet, their breath alone caused disease.
In 1607 Topsell wrote that the cat was "an vncleane and impure beast that
liueth onely vpon vermin and by rauening."[144] Contemporaries therefore rarely
ate cats, that is, except in Spain and Narbone where they cut off the head and
tail and hung the flesh in the cold air for one or two nights to get rid of the
poison.[145] In a poem on cats, Ronsard wrote of this fear:[146]

> Je hay leurs yeux, leur front et leur regard:
> Et les voyant je m'enfuy d'autrepart
> Tremblant de nerfs, de veines, et de member,
> Et jamais Chat n'entre dedans ma chamber.

Cats, partly nocturnal hunters, were also viewed as independent and rather
mysterious. They were also strongly territorial and content to stay at home.
Indeed, Topsell remarked that they would not leave a place "for the loue of any
man."[147] Dogs, on the other hand, were happy to accompany their master and
this "dogged" loyalty and faithfulness endeared them to their owners. As Topsell observed, "There is not any creature without reason, more louing to his
Maister, nor more seruiceable then is a Dogge."[148] In *La Franciade*, composed
in 1573, Ronsard addressed this subject:[149]

> Plus comme un chien au bon nez, qui du bois
> Ayant oui de son maistre la voix,
> Revient á luy, le reflatte et la touche
> Et sous ses pieds obeisant se couche,
> L'oeil contremont qui semble demander
> Si son seigneur luy veult rien commander,
> A sa parolle ayant l'oreille preste
> Sans sommeiller d'une pesante teste.

Even so, the old image of dogs as filthy scavengers did not completely disappear, continuing to exist in literary metaphors and popular proverbs.[150]

The Renaissance period witnessed considerable change in the way in which society used domesticated animals. At the opening of the period European farmers were giving greater priority to stock rearing as the decline in the population reduced demand for cereals and prices fell. In consequence, many more people were able to afford to eat meat and animal products and their diet improved. As population rose once more in the late fifteenth or early sixteenth centuries, the situation was reversed and real standards of living declined for most people. Yet mixed farmers could not do without animals: they provided the draft and their manure fertilized their corn fields. Animals transported all manner of goods on the roads. Regional differences persisted, though in general horses became more popular on the farms and roads of northern Europe and oxen (and cows) predominated in the south. In the southern uplands asses and mules were commonly deployed as carriage and pack animals and in places used on the farms too. The growth in Europe's population also promoted specialization in livestock husbandry as regions began to focus on producing those commodities best suited to physical and climatic conditions. Consequently, the number of domesticated animals continued to rise throughout the period.

Domesticated animals also served a social purpose. Ownership of a saddle horse, for instance, marked a real social divide. Naturally, the elite maintained stables full of valuable horses, each with their designated, often nonutilitarian function. Horsemanship was viewed as an essential attribute of a gentleman and to be seen riding a mettlesome steed in public was as much a political as a social statement. Control of such a noble creature clearly demonstrated the fitness of the upper classes to rule. At first, therefore, traditionally minded gentlemen were reluctant to be seen riding in a coach: it was unmanly and did not allow them to display their equestrian skills. On the other hand, it did act as a mobile indicator of their wealth and standing. Horses, together with hounds, played a vital role in hunting, a passion for which united the ruling classes throughout Europe. *Par force* hunting was the most valued form since it enabled participants to demonstrate their riding skills, their hardiness, and their courage in the face of dangerous quarry like the wild boar or hart. They treated their horses and hounds well. Increasingly people kept dogs—and cats and a variety of other animals—as pets. Dogs led the way, people valuing them for their loyalty and responsiveness to human command. Cats were accepted more slowly; apart from their independence, the notion that their breath caused illness acted as a deterrent. Their role as a companion, however, was graphically illustrated in the portrait of the third Earl of Southampton, depicted with his cat as a prisoner in the Tower of London.

CHAPTER FOUR

Entertaining Animals

TERESA GRANT

The Elizabethan antiquary William Lambarde, writing in 1576, made clear that, like many contemporaries, he viewed the sports of London's "liberties" as a package, differentiated but of the same type: "No more then suche as goe to Parisgardein, the Bell Savage, or some other such common place, to behold Bearebayting, Enterludes, or Fence playe, can account of any pleasant spectacle unless they first paye one pennie at the gate, another at the entrie of the Scaffolde, and the thirde for a quiet standing."[1] It is a commonplace that the proximity of the Elizabethan and Jacobean theaters to those other houses of entertainment, the bull and bear baitings, drew comparisons, particularly from detractors, between playing and baiting.[2] We read that the same crowds visited each in turn, and it has been surmised that one reason for the embargo on theatrical performance on Thursdays and Sundays was to protect the livelihood of the baiting houses. Later both entertainments were outlawed on Sunday, and Tuesdays were used instead. Certainly, it seems that Sunday had been the traditional day for baiting that gave many Puritans cause for self-congratulatory hand-rubbing when part of the old bear-baiting arena collapsed one Sunday in the 1580s, killing and injuring some of the spectators. John Norden's 1593 map of London shows the "beare house" and the neighboring "play house," the Rose, built in 1587 by Philip Henslowe, the manager of the Lord Admiral's Men.[3] In 1594, Edward Alleyn, who first performed such roles as Tamburlaine and Faustus, acquired an interest in the "beare garden" and his financial partnership with Henslowe (which lasted from 1591 until Henslowe's death in 1616) was cemented by his marriage to Henslowe's stepdaughter Joan. Lambarde's comment makes clear that the layout of theaters and baiting arenas was similar. And in fact, in 1613 Henslowe and Alleyn built the Hope on the site of the Bear garden, a "dual-function playhouse and baiting house."[4] These impresarios clearly understood that the proximity of the baiting houses and the theaters made good business sense, and indeed, between 1609–1611, polar bear cubs in their care "acted" in plays.[5] It may have irritated them, however, that the plays in question, *The Winter's Tale* and *Mucedorus*, were performed by a rival company, the King's Men.

CULTURAL GEOGRAPHY

> Of sports and pastimes in this Citie. Everie thing hath his time, a time to weep, a time to laugh, a time to mourne, & a time to daunce. Eccles. 3.
>
> Let us now saith (Fitz Stephen) come to the sportes and pastimes, seeing it is fitte that a cittie should not onely be commodious and serious, but also merrie and sportfull.[6]

John Stow's topographical survey of the city of London and its suburbs devotes a substantial section to Londoners' sports and pastimes, past and present, taking care to stress the continuity of festive tradition. Stow's decision to include what happens in London as well as its physical attributes indicates a keen understanding that places are made as much by their rules and customs as by their buildings. The physical location for all the events discussed here was London's "liberties," those suburbs (and isolated spaces within London's city walls) where, almost by historical accident, neither crown nor city could exercise effective restraint. Steven Mullaney notes: "Free, or 'at liberty,' from manorial rule or obligations to the crown, the liberties 'belonged' to the city yet fell outside the jurisdiction of the lord mayor, the sheriffs of London, and the Common Council, … constitut[ing] an ambiguous geopolitical domain over which the city had authority but, paradoxically, almost no control."[7] It was in these spaces—north of the city from Bishopsgate, Moorgate, and Newgate toward Hackney and Islington, and in Southwark, south of the Thames to the west of London bridge—that Londoners played. The kinds of play were many. Stow quotes William fitz Stephen's (*fl.* 1162–1174) "Description of London," and adds his own updates of Londoners' pastimes: "shews upon Theaters & Comical pastimes … for the acting thereof certaine publike places, as the Theater, the Curtine, &c have been erected"; cockfighting; ice skating; boar fighting (a twelfth-century pastime, it seems); bull and bear baiting "till this day much frequented"; tennis; wrestling; May Games involving may-poles and Robin Hood; and "many of the citizens do delight themselves in Hawkes, and houndes, for they have libertie of hunting in *Middlesex, Hartfordshire,* all *Chiltron,* and in *Kent* to the water of *Cray.*"[8] The specificity of place is important: as well as allotted times,[9] these sports had physical spaces proper to their exercise.

The liberties were not, therefore, places of anarchy; indeed sports and pastimes took place in these locales because it was ordained that they should. License, itself the result of custom, was given by legislation, as indicated by Stow's detailed description of the orders constituted by Parliament for the running of the "stewes" or brothels,[10] also in the Southwark liberties. Additionally the liberties accommodated prisons, hospitals, and lazar houses, undesirable within the city walls perhaps, but necessities over which the city sought some authority, even if it was limited.[11] My point is this: the activities that had been ordained for the liberties were those not thought to be "commodious and serious," either because they were unsavory (prisons, lepers, prostitution) or because, "merrie and sportfull," they required greater space than the confines of the city could afford.[12] This was often because they were spectator sports involving crowds—this was an issue both of physical space and the threat of lack of control—but also because many of the activities included animals, and not necessarily tame ones. Baiting was not the only entertainment offered by animals in Shakespeare's day. "Intelligent" animals were trained to do tricks. The monkey Ben Jonson's Stagekeeper mentions in the Induction to *Bartholomew Fair* was "a well-educated ape to come over the chain for the King of England, and back again for the Prince, and sit still on his arse for the Pope and the King of Spain."[13] Morocco, the most famous performing horse of his day, could also distinguish between friend and foe, and acted accordingly: he would also go into a trance, beat out the sum of dice with his hoofs, and was even supposed to have climbed to the top of old St Paul's steeple for a bet.[14] This was the cultural context in which the audience of Shakespeare's stage lived: a world where animal baitings, dancing bears, and performing monkeys were quite commonplace, particularly in London and nowhere more so than on Bankside. This represents both a historical and a geographical remove: the meaning of animals in the drama of the period depends upon its *place* of first performance, as well as its *time*. A right reading depends upon understanding the context of animal acts and their festive uses, so familiar to the audiences of stage plays of the period. We need to look at the acts themselves, but also the lore, classical and vernacular, that lay behind their performers.

As performing bears have attracted recent reinterpretation, this chapter investigates more workaday animal performers: the dogs of Jonson's *Every Man Out of His Humour* (1599), Marston's *Histrio-mastix* (1610), and Middleton and Dekker's *The Roaring Girl* (1611); and the horse in the anonymous *Woodstock* (ca. 1595–1610).[15] The spectral presence of Crab the mongrel in *The Two Gentlemen of Verona* will keep appearing in the discussion; the other dogs on the early modern stage must be situated in the context of two excellent studies of this play.[16] As Bruce Boehrer has pointed out, there is an "eternal triangle between man, hound and horse" that will be significant for the purposes of this chapter.[17] The plays concerned use the relationship between man, dog, and horse to make social comment particularly pertinent in the setting of the liberties. We have seen in Stow that each sport had its time and place and, especially in the sections he takes from fitz Stephen, that some customs were tied to a specific social group, such as schoolboys, scholars, citizens' sons, and courtiers. The *Book of Sports* (1618) continues this advice: some recreations are only appropriate to men, some to women, and "the meaner sort of people [are] by law prohibited [from] Bowling."[18]

The kind of dog a playwright uses is important. Marjorie Garber has noted that the early moderns transferred their social distinctions from man to dog; as Macbeth opined, about the First Murderer's assertion that they are men:

Ay, in the catalogue ye go for men,
As hounds and greyhounds, mungrels, spaniels, curs,
Shoughs, water-rugs, and demi-wolves are clipt
All by the name of dogs; the valued file
Distinguishes the swift, the slow, the subtle,
The house-keeper, the hunter, every one,
According to the gift which bounteous nature
Hath in him clos'd.[19]

Macbeth's point is that, as today, different dogs mean different things. Pit bull and papillon owners choose their dogs for different reasons, as did the playwrights of the period. In *Every Man Out* Puntarvolo owns a greyhound; Marston, Middleton and Dekker's citizens have water spaniels. In all these plays the type of dog is used with thematic force to reinforce characterization and to comment on social issues. And crucially, of course, both a man's and a dog's place in the world is ordained by "nature," according to his gifts.

DOGS: *EVERY MAN OUT OF HIS HUMOUR*

Nowadays *Every Man Out* is among the more obscure of Jonson's plays, its topicality of reference making it almost impenetrable to a modern audience. Very little "happens" in this "humors" comedy, which rests mostly on people's various ridiculousness rather than on comical situations. The main character is a knight called Puntarvolo who, mistaking his time, thinks he has a starring role in Malory's *Morte D'Arthur:* his "humor" is an exaggerated chivalry rather like Don Quixote's. Puntarvolo is overfond of his greyhound who accompanies him almost everywhere. The play uses the dog plot partly as a means of bringing the action to a close; when the envious Macilente poisons Puntarvolo's dog, this acts as the catalyst for most of the characters' loss of their humors. Baiting Puntarvolo, Macilente and Carlo (a malicious clown) suggest that he should have his dead dog flayed and buy a slightly smaller dog to fit in the skin.[20] The ensuing riot gets Fastidius Brisk, an exaggerated dandy, finally brought to

account for being a spendthrift and persuades Fungoso, a citizen's son trying
to impersonate a gentleman, that he has "done imitating any more gallants."[21]
Thus Carlo is forced to speak politely to Puntarvolo, who for the first time in
his life, loses his exaggerated chivalry, while Macilente's envy is satisfied (in the
Quarto) by the collapse of everybody's ideals: "I am as empty of all envy now, /
As they of merit to be envied at."[22] This denouement springs from the loss of
Puntarvolo's humor, of which the dog is not merely the principal objectifica-
tion,[23] but some kind of embodiment. In fact, the knight precipitates his own
downfall by falling short of chivalric expectations when he joins the party going
to mock a pretentiously witty gentlewoman, Saviolina. When abandoning his
dog to enter the court, he also temporarily loses his gentlemanliness. Thus it is
entirely fitting that the dog, the expression of this quality, be poisoned by the
likes of Macilente, as Puntarvolo has been by his association with this riff-raff.

Playgoers would have recognized Puntarvolo's greyhound as a peculiarly
English symbol. Keith Thomas notes that "there was a pronounced tendency
to regard the dog as the symbol of the nation. English dogs had been in demand from Roman times and in the Elizabethan age it was customary to claim
that they were better than those of any other country."[24] Humanizing of dogs
(as Launce does Crab in Shakespeare's *Two Gentlemen*) led to the association
of particular breeds with particular characters and classes. Dogs differed in status because their owners did; people tended to have dogs appropriate to their
social position.[25] Royal portraits included various pedigree dogs but never, of
course, anything not easily identifiable as classy. Daniel Mytens's *The King Departing for the Chase* shows Charles I and Henrietta Maria with the ubiquitous
King Charles spaniels and various show and hunting dogs (see Figure 4.1). But
the most aristocratic of all dogs was the greyhound: in Pisanello's *Vision of
St. Eustace* we see the patron saint of huntsmen with greyhounds and spaniels,
anachronistically recording the dog collection of the painter's patron, Leonello
d'Este, Duke of Ferrara (see Figure 4.2). Similarly, we can infer Puntarvolo's
social status from his greyhound.

John Caius's celebrated "catalogue" *Of Englishe Dogges* gives the following explanation of the derivation of the word *greyhound*:

> The Grehound called *Leporarius*, hath his name of this word, Gre, which
> word soundeth, Gradus in Latine, in Englishe degree. Because among all
> dogges these are the most principall, occupying the chiefest place, and
> being simply and absolutely the best of the gentle kinde of houndes.[26]

In the 1607 *Historie of Foure-Footed Beastes* greyhounds know their worth:
"they will not run after every trifling beast, by secret instinct of nature, dis-
cerning what kind of beast is worthy or unworthy of their labor, distaining to
meddle with a little or vile creature."[27] This association of hunting dogs and

FIGURE 4.1: Daniel Mytens, *The King Departing for the Chase.*

gentlemen was laid down by medieval game laws that restricted the ownership of dogs of "the gentle kinde" to those of above a certain social class.[28] Ian Mac-Innes has argued that the association of the mastiff with the English could be "justif[ied] … in humoral terms, [the dog itself] mirroring in body and mind the temperament attributed frequently to northern humans."[29] The greyhound's association with chivalry is also humoral, as he acquires the attributes of his lawful *gentle* master (or vice versa). This might prove particularly instructive in "humors" comedy such as *Every Man Out,* reinforcing its humoral reading of social class as both naturally imbued and fixed. Puntarvolo's dog becomes part and parcel of Jonson's essentially conservative social agenda.

Though dogs could also be a symbol of man's baser parts, the early modern hound, obeying the law that a dog is like its master, became an emblem of fidelity in a chivalric world where fidelity was the most highly prized of a knight's attributes.[30] Puntarvolo's obsession with his dog is yet another attempt to reinvent himself as a knight of a former time with all the attendant romantic allusions. After Puntarvolo, pretending to be a knight errant who has become (punningly) lost, woos his own wife up a ladder outside her bedroom window, Carlo reflects on "a tedious chapter of courtship after Sir Lancelot, and Queen Guinevere."[31] But Puntarvolo has become confused about his treatment of the dog. It is he who is faithful and loving toward the animal, rather than vice versa. Carlo claims that it is on account of belonging to such a quixotic figure as Puntarvolo that the dog affects melancholy. In fact, the dog's humor suits his master's temperament. Unlike Launce in *The Two Gentlemen,* who does occasionally manage

FIGURE 4.2: Pisanello, *Vision of St. Eustace.*

it, Puntarvolo seems incapable of separating himself from the greyhound. After he wagers that he will get himself, his wife, and his dog to and from Constantinople in one piece, his later attempts to maintain the health and security of the dog might seem to be in order to win. But Carlo and Fastidius make it clear that his soppy behavior predates any decision to undergo the journey. Of course, Puntarvolo's wager on the dog implies the misplacing of emotional ties; the dog is next to his wife in his affections. It sounds like they are going on a family holiday. Everyone enters into this spirit of conjugation. Instead of asking after Puntarvolo when they rendezvous, they enquire about his dog. One might suspect Fastidius of irony at 3.1.252 when he asks the knight "how does your fair dog?" but this echoes Sogliardo[32]—a foolish morris-dancing citizen trying to gentrify himself and the uncle of the dandy-in-training Fungoso—who is not one for intentional humor. Unlike Crab, who only after he is Crab is Launce's dog, Puntarvolo's nameless beast relies entirely for its character on being a refraction of him. Puntarvolo, threatened by the idea that Shift will teach his dog to smoke, uses the dog as an excuse for not dining with Shift: "Pardon me, my dog shall not eat in his company for a million."[33] Carlo and Sogliardo, who both have an interest in pacifying Shift, try to lessen the insult:

> *Carlo.* Nay, be not you amazed, Signor Whiff, whate're that stiff-necked gentleman says.
>   *Sogliardo.* No, for you do not know the humour of the dog, as we do.[34]

It is unclear about whom Sogliardo is speaking; characteristically he has conflated Puntarvolo's humor with his dog's.

Puntarvolo's assumption of his dog's personality implies a parallel blurring of the distinctions between his cat and his wife. That Lady declines to travel with the party on discovering that her affecting wooing scene with the "poore knight errant" was observed by all and sundry. Carlo thinks this is for the better, because the cat has eight more lives than Puntarvolo's wife.[35] Puntarvolo also considers the likelihood of seasickness less, but the parallels are enforced by the pointing out of these small differences. They are both female, whereas Puntarvolo and his dog are male. Of course, not all greyhounds were actually male, but they were gendered male in the same way as all spaniels were gendered female according to early modern materialist psychology.[36] Animals displaying certain "character traits" follow the "gender" of those traits. So while his wife sulks in her room, his cat is confined to hers with sore eyes and catarrh.[37] Jonson seems to have a fondness for poor cat jokes: "My squire has her there in the bag" refers to the practice of substituting a cat for a sucking pig in a bag at a fair and hoping that someone will be dim enough to buy it unseen,[38] thus reinforcing the comparison of the real thing (Puntarvolo's wife) with an imitation (the cat). This substitution of cat for person draws attention to the play's obsession with people masquerading as what they are not. Jonson particularly satirizes the upwardly mobile. Sogliardo buys his way into gentlemanliness, purchasing his arms and their patent for 30 pounds; we have seen Fungoso abandon his attempt to mimic gallants "in purse and apparel." But Jonson sends up others who would not be themselves; as Boehrer notes, "the goal that *Every Man Out* seeks to achieve is the exposure of affectation … some form of social pretence."[39] This also ties into the suggestion that Puntavolo, in order to fulfill the terms of the bet with Fastidius Brisk, should "flay … your dog presently … and stuff his skin well with straw … or get … somewhat a less dog and clap into the skin."[40] Carlo's absurd idea that Puntarvolo can cloak a new dog in an old skin, or merely stuff the old one, is intended to point out that most of the characters are pretending in some way to be something else. In a play that satirically insists with Sogliardo that if you have the sign (arms) of a gentleman then you are one—if you have a greyhound, are you then a knight? Boehrer rightly connects Puntarvolo's fantasy knight-errantry with the period's obsession with self-promoting travel,[41] but the demise of his greyhound and Puntarvolo's demotion to being the owner of a lesser dog also harps on another of Jonson's pet hates. Chapman, Marston, and Jonson, voicing Gertrude in *Eastward Ho!* (1605), lament the change that has come over England's aristocracy:

The Knighthood now a daies, are nothing like the Knighthood of old time. They rid a horseback Ours goe afoote. They were attended by their squires. Ours by their Lacquaies. They went buckled in their Armor, Ours muffled in their Cloaks. They trauaild wildernesses, & desarts, Ours dare scarce walke the streets. They were stil prest to engage their Honour, Ours stil ready to paune their cloaths. They would gallop on at sight of a Mo[n]ster, ours run away at sight of a Serieant. They would helpe poore Ladies, Ours make poore Ladies.

> *Syndefy.* I Madam, they were Knights of the Round-Tablet at *Winchester,* that sought Adue[n]tures, but these of the Square Table at *Ordinaries,* that sit at Hazard.[42]

There *is* something valiant in Puntarvolo's attempt to live up to the "knighthood of old time," but the times of *Every Man Out* and especially of *Eastward Ho!,* in its Jacobean "10 pound knight" setting, will not allow adventures to be other than mock heroic. Jonson's conservative social agenda, like many people's, is not one that can really conceive of a return to "better" times. Puntarvolo's real mistake remains his lack of chivalry at Saviolina's expense and it is this that does for his dog.

Boehrer has noted that for playwrights, perhaps especially for Jonson, there was a source of potential embarrassment in the connections drawn by almost everyone between the stage and the baiting arena.[43] But Jonson's classicism and his adherence to "high" culture did not stop him exploiting vernacular culture in, for instance, *Volpone,* which relies upon traditional fox lore for its central conceit.[44] Indeed the story of the fox feigning death to tempt carrion birds close enough to catch them demonstrates that much of the animal lore of this period was available in multiple sources—classical, medieval, and in Renaissance natural history. Edward Topsell's account clearly originates in Gesner's *Historia Animalium,* but can be traced as far back as the Greek writer Oppian (both books in Jonson's library), and it was a persistent theme throughout the intervening period, both in written and pictorial form.[45] In nearly all of the bestiaries derived from the *Physiologus,* the fox appears pictured in this guise, "shamming dead and being investigated by birds."[46]

So, because of the multivalency of source material, Jonson's very classicism could not necessarily preclude his use of vernacular traditions. If we note themes in *Every Man Out* that harken back to medieval English and continental folklore, we should not be surprised. Just as Stow's *Survey* updated fitz Stephen's London, so part of Topsell's project in the *Historie* was a redaction and correction of the medieval bestiary tradition. Richard Beadle has shown how Shakespeare's dog play, *The Two Gentlemen of Verona,* makes substantial use of popular comic traditions as well as classical precedents.[47] Both Beadle and Boehrer have noted that one of the important things about Crab in *The Two Gentlemen* is that he cannot be trusted to perform reliably either for audience or playwright: his part cannot require him to do specific tricks, including those that would be "natural" to a dog.[48] Boehrer recognizes that Crab's likely refusal to "perform" even bad behavior when required necessitates that Launce *report* his inappropriate antics (stealing food, farting, and "making water" on Silvia's farthingale) on their visit to Silvia: "not only does the dog threaten to frustrate Launce's metatheatrical moments; he also threatens to frustrate Shakespeare's frustration of these moments."[49] This off-stage metatheatricality is also present in *Every Man Out,* though differently refracted.

 Despite any embarrassment over the links to popular entertainment that it might forge, Jonson could not and did not avoid the homespun. With regard to the performance of tricks, there is some suggestion that that most noble of dogs, Puntarvolo's greyhound, was the canine joker in the pack. Though Fungoso brings back no more details to Puntarvolo of his poisoning than "your dogge lies giving up the ghost in the wood-yard,"[50] the audience witnesses Macilente administering the poison and could witness the death of the dog if the animal had sufficient skill to enact it. A story in Plutarch's *Moralia* is pertinent:[51]

> This dog served a plaier who professed to counterfeit many persons, and represent sundry gestures; & among sundry other pretty tricks which his master taught him, answerable to divers passions, occasions and occur-rences represented upon the stage, his master made an experiment on him with a drogue or medicine which was somniferous indeed and sleepie, but must be taken and supposed deadly; who tooke the piece of bread wherein the said drogue was mingled, and within a little while after he swallowed it done, he began to make as though he trembled, quaked, yea and staggered, as if he had been astonied, in the end he stretched out himselfe, and lay as stiffe as one starke dead, suffering himselfe to be pulled, haled, and drawen from one place to another, like a very blocke, according to the present argument and place required.[52]

Is this what originally happened onstage as Puntarvolo's greyhound died? Some versions of the text have the stage direction "Kickes him out" after line 85, which might suggest that the dog dies off-stage.[53] Even in the absence of an animal capable of such "prety tricks" this represents a determined nod in the direction of such antics on Jonson's part. We cannot rule out Plutarch as his source since Jonson probably knew the *Moralia* in Latin before its English translation of 1603. But this dog was just the earliest recorded of many, attached to clowns, in what became a healthy native tradition. Richard Tarlton, the Elizabethan clown, is described working with a performing dog in similar set pieces.[54] It is as likely that Jonson's allusion to this trick would remind his audience as much of *joculatores'* variety acts as it did of Plutarch.

 But, as Boehrer has noted in relation to *The Two Gentlemen,* the under-standable refusal on a playwright's part to *script* dog scenes is tacit acknowl-edgment of the limits of theater.[55] Usually, surely, *Every Man Out's* dog has to "die" off-stage (as it must in the absence of a greyhound trained to feign poisoning) and stage *reportage* of dog "tricks" takes the place of action. We have "a staged narrative representation of the failure of dramatic representation."[56] By admitting that the dog trick cannot always be played, Jonson draws attention to what Boehrer calls "the inability to progress from imitation to identity,"[57] crucial in a play so concerned with pretension and attempts to jump social classes. "Of course," Jonson argues in *Every Man Out*, "a leopard cannot change its spots," or, in the case of Sogliardo, a yeoman his rank. But what about a production where the animal has been schooled as Plutarch's dog was? Is it just a trick? Or does it intervene to suggest that if you *can* maintain your imitation it becomes your identity; that identity is merely imitation; or that there is something quasi-magical about theater?

DOGS AND CLASS: CITIZEN COMEDY

Cuddy in *The Witch of Edmonton* makes clear that, just as it was fitting for Puntarvolo to have a greyhound, water spaniels naturally belong to citizens: "neither is it a citizen's water-spaniel, enticing his master to go a-ducking twice or thrice a week, whilst his wife makes ducks and drakes at home."[58] Apart from its comic value, the reason for introducing the water spaniel and the duck onto the stage in Marston's *Histrio-mastix* (1610) is that they strongly characterize the citizens whom they accompany. Lawrence notes, "popular sport was exemplified in *Histriomastix*, a mystifying play in which Velure and Lyon-rash, when about to go duck-hunting, arrive on the scene with a water-spaniel and a duck."[59] This odd pageant-like play parades personifications of the Liberal Arts, Peace, Plenty, Pride, Envy, Warre, Poverty, and Astraea, the virgin goddess of justice, (to name but a few) across the stage. Velure and Lyon-rash demonstrate by going duck hunting how Plenty has afforded them leisure:

Come sirs, how shall we recreate our selves,
This plentious time forbids aboad at home.[60]

But Furcher and Vourchier tempt their friends to "meet some ten miles hence to hawke and hunt."[61] As a result of the "bounty of the time" they are, as Velure says, "Pancrace Knights." This is, of course, oxymoronic because St. Pancras fields, the right setting for fowling, a citizen sport, would be the last place you would expect to find knights. The disjunction of degree and recreation signals the disappearance of Peace and Plenty because it carries over into the citizens' feelings about their trades:

this plenty yeelds us choise of sports.
Our trades and we are now no fit consorts.[62]

Rather than using his horse as a mode of transport, Vourchier wants to "breath" (exercise) it as if he were a gentleman. Citizens may go "ten miles hence to hawke and hunt," but this is not a fitting pastime for nongentlemen and indicates that Pride and disaster are shortly to follow.

For this same reason, the water spaniels that belong to the citizens in *The Roaring Girl* are unremarkable.[63] Gallipot and Tiltyard are engaged upon a pursuit in keeping with their class, and water spaniels are the best type of dog for an afternoon's duck hunting. Issue must be taken with Wright's claim that "all of this is without any relation to the play, and is simply a variety show entertainment inserted extraneously."[64] He is quite wrong about both points: a structural pun in *The Roaring Girl* depends mainly upon this scene. At this very point in the text, Gallipot draws a significant parallel: "we'll show you the bravest sport at Parlous Pond … Here's the best duck in England, except my wife."[65] While he is setting his water spaniels to chase one of his ducks, Openwork's wife-duck is being chased for sport by a rather more predatory creature. Mistress Openwork initially enjoys the parallel that Goshawk's pursuit of her creates: "but, sirrah, this water-spaniel dives after no duck but me: his hope is having me at Brentford to make me cry quack."[66] Laxton refers to Mistress Gallipot as "wild fowl" at 3.2.238, continuing the suggestion that women are subject to the same treatment from men as ducks from dogs. But Trapdoor is sure of his species: he tells Sir Alexander Wentgrave that "For fetching, no water-spaniel is like me."[67] His engagement in double-dealing between Moll and Sir Alexander is typical of the "fawning" spaniel, with "a kind of sensational loyalty whose potential hypocrisy made it suspicious."[68]

The parallel between ducks and women, particularly citizens, is reinforced by the use of the word *trug* for the duck in *The Roaring Girl* 2.1.414. Cyrus Hoy cites several incidences among, apparently, many where the word *trug* is used to mean prostitute, and comments that: "I suspect that 'the trug' here represents some such cry as 'Hey, duck' in Davenant's 'The Long Vacation in London.'"[69]

> Ho, ho! to Islington ; enough!
> Fetch Job my son, and our Dog Ruffe!
> For there in Pond, through Mire and Muck,
> We'l cry, hay Duck, there *Ruffe*, hay Duck![70]

The poem is a verse burlesque on citizens' pastimes: aldermen play quoits, the lord mayor inspects Bartholomew Fair, attorneys and proctors take their bows and arrows to Finsbury Fields.[71] The sports they play reveal their social standing as do the places where they head ("Islington" and "Finsbury"), but no small part of their characterization is the proper accoutrements of these pastimes: the "canvas bow case" and "arrows";[72] the duck; the right sort of dog.

As in Stow's *Survey*, the topography is so important for physical and social placing: men are what they do, wear, pet.

Paul Mulholland thinks "the sense of Trug ('prostitute, trull') better accords with common associations of duck than with Stevens's suggestion that it was the name of the spaniel."[73] The structural pun in *The Roaring Girl*, which timetables that real duck hunt with Laxton's and Goshawk's attempts to seduce Mistresses Gallipot and Openwork respectively, is supported by the traditional view of citizen's wives as pathologically unfaithful to their husbands. Cuddy's comment, "whilst his wife makes ducks and drakes at home,"[74] uses typical language to describe such behavior, which in much City Comedy is influenced by the strong featuring of the Thames as a means of escape from everyday city life.

But Middleton and Marston must have hoped for some sort of sensation when they arranged for water spaniels and a duck to be brought on stage at the same time: the least that could be expected would be some sort of (in)appropriate interest in the duck on behalf of the dogs and consequent comedic value. But because you cannot risk scripting for this, as we have seen, each performance would be different. Of course, as dramatic theorists have long noted, *every* performance, scripted or not, is unique. The dramatic action takes place in real, unmalleable, time. Perhaps the crucial point is that the duck and water spaniel are commonplace, rightly inhabitants of the liberties, whose appearance on stage is a topical reference of much the same sort as references to specific places. But what is different from name-checking a specific ordinary, or even alluding to the fact that the action takes place in a specific theater, is that the dog, the duck, and Gallipot and Tiltyard are *at once* real and fictional. They are not allusions but illusions: they have a physical existence. This is a metatheatrical device: it points to the fictive nature of theater while recreating a very specific social scene, suitable for the locale. Because the playwright neither scripts nor do we expect a trick, this stage direction does not invoke Boehrer's formulation where an animal scene replayed in narration admits theater's lack of transformative power. A stage direction is something read or seen but, crucially, it can never be narration in the way that Launce's woeful tale of Crab's misdemeanors is. Stage directions do not draw an audience's attention to the limits of theater, even, as here, when there are intratextual implied stage directions "puh—pist—hur—hur-pist" to go with the actual "he spits in the dog's mouth."[75]

But this is not a "trick." The scene from *The Roaring Girl* has created problems for critics because they tend to misunderstand the nature of Tiltyard's spitting in his dog's mouth: "Gallipot [*sic*] has one of the dogs trained to serve as a cuspidor, for he spits in the dog's mouth, a scene which must have brought a storm of laughter from the groundlings."[76] In fact, they probably thought this a quite normal way to behave around a dog, as did William Fennor in *The*

Compter's Commonwealth (1617): "when a poore man comes nigh a churlish mastiffe he must not spurne him if he mean to go quietly by him, but flatter and stroake him on the backe, and spit in his mouth."[77] Spitting into a dog's mouth linked specifically to water spaniels is demonstrated in Ulpian Fulwell's 1579 *Ars Adulandi:* "I think those men of Honour and worship, use you as men use their waterspaniels: that is, they make you their instrument to fetch and bringe unto them such commodities, as you by the corrupting of your conscience may compass, and … for your labour they spitte in your mouth."[78] Cyrus Hoy comments rather bemusedly that:

> noting the obscurity of the reason for this action, A. Gomme in his New Mermaid edition of *The Roaring Girl* quotes T. R. Henn's suggestion "that it may have been a device to ensure that the dog memorized its master's scent." … Perhaps so; but other evidence suggests that the action betokens some odd sign of affection bestowed on a pet.[79]

Apart from the examples given by Mulholland above of this sign of affection, Marston suggests in *The Malcontent* that it is as common as patting a dog:

> PASSARELLO: Well, I'll dog my lord, and the word is proper; for when I fawn upon him he feeds me; when I snap him by the fingers, he spits in my mouth. If a dog's death were not strangling, I had rather be one than a serving-man.[80]

Marston and William Fennor indicate that spitting in a dog's mouth was less a sign of affection than a means to pacify an unruly dog. Passarello word-plays on snapping his fingers for his master and snapping, dog-like, at his master's fingers; the former meaning results in his master dancing to his tune, but the latter implies that his master spits in his mouth in order to calm his dog-servant. However, in Daniel's *The Queenes Arcadia,* Cloris, by report, uses the spitting device to try to seduce her eventual lover's dog to follow her:

> *Amyntas.* And if she meete but with my dog, she takes
> And strokes him in the head, playes with his eares,
> Spits in his mouth, and claps him on the back,
> And sayes, come, come, *Melampus,* go with me.[81]

Coaxing the dog might be rightly read as appropriate to a girl, and, certainly, the not-so-hidden agenda to seduce the master as well as the dog is more likely to succeed by charming than calming. Cuddy in *The Witch of Edmonton* considers that he owes it to Tom as a reward for his excellent invisible performance: "I am bewitched, little cost-me-nought, to love thee—a pox, that morris makes me spit in thy mouth."[82] Widespread the motif certainly is, and if one accepts that this is a commonplace of Renaissance dog handling, whatever its calming or affectionate purpose, then the water spaniels in *The Roaring Girl,* therefore, are no more there to perform tricks than Crab.

HORSES: *WOODSTOCK*

Everyone knows that to be a proper king you have to cut a dashing figure on a horse: an English Civil War substitution of Cromwell for Charles in the same equestrian picture shows (somewhat ironically in this particular case) the symbolical strength of the mounted leader.[83] The mounted king was very common in Renaissance art: Frederick II of Denmark had himself done in alabaster, Charles V famously was painted by Titian, and Charles I by Van Dyck in the portrait known as *Charles I on Horseback with Seigneur de St. Antoine* (see Figure 4.3). This portrait uses the King's horsemanship to underline his majesty: Seigneur de St. Antoine was a well-known riding master whose presence in the picture, *leading* the King's horse, emphasizes Charles's superiority in horsemanship even to the most skilled exponents of that art in England. Charles's excellent horsemanship is supposed to be emblematic of his kingship: he rides the country as he does his steed (in retrospect one can't help suspecting him of trying to force his horse, and the country, over fences). The frequency of the horse image in the history plays of the period primarily exposes a practical use—as a mode of transport horses were part of the machinery of war. But kings and nobles, the protagonists of this genre, not only ride horses but invest their own and others' steeds with properties reflecting their status and welfare. Horses act as indices of wealth and power and literally represent one's ability to best the enemy in battle and to govern the country.[84]

The appearance of the real horse in *Woodstock* is primarily a joke.[85] The register of this scene is unstable but stage tradition, more than anything else, suggests how it should be read. Critics have endlessly discussed the possibility that the early modern stage employed real horses in performance. Harry Levin sees the persistent unmountedness of the fat knight Falstaff and the hand-to-hand fight in which Hal defeats Hotspur as ironic gestures toward the dearth of horses on stage, unfeasible because of their large size and, according to Lawrence, their attacks of stage fright.[86] Furthermore, the (very useful) Prologue to *Henry V* disclaims any such phenomenon and urges us to use our imagination:

> Think, when we talk of horses, that you see them
> Printing their proud hoofs i' th' receiving earth;
> For 'tis your thoughts that now must deck our kings,
> Carry them here and there.[87]

FIGURE 4.3: Anthony Van Dyck, *Charles I on Horseback with Seigneur de St. Antoine.*

Levin remarks: "we find so many characters walking on with the announce-
ment that they have just dismounted, or walking off with the declared intention of mounting a steed, that we are justified in recognizing the observance of
a convention."[88] It is this stage convention that the appearance of the Courtier
in *Woodstock* transgresses; the dialogue between Woodstock and his servant
makes this abundantly clear:

(Enter a Servant)

Woodstock. How now? What news?

Servant There's a horseman at the gate, my lord,

He comes from the king, he says, to see your grace.

Woodstock. To see me, sayst thou? A God's name, let him come

So he brings no blank charters with him.

Prithee bid him 'light and enter.

Servant. I think he dares not for fouling on his feet, my lord. I would

have had him 'light, but he swears as he's a courtier he will not off on's

horse-back till the inner gate be open.

Woodstock. Passion of me, that's strange. I prithee, give him satisfaction.

Open the inner gate. What might this fellow be?[89]

An audience expects the horseman to be at the gate rather than actually on the stage, and for him to walk on, as did Robin Hood and his servant in *Look about You*, "with riding wands in their hands, as if they had been new-lighted."[90] Woodstock clearly expects this too, as does his bemused servant: "I would have had him 'light" bears a defensive tone, perhaps in response to Woodstock's "Prithee bid him 'light and enter." The ridiculous Courtier is so fine that he dare not alight in the muddy road—which gives the audience a splendid opportunity to laugh at him and to marvel at the real horse he brings on stage. The double audacity of the Courtier refusing to dismount outside Plashey and of the playwright daring to employ an equine actor has been set up by Woodstock's final "Passion of me, that's strange." And it is. The splendid spectacle of the Courtier "attired very fantastically" *and* his mount, actually on stage,[91] was bound to raise a laugh from the audience in a play of intentional jokiness, as the scenes with Nimble attest. The following conversation, where the Courtier mistakes Woodstock for his own groom, would add to the sense of comedy as would Woodstock's decision to address the horse. All the dealings with the Courtier are hilarious; even when he finally realizes who Woodstock is, he is consistently led off track by Woodstock's mock admiration of his shoes with their "Polonian peaks" and the "most fashionable chain which links as twere / The toe and knee together—."[92]

The writing is extremely clever here, since it is funny, whether a real or a pantomime horse were to be used. The dialogue sets up the appearance of a real animal, but works well if, instead, the fake animal were to be used as if it were real. While the actor pretends to take the fake horse for flesh and blood he manages to make the audience laugh, not at his stupidity, but at his ironical adeptness. If we are disappointed by the nonappearance of the real horse, at least we can laugh at our own gullibility and at the ridiculous figure both Woodstock and the panto steed cut during their conversation. This is one of the few places in early modern drama where a pantomime horse would work. Lawrence vilifies Barrett Wendell's endorsement of hobby horses in the latter's imagined scenario (which *does* seem strange):[93]

> As to the riding, Macbeth and Banquo probably made their first entry with wicker-work hobby horses about their waists, with false human legs, of half the natural length, dangling from the saddles, and with sweeping skirts to hide the actors' feet. Monstrous as such a proceeding seems, it might still occur in serious tragedy on the Chinese stage, and the Chinese stage is very like the Elizabethan.[94]

Lawrence quite rightly points out that this implies that the Elizabethans had "no sense of the ludicrous," and "it is difficult to know how Shakespeare ever came to write his burlesque of Pyramus and Thisbe" if it is true.[95] In *Woodstock* the comic tenor of the scene could encourage two men to impersonate the horse, as might Woodstock's words on the first departure of the Courtier: "O strange metamorphosis! / Is't possible that this fellow that's all made of fashions / should be an Englishman?"[96] Woodstock introduces the idea of disguise and *metamorphosis,* a term specifically used for the changing of men into animals, at exactly the point in the text that he turns to address what might be a pantomime-horse costume over two men. He has himself already been congratulated on his "golden metamorphosis / From homespun housewifry" by King Richard at 1.3.75–76, when he dons rich attire for the coronation. But it is a transformation that Woodstock makes clear is only temporary: "Should this fashion last I must raise new rents, / Undo my poor tenants, turn away my servants / And guard myself with lace."[97] The Courtier's fineness, though, is deceitful, like the manmade horse, because it sets itself out as real when it is not: the Courtier is English, just as the horse is fake.

One might object that sharing the stage with a pantomime steed would undermine the dignity of Woodstock's position, and so reduce the seriousness of his tragedy. However, Woodstock spends most of the play having his plainness mistaken for lack of dignity: even his brothers are shocked at I.I.206 at his avowed intention to turn up at Richard's wedding wearing unglamorous frieze:

> My heart in this plain frieze sits true and right.
> In this I'll serve my king as true and bold
> As if my outside were all trapped in gold.[98]

Woodstock gives into their entreaties not to "so disgrace the state and realm,"[99] but makes it clear that he does so reluctantly, and would not have given in to the King's demands to do so: "Afore my God the king could not have entreated me / To leave this habit."[100] What sounds like treasonable stubbornness is a deliberate attempt to define himself against the prevailing fashions of the day: Woodstock is afraid that if he were to give in to the King's demands to beautify himself, he would be aligning himself with the new dispensation, against the dictates of decency and order. His insistence on the inner man over the outer shell demonstrates that lack of patience with appearances that so often lands him in trouble. His willingness to entertain the horse in 3.2 indicates an equal lack of false pride consistent with his sumptuary inclinations, which have left him undisguised, he claims, for the best part of twenty years.[101] When Richard's favorites note his transformation at the wedding, and mock Woodstock for his habitual fashions, he makes explicit the point that he always intends his "tother hose" and "frieze coat" to carry: "There's honest plain dealing in my tother hose."[102] Woodstock is a play about appearances in many senses: it constantly jokes about ridiculous fashions, as we have seen; its horrifying masque-kidnap of Woodstock depends upon the disguises of the conspirators led by Richard; even the low comedy of the scenes where Nimble arraigns innocents on charges of treason depends upon the misrepresentation of the appearance of a whistle. Though he claims that he is "no stoic ... / to make my plainness seem canonical,"[103] he is trying to make a point about his lack of fineness: "Scoff ye my plainness, I'll talk no riddles, / Plain Thomas will speak plainly."[104] He is particularly angry with the favorites for mocking his plainness because his present finery seems to have undermined his reputation for plain-speaking.

Unlike the groom in Every Man Out, who objected to being Puntarvolo's dog keeper even for a minute, Woodstock does not mind being demoted to the position of his own groom because it sets him aside from the kind of men, like the spruce Courtier, he despises. His attention to the needs of the "Commons" is based on a worldview that sees honesty, not wealth and finery, as the true indication of a real man. However, it would be wrong to make proto-Marxist claims for the author of Woodstock: Woodstock thinks the responsibility of his class is to fend off the worst economic and social threats to the ordinary Englishman, not to level the playing field. His amusement at, and ironical acceptance of, the Courtier's mistake is reinforced by his wish to be nothing like the Courtier. A pantomime horse lends Woodstock a visual reminder of the Courtier's spurious spruceness, by differentiating Plain Thomas in his frieze coat from an absurd creature that mocks its master's unseemly fineness of disguise. We know little about the performance history of Woodstock, but must assume that the play was given more than a single airing on the boards. Lawrence is right, of course, in supposing that the internal jokes about the horse argue for a real animal in the first performance, but the performance conditions that would have made this possible (in the case of a horse, strong boards and no stairs) could not necessarily be replicated in later stagings of the play. The author must have understood this, and it may account for the way the jokes in the horse scenes glance at the real and the costumed. In performances where a real horse could be used, the audience could not avoid comparing him to costumed animals, which were used on the stage in comedy, at least. Equally, if a costumed horse had to be used, the joke operated on the basis of the audience's memory of real horses, perhaps even, by reputation, of an earlier real equine actor in this very part.

However, Woodstock's conversation with the horse is not only a comic gesture. It tries to make a serious point as well, just after Woodstock has expressed in soliloquy his fears that he has "no eloquence / To stay this uproar [of the Commons],"[105] who are, not unnaturally, in revolt over the blank charters they are being forced to sign to levy taxes. Perhaps his assessment of the horse's intelligence does not suit our modern ideas either about the intelligence of horses or of the "Commons," but the conversation with the horse is the one he would like to have with the people and cannot, for fear of provoking all-out rebellion. Like Master Ignorance the Bailey of Dunstable (who appears in the very next scene), the horse, according to Woodstock, has "sweat hard about this haste, / yet I think you know very little of the business"; Woodstock has no illusions about the "indifferent beast" that is the people, which will "follow any man that will lead you."[106] Woodstock understands that the king/rider must lead the people/horse gently and kindly. In *Woodstock,* the behavior that loses both crown (and roan Barbary in *Richard II*) to Bolingbroke is apparent to its hero in the court's treatment of horse and Commons alike: "You're pricked more with the spur, than the provender ... I see that."[107] Woodstock's comment that the horse's "dwelling be at Hackney when you're at home, is't not?" puns on the word:[108] while the audience would no doubt think of the London suburb, the word also describes a horse of exactly the type we expect:

> Hackneys, a word derived from the French *haquenée,* and the Italian *achinea,* a little nag ... were ridden in marches to ease the war-horses.[109]

If there is a hidden irony in riding the common people while giving the King's cronies a rest from taxes, then we can be sure that the audience would have seen it. Like Master Ignorance in the play, the horse is forced to put out his labor to the highest bidder because his master wills it, in spite of any repercussions for himself or his fellows. The Commons "feed not in Westminster Hall adays" with Richard and his crew, and this banqueting may well result in them being eaten by the feasters in the end.[110] When Woodstock demands of "vulture England, wilt thou eat thine own?"[111] and apostrophizes the favorites as "kites ... enjoy[ing] the eagle's prize,"[112] it is a theme he elaborates upon with the prospect of the horse being eaten along with all the rest of the sheep and oxen. Symbolically, the eating of the Commons thrives if the horse is a pantomime horse because of the irony that his constituent humans might be fit to eat—as fit, at least, as the beleaguered Commons of the late fourteenth century.

It is, of course, also a dig at the repulsive French habits of the English court run by Richard of Bordeaux: they dress in fancy clothes, their women ride side saddle like Richard's Queen,[113] and they eat horses.

As Bolingbroke's uncle (the shadow of *Richard II* is always here) Woodstock has much in common with him: as well as both being gentle riders, the idea of usurpation is on the edge of their consciousness. Bolingbroke, one might argue, is prepared to see through the idea that Woodstock merely entertains when he pretends to tempt the horse's allegiance to its master: "Faith, say a man should steal ye—and feed ye fatter, could ye run away with him lustily?"[114] At the end of a soliloquy that constantly equates the horse with the Commons, this has one primary meaning. Whether Woodstock thinks he should stand in place of Richard, or whether his teasing comment indicates his fears of what might happen if the King's behavior does not improve, it stands as overtly premonitory for an audience, familiar at least with the stories in Holinshed, who knew the outcome of the tale.

Woodstock is a tragedy, but its comic relief has what Moelwyn Merchant calls a "characteristic choric function."[115] The horse may be a simpleton, but he exposes the essential wrongness of Richard's behavior by allowing metaphor to mediate between truth and the commonplace. Throughout history, the Commons have complained that their king and his noble friends abuse and exploit them; the comical horse (real or pantomime) provides a living proof of that exploitation without allowing the Commons to say one word, or, therefore, to tell one suspected lie. Woodstock's conversation with the horse is a revelation of otherwise hidden facts; it is only the soliloquizing nature of the conversation that makes it safe for Woodstock, but the presence of the horse provides a useful vehicle for the tenor of his words. The horse gives his fears form, and words.

Furthermore, in the minds of the audience there may have been a precedent for talking to a horse about the state of the nation. The most famous stage horse of all, Morocco, appeared in a 1595 pamphlet purporting to detail a conversation that the authors overheard between Banks and his horse. Like Jonson's play, the pamphlet makes persistent topical and topographical reference: the conversation takes place at the Bel Savage Inn where plays were staged and the horse is said to have performed;[116] the "poxe" grows at "Shordich and Southwarke" and initials are used tantalizingly to suggest real people.[117] The authors' expressed purpose is "Anatomising some abuses and bad trickes of this age."[118] Of course, the exposing of tricks keyed into the act itself, which was so convincing that Banks was imprisoned and the horse impounded by the French on suspicion of witchcraft.[119] But the tract is also concerned with abuses in London, particularly those relating to landlords and tenants: "But the covetous Landlord is the caterpiller of the commonwealth, hee neither fears God nor the devil, nor so hee maye racke it out, cares not what Tenant he receives."[120] This is verbally reminiscent of both *Woodstock* (1.3.157; 3.3.145) and, especially, *Richard II* (2.3.166). By 1595, as an elderly Queen Elizabeth was finding it more difficult to keep her faithful Commons happy, public discontent was at its highest in her reign. Essex avowed that the aim of his 1601 rebellion was to rid Elizabeth of her exploitative favorites and the Queen identified herself to William Lambarde as Richard II.[121] In this context, the local crimes detailed by Morocco should also be read macrocosmically onto the state of the nation. And if Woodstock is an Elizabethan play, the Duke's assessment of the treatment meted out to the horse by his rider, and to the country by the King, comments on public dissatisfaction of the 1590s. But P. MacDonald Jackson has plausibly identified Samuel Rowley as the author of *Woodstock* and suggested that we redate the play to early in James's reign. The conversation with the horse resonates similarly in connection with James, to whom "advice" was meted out by playwrights soon after he arrived in London. There was a curious mixture of warning, exhortation, and praise implied in the comparisons to earlier monarchs' reigns.[122] But the extravagance criticized in *Woodstock* (see I3.1.81–95) fits James's glamorous early English years much better than it does Elizabeth's famously stingy court and, as such, strengthens Jackson's claim for a later date of composition.

RECREATION AND REPRESENTATION

There was, of course, a pun I didn't note in Velure's question in *Histrio-mastix* about how he should "recreate" himself. The potential for transformation afforded by Peace and Plenty allowed many people also to "re-create" themselves, moving to a different social station. All the plays concerned express anxiety about the threat to the old social order that these "new men" pose, and their use of animal iconography is a major feature of their method. Metonymically using breeds of dog, understood to be *naturally* imbued with certain qualities, Jonson and Marston satirize social climbing and expose it as unsustainable performance. *Woodstock*'s hackney, riffing on the emblematics of horsemanship, interrogates the ongoing negotiation (which collapsed in 1642) of the relationship between king and country. The plays' insistent topographical placing of themselves in the liberties stresses not only the link between animal and human acts, as has always been understood, but also argues for Stow's ordered social arrangement where every re(-)creation has its rightful place, laid down by custom and its resulting legislation. And plays that have this social agenda use productively the coincidences between performance and rank: players' costumes draw attention to the tricks appearance can play in real life. Puritan objections to theater made much of the unnatural disfigurement of one's God-given image, especially insulting when the player impersonated an animal. Ironically perhaps, the 1572 Act for the Punishment of Vagabonds encouraged the dressing of players in liveries, giving them a fixed sumptuary identity at variance with their shape-shifting trade.[123] In *Woodstock* the possibility of a costume horse reinforces this joke; but plays that use real animals, as Boehrer has argued, run the risk of admitting the limitations of theater. In the case of stage dogs, though, this is useful anti-metatheater: the real dogs cannot help but be what they are, despite theater's transformative power. This boosts an agenda that sees nature as preordained, class as fixed, and an idealized status quo as desirable.

The Relationship between Text and Illustration in Mid-Sixteenth-Century Natural History Treatises

PHILIPPE GLARDON
TRANSLATED BY SUSAN BECKER

Despite obvious weaknesses that many see in the illustrations of sixteenth-century natural history studies, scientific historians often consider those illustrations characteristic of the new resolve to surpass what ancient Greek science had been able to accomplish in the complete and objective description of nature. In this chapter, I hope to show that the relationship between text and image in these treatises needs reevaluation from a less anachronistic perspective. To do so, I will examine what, from our modern perspective, we call "imperfections" in the zoological and botanical illustrations of the Renaissance.

Examples of such "imperfections" are not limited to images of monsters, but include pictures built from textual descriptions, repeated illustrations of the same animal and, conversely, the absence of any representation of a number of species. In the following section, I will briefly examine the definition of natural history during the period in question, a matter crucial to understanding the epistemological value of the treatises and their iconography. In the third section, I will look at the function of the classical texts, particularly as it concerns the descriptive method, which lies at the heart of the Renaissance naturalist's deliberations. In the fourth section, I will enumerate disparities and incoherencies in the illustrations and then, in the fifth, relate these to the general discourse on nature. This will lead us, in section six, to reassess the status of the Renaissance naturalist, a status that cannot be reduced to that of a precursor of the eighteenth-century taxonomist.

For several reasons, it is possible to speak of a real natural history in the sixteenth century. First, the authors themselves consider their work different from the nature writings of previous centuries. As doctors and physicians in the Aristotelian sense—that is, natural philosophers—they consider their work superior to such things as simple technical treatises on the medical virtues of plants. Thus, they propose to go beyond medieval writings on the philosophy of nature such as the paraphrases of Aristotelian zoological treatises by Albert the Great, later widely repeated in the form of summaries or *quaestiones*. According to Conrad Gesner (1517–1565), the first author to produce a text that met these expectations was Paolo Giovio (1483–1552). With his *De romanis piscibus* (1524),[1] he was "the first in our century to shed light on the natural history of fish."[2]

From this date on, the production of works of natural history increases steadily. Between 1530 and 1536, Pierre Gilles (1489–1552) and Otto Brunfels (1488–1534) publish their books, about aquatic animals and plants, respectively. During the following decade Leonhart Fuchs (1501–1566) edits his essential work, *De natura stirpium,* in 1542; William Turner (1500–1568) the *Avium praecipuarum [...] historia* in 1544; and Michael Herr (1485–1550) his *Liber de quadrupedibus* in 1546. The maximum occurs between 1550 and 1558, when Edward Wotton (1492–1555), Adam Lonitzer (1528–1586), Guillaume Rondelet (1507–1566), Pierre Belon (1517–1564), Conrad Gesner, and Ippolito Salviani (1514–1572) edit their works in England, Germany, France, Switzerland, and Italy.[3] With the exception of Wotton's *De differentiis animalium* (1552), the works are richly illustrated. Subsequently, they will be copied, summarized, and used as references until the end of the following century, and even beyond.[4] Their illustrations clearly show that the scholars carried out extensive exchanges of material concerning plants and animals, not just pictures but skeletons, feathers, shells, leaves, and dried flowers, as well.

Despite the indisputable originality of their work, the naturalist doctors recognize their debt to the ancients. They venerate not just Aristotle, Pliny, and Dioscorides, but Galen, Athenaeus, and poets such as Homer, Oppian, Ovid, or Virgil as well. Here, we will discuss the relationship between these men and their illustrious predecessors only as it concerns points directly related to our subject.

Among those points is the need to summarize briefly the ancients' teachings on the existence of a natural phenomenon and the image's role in the protocol for its verification. There is no doubt pictures were used in teaching anatomy, but what of their ancient use in the specific identification of plants or animals? This question is important to the naturalist doctors of the Renaissance, who champion the heuristic value of individually describing plants and animals: Rondelet's *particularium exercitatio*.[5] Viewed from the perspective of a factual history of science, this has an epistemological value that explains why modern scientists think of Fuchs, Gesner, and their colleagues as direct predecessors and celebrate their progressive inspiration.

Earlier, Aristotelian zoology is credited with laying the foundations of taxonomy by defining genus and species, although the Greek philosopher made no effort to apply this theoretical knowledge systematically to concrete reality.[6] Still viewed from the continuist perspective of a factual history of science, Renaissance scholars go one step further by emphasizing specific differences. There can be no doubt the naturalist doctors want to distinguish themselves from their ancient predecessors, as in the example of Leonhart Fuchs:

> Assuredly this description is quite brief and imperfect [...]. We might thus have good reason to accuse D. [Dioscorides] of negligence here, as one who has wished to leave to his posterity numerous stories lacking their perfect description. This notwithstanding, if one is willing to pay particular attention to the few indications there are, certainly he will find that the herb described here is the true *Petroselinon*.[7]
>
> And Pliny, who translated what Aristotle had written about them ["birds of prey"], adds six more, but doesn't specify all of them. In any case, neither the one nor the other has left sufficient signs to let us know of which they wished to speak. As a result it is quite difficult to fit them with the names which they have acquired in our French, unless by hints we can divine these.[8]

An attentive examination of Renaissance natural history texts and their illustrations will show that the relationship between those texts, the ancient texts, on one hand, and nature itself, on the other, is considerably more complex than this linear vision of continuous progress since the origin of "Science" would lead us to believe. The usual position adopted by scientific historians concerning the illustrations attributes to the doctors of the Renaissance the same point of view as our own on the function of the illustration and its relationship with the scientific text: the artists and woodcutters of that time supposedly "established a tradition traceable to our times."[9]

However, it is obvious that Renaissance natural history cannot be compared without qualification to our biology or even to an early stage of it. We would do better to consider it a specific view of nature, which examination of both the natural history treatises themselves and their prefaces will demonstrate.

NATURAL HISTORY IN THE SIXTEENTH CENTURY: THEORY AND DEFINITION

A complete understanding of the development of natural history in the sixteenth century would take us too far from our subject, requiring us to examine such elements as the education of the doctors who conceived it or the legacy of medieval thought and its influence on the university system. The general cultural and socioeconomic context is quite important as well. A doctor is not at all certain of finding a position other than a theoretical university career. Positions as town doctor are rare, often temporary and, furthermore, dangerous due to the high risk of contamination from the sick in one's care. The most highly prized position is that of private doctor to an important person: courtier, churchman, prince, bishop, or cardinal. Publishing works on natural history can be considered in the light that dealing with natural questions and, more exactly with plants and animals, offers an opportunity to participate in the general wave of interest in many ancient literary themes: medicine and dietetics, certainly, but also poetry or mythology. The author of a work on natural history can prove his competence as a doctor in the purest sense of the word, a guardian and preserver of health, and at the same time present himself as an erudite courtier. Pierre Belon offers a good example of this strategy with his first ichthyologic book, *L'Histoire naturelle des estranges poissons.* Belon himself suggests that this little work, made up of small, varied, and attractive chapters, was conceived to be read aloud to the patron:

> Knowing well that you have no greater pleasure than to spend the necessary time hearing things drawn from the intimate knowledge of natural history and that you gladly give a few hours of the day after meals to devising and hearing erudite discussions not overtaxing to the mind.[10]

Belon, like Rondelet, uses the expression *histoire naturelle,* equivalent to the term *historia naturalis* contained in most of the Latin titles. The general recourse to this expression suggests the existence of a stable and clearly defined concept, which we must make explicit.

In Aristotelian heuristics, *Historia* has an essential signification central to the sixteenth-century doctors' approach to natural phenomena. As Pierre Louis has demonstrated with regard to Aristotle, ἱστορία primarily signifies "inquiry into specific and concrete facts."[11] Depending on context, the word has been translated as "research" or "knowledge." Composing ἱστορία primarily consists of collecting specific data. This is doubtless the meaning Pliny has in mind when titling his *Natural History.* Though history, thus defined, is inferior to poetry, P. Louis reminds us that ἱστορία and ἐπιστήμη have a common etymology and that, consequently, the "historical" approach to natural facts allows philosophical exploitation of the data.[12]

Conrad Gesner is one of the most articulate of these authors on the subject of "scientific" method. His prefaces to the different volumes of *Historiae animalium* are quite revealing on this point and we also find a summary of his reflections in the *Ad rei medicae studioses praefatio* of Gesner's 1552 edition of Hieronymus Bock's *De stirpium maxime earum quae in Germania nostra nascuntur.* According to his precepts, the treatment of a subject can be:

- *Grammatice,* "as in our catalogue, where we only interpret names" [*"Ut in catalogo nostro ubi nomina solum interpretamur"*].
- *Historice,* "in the manner of Oribasius and Dioscorides, and our own, in our history, as well, giving only descriptions of it, but leaving out the properties" [*"Ut in Oribasius et Dioscorides: et nos quoque in historia nostra, descriptionibus tantum expressis"*].
- *Modice,* like Galen and Aetius, who "almost exclusively presented virtues and properties" [*"... vires et facultates ferme tantum exposuerunt"*].
- *Philosphice* and *Physice,* like Theophrastus and Aristotle.
- *Rustice,* used by authors dealing with agricultural questions.
- *Magice* and *Superstitiose,* the most harmful, "like Orpheus and Democritus, whom Pliny often mocks and who are not worth mentioning" [*"... ut Orpheus et democritus, quem saepe deridet Plinius, indigni sunt mentione"*].[13]

But Gesner makes clear that the description is twofold in *Physice: historica* when the authors have "distributed the plants' genus, species, differences and secondary parts according to the *loci communes*" [*"plantarum genera, species, differentias, et partes secundum locos communes distribuerunt"*]; *aetiologica* when they have "inquired into causes" [*"aut causas investigarunt"*]. And, Gesner adds, "Theophrastus, following Aristotle's lead with animals, used both modes in dealing with the history of plants" [*"Utroque modo ut Aristoteles animalium, sic Theophrastus stirpium historiam prosequitur"*].

We note here that Gesner is aware that, though *historia* concerns concrete facts, it can also prove useful at the highest level of knowledge, in a philosophical approach leading to a general understanding of nature. This allows us to understand the principal justification that Gesner and his colleagues set forth in all their prefaces: knowledge of physical phenomena can lead to God, since God's work is visible and perceptible in earthly creatures.[14] The theological interpretation of nature is the fundamental key to defining the concept of natural history in the sixteenth century and our purpose will be to understand how this interpretation decisively determines analysis of the illustrations in the treatises we will examine.

THE ROLE OF ANCIENT TEXTS

We have read in Gesner's commentary that even if the manner of describing plants and animals in the sixteenth century is distinct from ancient practice, the naturalist doctors are still greatly indebted to their predecessors. The first element to note on the subject of description as revealed in Renaissance texts is its "grammatical" dimension: onomastic investigation including the question of etymology.

The naturalists' responsibility is to recognize the plants by combining etymology and direct observation. Identifying plants and animals described by Aristotle, Pliny, Dioscorides, and others is essential. Identifying plants in the works of Pliny and Dioscorides opens the door to exploiting their botanical virtues. As for Aristotle's "zoological" treatises, their descriptions require special attention since they have a didactic function in demonstrating the organization of the physical world. This is why Rondelet and Belon do their best to follow Aristotle's choices, concentrating on the animal "parts" to which Aristotle directed his attention, and often neglecting the others.

The fish's swim bladder is a good example of this selective view of animal morphology and anatomy. Not mentioned by Aristotle in his inventory of the viscera, this organ was known to Belon and Rondelet, as was its function. The former wrote:

> [*Callarias*] possesses the same sort of bladder as the other species of *asini*, like a double pocket attached to the back. Its role seems to be to facilitate swimming.[15]

Belon mentions it briefly from time to time, but makes no point of its discovery and takes no issue with Aristotle for not having identified it. Rondelet also describes it, omitting its function, in the general inventory of the "parts" of the *aquatilia* in the first book of his *Libri de aquatilibus*. The organ is, to all appearances, of no interest since it is not the determining characteristic of any genus. Comparison is easy with the organs described by the Stagirite and almost invariably examined by the naturalist doctors of the sixteenth century: the liver, the gallbladder, the intestine, or even the pyloric caeca, characteristic for a number of fish.

It seems that the Renaissance naturalist doctors' respect for the authority of the ancients derives principally from their belief that the Greek and Roman authors had been able to put their finger on the original organization of the physical world. It is easier to understand, from that point of view, that it should be considered useless to develop areas passed over by ancient science.

Aristotle embraces the entire physical world in his system of thought, but other authors in antiquity also exhibit an interest in nature and natural philosophy. Principal among them is Cicero; a fact important because of his authority over Renaissance philosophy. Through Rudolph Agricola's works, the doctors of the period borrow Cicero's concept of *locus* as an instrument of scientific demonstration, and his image of the *orator philosophus,* whose knowledge includes natural facts.[16] With the Friesian philosopher's *De inventione dialectica,* the naturalist doctors have at their disposal an instrument to provide theoretical basis and legitimacy to their enterprise.

Agricola supports the position that a philosopher must know the facts, *res ipsas,* in order to reach the essential. Once these facts have been organized according to position (*loci*) the philosopher can lead the reader to conviction and knowledge. Obviously, the naturalist doctors are receptive to this didactic concept, which plays a role in all Renaissance intellectual activity, including poetry and painting.[17] For these "physicians, the rhetorical method with its goal of convincing is not limited to showing the correspondence between real plants and their ancient names"; it is used also in relation to the theological dimension of natural history treatises, to proclaim and illustrate the magnificence of Creation.

> Well-born men, endowed with greater courage, doing virtuous deeds and works worthy of their immortality, have no difficulty bowing in contemplation of the high deeds of the Almighty who has created all things, knowing that the principal duty of man is to praise His deeds and with admiration consider the excellence of His works and never to cease to magnify those things which he understands exceed the capacity of his understanding, those the providence of this great Architect has willed to be done for the use of human life and of other animals.[18]

THE UNEQUAL QUALITY OF THE ILLUSTRATIONS

We can now concentrate our attention directly on the illustrations. In general, their quality is striking, particularly compared to that of early printed works, such as *Hortus sanitatis* or Conrad Megenburg's *Buch der Natur,* which still remain quite close to medieval manuscripts, where the pictures are usually crude and oversimplified. In sixteenth-century treatises, on the other hand, Brunfels's or Bruch's plants, Rondelet's, Belon's or Salani's fish are rendered individually, often with enough precision to make it possible to identify them. Thus the authors are convinced of the necessity of illustrating their works. They emphasize the likeness between the model and its *pourtraict.* According to the subtitle of Leonhart Fuchs's *De natura stirpium,* the *imagines* are *vivae.* In the French translation, the *effigies* are *au vif.* In Belon, the *naifs pourtraicts* are painted *au naturel.* This ambition seems great, reminding us of the theoretical discussion among painters of the problem of mimesis. Scientific history considers the naturalist doctors' assertion the best proof that scientific progress is taking place beneath their pens.

In fact, the naturalist doctors' interest in direct observation is more visible in their illustrations than their texts. While the texts are criticized because, too often, the authors base their remarks on ancient descriptions, the illustrations, by contrast, are seen as opportunities to develop the budding project of describing nature objectively, beyond the authority of the Greek and Latin authors. But science historians are forced to admit that there is a gap between the project they would like to see correspond to the premises of modern science and the reality shown in treatise illustrations marred by odd weaknesses. Among these inconsistencies, monsters cannot fail to attract attention since, although nearly all the naturalist doctors condemn the fictional nature of some creatures, numerous others continue to be treated as totally real in the treatises (see Figure 5.1).

FIGURE 5.1: "The sea monster clad like a monk," Belon, *La nature et diversité des poissons*, p. 33.

While the sea monsters are notorious, mention can also be made of an extraordinary bird, the phoenix, that appears in *L'histoire de la nature des oyseaux*.[19] As a general rule, science historians explain the presence of monsters by the naïveté of the authors. Much having already been written about these creatures, we will only add a few remarks directly related to the subject at hand.

First, we must reconsider the criteria for accepting a species as real. Rondelet and Belon both reject monsters that are the fruit of human imagination, but accept others if trustworthy testimony proves their existence. This issue of testimony leads us directly back to Aristotelian rhetoric.

In *De rhetorica,* Aristotle establishes a hierarchy of the value of those testimonies that have the status of inartificial proofs, as do laws, contracts, tortures and oaths, if the credibility of their author is assured. The most reliable witnesses are "poets and men of repute whose judgments are known to all"—the most worthy of faith because they are incorruptible.[20] On this point picture and text line up exactly: in the example of Rondelet's *Libri de piscibus marinis* both denounce the *scolopendra marina* as imaginary but, on the other hand, accept the *piscus monachus* as *mirabilium.* The principal function of the image, therefore, is not to be the representation of some hypothetical objective reality, but an instrument for demonstrating a divine power, which must not be usurped by man.

If a physician whose authority is unquestioned presents a creature, no matter how extraordinary it may be, there is no reason to doubt its existence. This explains the uncritical transmission of portraits of fanciful animals until late in the seventeenth century, not simply for technical, economic, or iconographic reasons but because the naturalists have attained the authority of trustworthy witnesses, whose works—and opinions—prevail over ocular verification.

We must pursue this further. Faith in pictures does not appear to be as unshakable as the enthusiastic proclamations in the titles would lead one to believe. Pietro Andrea Mattioli (1500–1577) explains that the task of recognizing plants by means of illustrations is almost impossible because of the variations observed in each species:

> No one would be able to arrive at a true and perfect knowledge of medicinal simples by their pictures, their diversity being so great that one would not be able to include it in one portrait: for a budding herb does not have the appearance of a larger one, nor the larger of one which is wilting.[21]

It is interesting to note that Mattioli justifies the presence of illustrations by their popularity with readers rather than by their scientific efficacy itself.

> But seeing the undertakings of others, which feature portraits, to be praised by almost everyone and increase from day to day, having known

this all from experience and diligently considered it, I have not wanted to fail to do my will in this area.[22]

The scientific value of pictures depends greatly on their quality and size. Mattioli underlines this when he denounces an illicit edition of his works.

Cottier, the Lyon printer who had the aforesaid portraits printed in the French translation of Dioscorides, is more to be chastised; because, more interested in gain than in the profit of those of his nation, he has reduced the portraits of the plants to such small form that it is not possible to profit from them, neither the appearance of the leaves, nor the flowers, nor the fruits, nor the roots being depicted adequately, thus all is muddled, imperfect, and corrupted.[23]

Mattioli's arguments offer us a first indication that, for the naturalist doctor, human means do not suffice to represent nature perfectly. The criticism of technical imperfections in engravings is constant. Gesner gives several examples of it (see Figure 5.2):

I think that Rondelet's is better, which shows the teeth in the mouth, the scales on the whole body and the dorsal fin which is not the same for its entire length but divides in the front into distinct spiny points though not in its posterior part.[24]

These imperfections can be attributed to editorial negligence and to the loss of quality sustained during the involvement of different artists: painter, copyist,

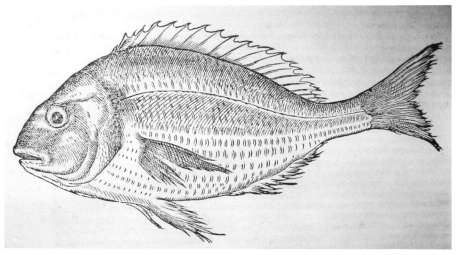

FIGURE 5.2: "Aurata" (Gilthead, *Sparus aurata*), Gesner, *Historiae animalium, liber IV*, p. 128.

sketcher, or engraver. More profoundly, the explanation lies in the difficulty of the task and the philosophical motives of the author.

The difficulty of the task can be dealt with in various ways. One is the duplication of several images of the same species, so as best to highlight its determining characteristics. Gesner's or Aldrovandi's habit of accumulating material, sometimes negatively referred to as the principle of "compilation," was not intended to attain exhaustivity, but to vindicate human limits. In Aldrovandi's *Ornithologiae,* we find, for instance, three engravings of the *bubo* (Eagle Owl, *Bubo bubo*), a very significant bird, the nocturnal equivalent of the eagle (see Figures 5.3, 5.4, 5.5). The first is a copy of Gesner's illustration; the second has smooth legs and small feet (*"tibias minime hirsutas habet, sed quemadmodum et pedes, debiles"*). The third, necessary to fill out the information on the species, was sent to Aldrovandi: *"Is vero cujus tertio loco iconem spectandam dabimus, iconem, etiam pro Bubonis imagine mihi misa fuit."*[25]

The principal reason for the various shortcomings of the illustrations is thus that man is incapable of representing either the perfection or the complexity of nature, so visible in the multiplicity of living beings. In this sixteenth-century science obviously differs completely from Linnaeus's taxonomic system. In botany, there is no place for the idea of a progressive inventory of all plants. That fact is very much on Pierre Belon's mind. There must be boundaries to human investigation:

> If someone proposed that there are two thousand kinds of bird it would be like him who would say that there are several worlds, and that there is a sun and a moon in each world, which is a totally unbelievable thing. [...] The man of good judgment [...] foresees a limit to certainty in the knowledge of natural things. For which reason we say freely [...] that it is beyond the power of man to find more than about five hundred species of fish, more than three hundred sorts of birds, and more than three hundred quadrupeds and more than forty diversities of snake. [26]

This sentiment, reinforced by the discovery of the totally unknown American fauna and flora, is particularly intense with regard to aquatic animals:

> The immense and so admirable divine power and ingenuity manifest themselves in celestial phenomena, those which occur in the air and on land, but nowhere more than in the seas, where the forms of things one sees are so varied and stupefying that their inventory and their contemplation can never be complete. A good example of that can be what we propose here.[27]

Not only the number of beings but also the complexity, the refinement, of their configuration (their *fabrica*) are beyond human capacities. Many of the creatures

FIGURE 5.3

FIGURE 5.4

FIGURE 5.3, 5.4, AND 5.5: "Bubo" (Eagle owl, *Bubo bubo*), Aldrovandi, *Ornithologiae*, pp. 509–511.

are too beautiful to be described other than by hyperbole. Belon expresses his perplexity before the mouth of the *chabre* (Edible Crab, *Cancer pagurus*):

> If you open its mouth, and contemplate each thing in turn, you will find so many little secrets, layers, other little jumbles, that in spite of yourself you will say that the ingenuity of nature is almost unbelievable.[28]

Here we should mention another, rather rare, case of duplication: that which has a laudatory function. Once a described species has been illustrated, it is possible to give a supplementary "portrait" of it, not with the goal of making identification easier but to show its beauty, as Aldrovandi does for the *Gyrfalco* (Gyrfalcon, *Falco rusticolus* [see Figure 5.6]). The specimen represented is identified, placed in a precise context, and Aldrovandi explains its unusual posture (*"statura habituque pulchre composito"*). Such an addition can be compared to a poetic digression, a concession to the beauty of Creation,

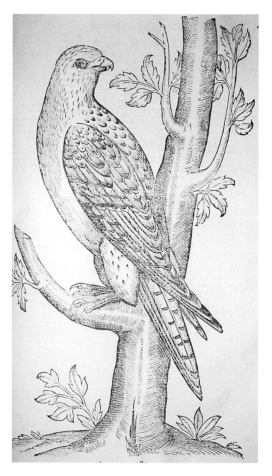

FIGURE 5.6: "Gyrfalco" (Gyrfalcon, *Falco rusticolus*), Aldrovandi, *Ornithologiae*, p. 472.

and must be seen as more than just an anecdote given its underlying theological foundation.[29]

In the fourth volume of his *Historiae animalum,* Conrad Gesner presents an even more striking example of poetic digression. He shows a magnificent lobster claw (see Figure 5.7).

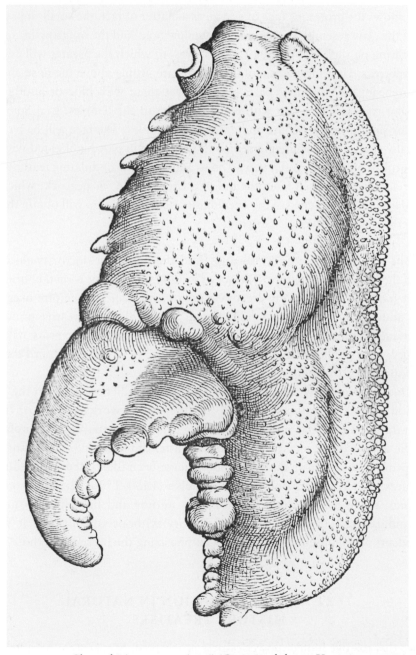

FIGURE 5.7: Claw of "Astacus marinus" (Common lobster, *Homarus gammarus*), Gesner, *Historiae animalium, liber IV,* p. 119.

We might expect a lengthy and detailed anatomical description of it, but the associated text is surprising and requires that one view the engraving vertically to grasp its full scope and flavor.

Claw of *astacus marinus,* such as I have at home, although slightly smaller. It can be represented thanks to the artist's skill in such a way that it shows the grotesque face of a man; as a matter of fact, the smallest part of the claw resembles an enormous aquiline nose and the outgrowths appearing on the edges of the two sides, eyes, to which the painter will add eyebrows. Up to four sorts of little horns are visible above the nose and forehead, on the upper part; he will cover them with blue or another color to resemble a cap with earflaps falling to the temples. [...] Some hair should bristle behind and around the temples. The face will be partially coated with white pigment, and should be in part highlighted with purplish pink. [...] And if you go on to add a crest of undulating feathers, preferably borrowed from the tail of a cock, capon, or peacock, which you will have attached in the opening situated on top, you will obtain the perfect face of a terrible Gorgon.[30]

The monster appeared by surprise, and the naturalist doctor could only echo the creativity of nature. The act of writing or painting is metaphoric for what happens among living creatures: nature establishes its empire over beings and combines the "parts to its liking." This unlimited creative principle of divine origin explains the apparent "naïveté" of sixteenth-century natural history: why should a "monster in monk's habit" be any more absurd than a hippopotamus, flying fish, whale, or seahorse?

One question now reemerges, that of the contradiction between the perfection of the illustrations touted in the titles of the works and the obvious limitations of the final result. The answer seems inescapable: the emphasis on the quality of the engravings is only a matter of marketing. The history of the printed book shows that since books have been illustrated with realistic pictures, that is to say, since Otto Brunfels's (1530–1536) *Herbarum vivae eicones,* it has become impossible for an author and his editor to imagine publishing a treatise on natural history without embellishing it with woodcuts and, consequently, without emphasizing the presence of those pictures.[31]

TEXT AND ILLUSTRATION IN NATURAL HISTORY TREATISES

Once this relative human powerlessness is accepted, it may seem paradoxical that the naturalist doctors of the sixteenth century can claim man's legitimate dominance over Creation. This is particularly true in the case of botanists, who justify their work by saying that nature furnishes man everything necessary for his health and his comfort. On reflection, however, this does not contradict what we have put forth: the botanists are primarily interested in useful and spectacular plants; to embrace the totality of the vegetable world is both vain and impossible. Confirming this fact is at the very heart of natural history discussion and I now intend to demonstrate that the textual architecture of the treatises we examine and the image of the authors emerging from it are both coherent and specific expressions of Renaissance thought.

From our modern point of view, another weakness of "scientific" illustration in the Renaissance is its variable relationship with the text. A brief list will give some idea of the different bonds that can exist between text and image, before we go into further detail.

1. An illustration can complete a written description: "Their portrait will show the rest."[32]
2. An illustration can be necessary to fully evoke a species insufficiently described by the text: "The following figure will show it better."[33]
3. An illustration can be almost redundant when it simply confirms the written description: "As it looks in its portrait."[34]
4. The illustration is even rendered superfluous if a determining characteristic already appears in the text: "the mouth of the Achon is a sufficient sign to make it recognizable."[35]
5. Inversely, a precise illustration can make a text useless: "I do not want to consume time now by describing this tree, but I did want to give the portrait to show it."[36]

Now, we must look at an example more closely: the case of Belon's strange "sea wolf," whose written description is as follows (see Figure 5.8):

For as much as the English have no Wolves on their land, nature has supplied them with a beast on the banks of their sea so strongly resembling our Wolf, that if it were not that it throws itself rather on fish than on *ouailles* [sheep], one would say it was just like our very predatory beast when one considers its build, fur, head (which is all the same quite large) and tail closely approaching the terrestrial Wolf: but because this one (as has been said) only lives on fish, and has not been known at all by the ancients, it has not seemed less notable than the double-lived animals alleged above. For which reason I wanted to put in the portrait.[37]

Belon's explanation is interesting. There is a sort of natural necessity for the presence of the "sea wolf" in England, perhaps to remind people of the

FIGURE 5.8: "The sea wolf," Belon, *La nature et diversité des poissons*, p. 29.

omnipresence of evil. This together with the physical resemblance to the land-dwelling wolf justifies Belon's choice of name. On the other hand, the creature's lifestyle explains why it is ranked among the amphibians, beside the beaver and otter. After this detailed presentation, the reader discovers the figure of a totally imaginary animal.

In this case, the name *lupus* and the written description have determined the engraving's creation, although the description clearly makes one think of the seal, which is described elsewhere in the treatise. The awkward representation of the animal's lifestyle is noteworthy. It is literally half on land and half on top of the water, giving the impression that it is walking on the water.[38]

We must conclude from this that the visual establishment of a fact, as embodied by the picture, is not necessarily among the conditions required to verify the phenomenon. The written words take the role of proof and, as a result, direct the composition of the picture. Many cases of the ascendancy of description over picture can be cited, which must be interpreted as that many manifestations of the naturalist doctors' heuristic methodology. We cite a new example taken from Gesner, whose *lagopus* really has hare's feet (see Figure 5.9).

This corresponds exactly to what we pointed out regarding monsters: a serious testimony is considered convincing and written words make direct examination unnecessary. In the case of the sea wolf it is quite probable that Belon received the description from an English doctor friend.

It is possible to complete our response to questions regarding the system of verifying and describing nature. The first explanation was historical: Aristotelian rhetorical thought still dominates the sixteenth-century doctors' education and the entire scientific culture of the period. The other, theologically

FIGURE 5.9: "Lagopus" (Ptarmigan, *Lagopus mutus*), Gesner, *Historiae animalium, liber III*, p. 554.

based, explanation is to be found in the omnipresent religious preoccupation of Renaissance man. Thus Gesner, Belon, and their colleagues are intimately convinced of the insufficiency of the means at man's disposal for understanding the real world, that is to say his sensory perceptions. Since it is legitimate, nevertheless, to describe nature in the framework of their eulogistic project, the naturalist doctors try to associate textual and visual productions whose information combines to offer as coherent and satisfying a message as possible. The consequence of this choice manifests itself concretely in a chapter organization bringing together on one page a descriptive text and illustration for most species present in a work.

We must now apply ourselves to the text to see whether the relationship between word and image is as complex and important as we suppose and to analyze more closely its origin and epistemological meaning.

One important element is that the naturalist doctors often resort to ambiguous expressions to qualify the act of description. Fuchs uses *delineatio*, which means "sketch" or "outline" in classical Latin, in the same sense as *descriptio*, for both the written description and the illustration of a species.

The two terms have a French equivalent in translations:

[The *arum*] has a white root, comparable to that of the *Dracunculus*, but less bitter. It is eaten cooked. Surely these descriptions correspond to our *arum*, without any possible doubt.[39]

More than complementarity, we must speak of fusion between the written and drawn elements, between *delineatio/descriptio* and *pictura*.

> This description represents so well the plant whose picture we present that one egg could not better resemble another.[40]

In these sentences about the relationship between text and image, the adverb *graphice* plays an important role. In classical Latin, it has two meanings: "artistically"/"elegantly" and "completely"/"entirely." This latter sense interests us, because it appears in Aulus Gellius, a Stoic author who figures among the philosophers Gesner praises for their erudition.[41] Let us examine some examples of sentences containing *graphice,* in chronological order, from Leonhart Fuchs (1542), William Turner (1544), and Guillaume Rondelet (1554):

> [The arum] also has a white root, which recalls that of *Dracunculus,* as the illustration shows perfectly (*graphice*).[42]

> The *curuca* would not be nearly unknown by all today if this same Aristotle, who described the cuckoo for us with adequate precision (*graphice*), had depicted it with the same care.[43]

> In fact, he undoubtedly calls *echeneida* because of its power [to stop ships] that which we name *lampetra,* and which he describes with such precision (*graphice*) that no person of sound mind would fail to recognize it for the *lampetra*.[44]

The first fact to note is that a word that derives from the act of writing is being applied indifferently to written description and picture. It is equally quite significant that Fuchs's two translators, Guillaume Gueroult and Eloi de Maignan, both resort to the expression *au vif*: the word and picture ally to supplant nature's power to evoke the thing.[45]

If we turn to the history of vocabulary, the fact that the adverb *graphice* is absent from Medieval Latin leads us to believe that the naturalist doctors are making a notable effort to renew the theoretical lexicon. The question of their choice of words must be briefly reconsidered in its intellectual context.

Even though the sixteenth- and seventeenth-century university system is still very much under the domination of the medieval model, scholars, and among them doctors, have the right to proclaim their intention to surpass their predecessors. In the case of the naturalist doctors, authors who devote themselves to the description of nature construct a discursive system that differs radically from the medieval vision of nature. The terms I have chosen to examine are typical of the Renaissance mindset: the lexicon is taken from Greek and Latin philosophy, but the content of the terms is modified. The naturalist doctors' deliberations are so careful that we can rely on lexicological analysis to make the epistemological content apparent. This brings us back to the association between text and picture, from the linguistic point of view.

If we consider the development of the discussion on discourse, it seems out of the question to speak of confusion between word and picture, or to put forth an explanation that assimilates all signs, following the "Foucauldian" model of "correspondences." The general Renaissance interest in languages of whatever nature, secret codes, rebuses, pictograms, or hieroglyphics must not be interpreted simplistically.[46] Like other scholars, the naturalist doctors are doing their best to develop an extremely rigorous descriptive method, one of the foundations of which is the concept of *nota*, which I described in my thesis.[47]

I have tried to demonstrate that *nota* (*note, enseigne, marque*, or *merque* in French translations) was the word used to designate the distinctive determining characteristics of plants and animals, particularly when the scholar is comparing a real species with an ancient description. *Nota* has a close relationship with Rudolph Agricola's theory on the subject of rhetoric, a theory aimed at enriching the "store of arguments," the "wealth of knowledge" indispensable to the Ciceronian *orator philosophus*. Consequently, in the naturalist doctors' system *nota* becomes the decisive argument that proves the identity of each species.

Here we return to our question about the relationship between picture and text since *nota*, as an argument, can be a distinctive plant or animal characteristic appearing as easily in the text as in the illustration. This suggests that, in the minds of the naturalist doctors, nature can be read directly. There is a natural discourse, comprehensible to the erudite, the "contemplative philosopher." This conception is completely compatible with the relationship between man and nature as perceived in the Renaissance. As a work of God, the Creation communicates its secrets to whoever is capable of reading them.

This deepens the association between word and picture in the sixteenth-century natural history discourse. The distinctive characteristics of plants and animals are obviously not written in real script, but nature is capable of writing actual Hebraic characters—Hebrew is still sometimes considered the original language—as Belon notes beside the Red Sea:

> We found a round stone on the bank, fat and round as a *teston* piece, which we believed to be a medal (for it resembled iron), where some Hebraic letters were naturally written.[48]

In the example of the fish, *achon*, we saw that *nota* can be present in the text as well as the picture. More than an analogy, there is an identity between the organization of the language of nature, so to speak, and all human discourse, with regard to their essential function: both are conceived for the instruction of man.[49] Nature delivers signs that render its organization and underlying divine principles intelligible. But nature's messages also relate to the legitimate exploitation of its resources. This point is very important in understanding the relationship between the naturalist doctor and the world he describes. The Renaissance attitude is not dominating, in contrast to that of the eighteenth-century taxonomist projecting his classificatory grid on all living beings. We must imagine Gesner and his colleagues listening, or better, reading endlessly from the book of nature, in an attitude of humility dictated by the constant appearance of new signs of limitless divine power.

THE SIXTEENTH-CENTURY NATURALIST DOCTOR AS INTERPRETER OF NATURE

Now, we understand the ambiguous position of the sixteenth-century naturalist doctor or philosopher physician and cannot help thinking of the cliché about Renaissance man returned to the center of the universe. The naturalist doctors vie in their prefaces to assert that man is a privileged creature, authorized to dispose of everything on earth. But we must go more deeply into the question of man's status in Creation, and not be satisfied with the overly sketchy image of a free-thinking Renaissance philosopher still being given by Eugenio Garin:

> He is no longer, or not necessarily, a schoolmaster, nor bound by orthodoxies of any sort; he is rebel to all hegemonic pretension, critic by vocation and often rebellious, an unsettled seeker and experimenter in all fields.[50]

We have seen the importance of religion for the naturalist doctor. That fact greatly nuances Garin's vague and nearly anachronistic portrait of the philosopher, for which we find it appropriate to substitute the figure of the interpreter, the perfect incarnation of which, to our way of thinking, is the naturalist doctor.

For Pietro Andrea Mattioli, it is "impossible that a similar and equally magnificent science, and equipped with so many virtues and mysteries, can otherwise than by divine revelation take its beginning: [...] it is not permitted to human sense and intelligence to acquire and know the natures, virtues and properties of the Simples, if first it is not given from above."[51] The mission of the naturalist doctor is sacred and brings him closer to the Renaissance poet than to the modern man of science. Following the example of the former, the physician, the naturalist doctor, is supposed to reveal facts hidden from common mortals, elicit an emotion, or even simply praise the beauty of nature, after having rooted it out of the confusion of things. Again, like the poet, the naturalist doctor is confronted by the dual problem of imitation: imitation of nature and imitation of the ancient model.[52]

This point is linked closely to another we have discussed rather broadly: the attitude of the naturalist doctor before the languages of nature. Here again, we must distance ourselves from Garin's position on the emancipation of Renaissance thought: the ancients, thanks to the perfection of their language and their intelligence, were believed to have come much closer to the truth than the naturalist doctors could do by means of their own linguistic instruments.

In his subtle analysis of the term *inventio* and its value in the Renaissance, Grahame Castor underlines its Ciceronian content: it signifies "investigation of that which is not immediately perceptible." The action of "the inventor" consists in revealing that which was hidden and giving it the capacity to persuade. Thus the poet is not the genius who announces his introspective reflections, while the naturalist doctor is not the inspired discoverer, who would single-handedly revolutionize common knowledge despite a still dominant obscurantism.[53]

The *differentiae,* which allow us to understand the natural order, preexist the action of the observer, both in nature and in ancient literature. In describing the work of Valerius Cordus, his German master, Belon writes that Cordus "demonstrates and interprets the plants of Galen, Theophrastus and Dioscordes."[54] For the naturalist doctor, the dilemma is to show his personal talent as an orator by appearing convincing, indeed even brilliant, but without compromising the meaning of the natural messages.

Without straying too far from our subject, we must mention how close these issues are to the translation studies so important to the humanists. The considerations and even the polemics are exactly identical, whether concerned with finding the right word to render the sense of an ancient text, a Biblical message, or the harmony of Creation. Faced with these difficulties, the naturalist doctor, first having set forth his duties and moral engagement in his preface, considers himself empowered to make personal choices in presenting the material. Far from seeking to free himself from his intellectual environment, it is within this space that he will legitimately claim relative personal freedom as a theologian of nature.

The subject of illustration choice will furnish us new information regarding the representation of nature in the Renaissance. From the perspective of modern biology, another deficiency in the illustrations of these natural history treatises is the relatively small number of images compared with the number of species described in the text. The explanation of this fact is in part of an economic order; engravings represent a considerable portion of the total cost of an edition. Still we must not stop there; more enlightenment will appear if we inquire into the species represented.

To see this more clearly, we have chosen to examine Belon's *De aquatilibus* and its French translation (*La nature et diversité des poissons*). First we must remember that for economic reasons, and perhaps to precede his rival Rondelet's *Libri de piscibus,* Belon wrote *De aquatilibus* in great haste, with limited means. The reduced-format work has only 176 engravings (181 in *La nature et diversité des poissons*) although it describes, or at least cites, more than 300 species. These circumstances make analyzing Belon's ichthyologic work particularly fruitful, since Belon had to make a choice of which species to illustrate and felt the need to justify that choice.

Besides the case, mentioned earlier, of a superfluity of pictures next to certain descriptions, one can view an illustration as redundant for four other reasons:

1. When a fish is assumed to be known by everyone, as, for example, the eel.
2. When species are very similar to each other, for example, the "flat fish" (turbot, flounder, plaice, etc.). The absence of an engraving may even emphatically underline the resemblance between two species. [*Channus*] is smaller than a sea perch, greatly similar to *Orphus* and *Hepatus:* so much so that being grouped together they could be sold the one for the other: in sum, having so great a similarity that I have not at all caused the portrait of *Channus* to be drawn, wanting it to be known to be just like the sea perch.[55]
3. When a fish exists in Europe and has an "equivalent" elsewhere. Of *callarias* (*Lote de mer*) and the Egyptian *Claria nilotica* (*Lote du Nil*), only the former is represented.[56]
4. When too many similar species exist for all to be mentioned, which is the case, for example, with the "little fish" (*pisciculi*).

The three last cases, in particular, are important to understanding Renaissance "zoology." We read similar explanations in Gesner and Rondelet, with regard to "little fish," and in Belon's *L'Histoire de la nature des oyseaux,* on the subject of little birds:

Who would record the portrait of a little bird, could easily make it hold for thirty others, as long as one adjusted the correct colors: for almost all have legs, claws, eyes, beaks and feathers the same: and only appear different to the view in color alone.[57]

For Gesner, the *pisciculi* do not belong to any established "genus" and "cannot be grouped according to any characteristic."[58] In the first place, given that the object of natural history is to serve man, it is useless to describe things in too much detail or to represent a fish too similar to another, if its dietetic or gastronomic virtues are the same.

The absence of other pictures reveals the natural hierarchy illustrating the fact that a global classification of all the creatures is both impossible and

useless since certain animals or plants are literally insignificant. This is why nature equipped them with secondary marks (*notae*), their colors, there being no
value in documenting their diversity. On the level of art history it is worthwhile
to note that the broad debate taking place on this subject between the authors
and artists involved in producing natural history treatises echoes the old rivalry
between color and line.

Returning to our subject, we can assert that one of the keys to many of
the naturalist doctors' choices is the concept of natural hierarchy, a complete
description of which would be too long to present here. I will simply give some
examples of the considerations this principle elicits.

Notable are the various ways of organizing the works besides the alphabetical order of Gesner's *Historiae animalium*. In *Nomenclator aquatilium animantium* the latter begins by discussing the "little fish" in order to move from
beings hardly distinguishable from the original material to arrive progressively
at the superior, organized beings. Belon, Rondelet, Salviani, and Aldrovandi
each adopt their own system of representing the natural order according to
dignity (*dignitas*). In ichthyologic works, the dolphin often wins the first-place
honors. He is the king of the fish in Belon's *L'Histoire naturelle des estranges
poisson marins*. The largest cetaceans appear at the beginning of the latter's
two other treatises (see Figure 5.10).

Cleverly, Rondelet begins the *Libri de piscibus* with the *dorade* (Gilthead
Bream, *Sparus aurata*), which, for him, is the noblest. Much appreciated by
the ancients, this fish is concretely and metaphorically crowned with gold. All
these systems show the naturalist doctors' eagerness to elaborate and then defend their points of view, their personal "interpretations."

All their decisions betray an anthropomorphic and Eurocentric perspective.
The social order is to be read in nature and the European species are arche-
types, whose "quality" is superior to exotic beings of any origin. That is true

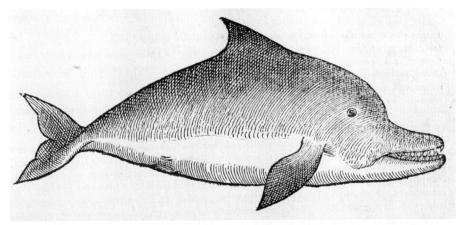

FIGURE 5.10: "Balaena" or "Cete," Belon, *La nature et diversité des poissons*, p. 5.

a fortiori for the species of the Americas. The discovery of the New World and its innumerable unknown animal and vegetable species will progressively ruin the Aristotelian system; but that will take place much later, beginning in the second half of the seventeenth century. The American flora and fauna will long be considered merely *profuse simulacra* of European nature, proving that natural history in the Renaissance constituted a coherent system that deeply influenced the way voyagers to the New World viewed nature.[59]

Finally, this anthropocentric perspective explains the apparent carelessness with regard to "inferior" creatures. Lexicological examination shows an interest principally concentrated on the comparison of organs with those of man, the divine masterpiece. The paucity of pictures devoted to animal anatomy strictly speaking, outside of some of Aldrovandi's engravings, confirms this for us. The examination of animal anatomy is far from systematic. Other than its comparative role, its foremost function is to illustrate meticulously the divine genius. Here again the author's freedom is limited and the great risk for him is to stray from his initial goal.

CONCLUSION

If my objective has been to contest the idea of the "modernity" of sixteenth-century natural history, it nevertheless has not been to contend that this differed in no way from the medieval view of plants and animals, nor that it espoused all the features of the classical model. It is undeniable that Fuchs, Gesner, and their colleagues elaborated a method of meticulous examination of nature that shows common points with the zoology of the following centuries. But a misunderstanding arises when we try to extend the comparison. We have seen that some aspects of sixteenth-century natural history can be reduced to weaknesses, to incomprehensible gaps or clumsiness in the iconographic cohesion of the treatises; however, our task as historians has been to go beyond these prejudices to achieve an overall understanding of a concept that absolutely cannot be considered an early form of modern biology.

The notion of natural hierarchy, for example, is a very important specificity of sixteenth-century natural history, inherited and adapted from the preceding centuries. Far from being torn between past and modernity, Renaissance natural history has shown solid principles of coherence, wedding theological constraints to rhetorical principles. The best illustrations of this have been limitations due to the rhetorical requirement for variety and submission to the divine as observed in *Naturae sagacissimae misteria*.[60] The main objective of the discourse is to instruct, notably by reference to the notion of pleasure, a thing incompatible with the monotony an overly detailed inventory of species would cause.

One consideration, which exceeds the framework of our study, remains to be developed, that is, the evolution of the picture in natural history at the end of the sixteenth century and in the following decades. Such an overview would show without doubt that there is no linear progression in the function of the zoological illustration, and that it is urgently necessary to take into account economic, social, and religious context when undertaking an analysis.

Two French researchers, Claudie Balavoine and François Lecercle, have demonstrated that the picture loses its central position in late sixteenth-century emblem-books.[61] Its semantic use weakens to the profit of the impact of the text. One explanation for this is the combined influence of the Jesuits and the Protestant reticence with regard to the power of the picture. Does this phenomenon have anything to do with the general ossification of the picture in natural history treatises, which for the most part draw their illustrations from the works of Gesner and his peers, to reduce them, as it were, to mnemonic signs? This may be an accepted fact and, in any case, demonstrates the strength and originality of the mid-sixteenth-century treatises, even though their content does not correspond to our retrospective modern expectations.

CHAPTER SIX

Philosophers and Animals in the Renaissance

STEFANO PERFETTI

Several factors determined a deep renewal of philosophical consideration of animals in the Renaissance. Humanist editions and translations had enlarged the canon of readings, and new books and reappraisals of ancient works crowded the bookshelves and the working desks; not just Aristotle's zoological treatises (which, although already Latinized in the thirteenth century, were newly translated with elegance), but also works on animals by Pliny, Aelian, Plutarch, and others were edited, translated, and circulated. Thus, when professional Aristotelians at the sixteenth-century universities resumed a tradition of commenting on Aristotle's books on animals (a tradition that had been neglected in the previous two centuries), they had to take into account this enlarged canon of authoritative readings. Soon after, geographical explorations produced a rich travel literature with descriptions of novel animals. These too asked for admission within the bookish science of animals of the university professors. Faced with all this new material, professors of natural philosophy at first tried to incorporate it within the traditional Aristotelian commentary format. But very soon, approximately around 1550, it became clear that it was impossible to keep everything together. Thus the science of animals found its expression in new literary genres and epistemic practices.

What happened was a passage from an age of commentaries on Aristotle to the age of Renaissance zoological "histories." While the Aristotelian tradition had emphasized knowledge of the physiology of animals and the structure and function of their parts (in relation to the nature or "essence" of the whole animal), an alternative view, emphasizing the rationality of animals and their uncorrupted moral virtue, will be advocated by the end of the century by Michel de Montaigne.

HUMANISM AND ANCIENT BOOKS ON ANIMALS

The first step had been taken in the second half of the fifteenth century, with the humanist rediscovery and/or reappraisal of a great number of ancient texts on animals and plants, and with the lively, at times red-hot, debates around them. A good example is Pliny's *Naturalis historia,* of which several editions were printed, provoking endless debates halfway between philology and philosophy of nature (the discussion took the start from Niccolò Leoniceno's *De erroribus Plinii* and Ermolao Barbaro's *Castigationes plinianae,* both printed in 1492).[1] Similar considerations, on a smaller scale, though, could be extended to Aelian, Plutarch, Oppian, and so on.

Far more important to us is the reappraisal of Aristotle's major zoological treatises (*History of Animals, Parts of Animals,* and *Generation of Animals*). These works had been rarely commented on by scholastic masters of the thirteenth century, when they were Latinized for the first time (one notable exception was Albert the Great). Even worse, fourteenth- and fifteenth-century commentators, as far as the extant documents tell us, seem to have completely neglected these books. It comes as no surprise, then, that they received a genuine reappraisal from humanists outside the university world. Within the project promoted by Pope Nicholas V (the humanist Tommaso Parentucelli) of rendering into elegant Latin a certain number of ancient natural history works, Aristotle's zoological treatises were translated twice into Latin in the 1450s by two Byzantine émigrés. The first translation, by George of Trebizond (Trapezuntius), stylistically old-fashioned and unelegant as it was, proved really disappointing to its commissioner (and never reached printing). Thus the pope entrusted a new version to Theodore Gaza (a protégé of Cardinal Bessarion). This elegant Latin translation (presumably completed in 1459) was printed for the first time in 1476 and soon became the reference version for humanistic circles.[2]

Theodore Gaza introduced his translations with a preface that offers a philosophical evaluation of Aristotle's zoological works and suggestions for their use in philosophical and theological curricula. First, these treatises allow a complete recapitulation of the science of nature, from its first and general principles down to the smallest details of animal behavior:

The rational inquiry of nature proceeds in order through all the distinctions which nature has made [...]; it distributes genera in species and describes them one by one (and these books contain some five hundred of them); it continues by explaining in which way each one reproduces (both terrestrial and aquatic species), of which limbs it is constituted, by which aliment it feeds, by what it is injured, what are its customs, how long it is allowed to live, how big its body is, which one is the larger and which the smaller, and the shape, the color, the voice, the character and submissiveness; in short, it does not neglect any animal that nature generates, feeds, grows, and protects.[3]

Then, knowledge about animals, even the smallest ones, is not mere curiosity, because, as Paul the apostle says, "the invisible things of Him from the creation of the world are clearly seen" (Rom. 1, 20). Therefore:

We shall not listen to those who say that Aristotle said many things about the fly, the tiny bee, the worm, but few about God: he speaks of God much, who by means of an accurate study of the created things, lets the creator himself be known; [...] nature's ingenuity must be contemplated in the most minute details.[4]

Finally, the study of animal behavior provides immediate, constant, and genuine illustration of moral values. Indeed, the animal world is full of examples of social solidarity, family piety, and generosity (often performed by beasts better than men):

Who is ever an enemy of his own kind with such perverse character that he cannot be corrected and appeased, when he understands that no animal is ever killed by a member of its kind? Who is ever so lacking in piety to his parents that he cannot be brought back to piety, when he learns of the piety of the stork or the bee-eater to their parents?[5]

It is apparent that Gaza here provides several different reading keys for these treatises. Not only is there the physiological analysis of animals' parts and functions in strict Aristotelian terms, as one could expect, but also a theological and, particularly, a moral reading key, the latter heavily indebted to Pliny. Most sixteenth-century professors of natural philosophy will adopt and develop the Aristotelian line of approach. Nevertheless, the Plinian hints, reinforced with the theses of Plutarch on the cleverness, rationality, and uncorrupted natural morality of beasts, will be revisited at the end of the century by Michel de Montaigne.

UNIVERSITY COMMENTARIES ON ARISTOTLE'S ZOOLOGICAL TREATISES

Novelties in style and tone kept the new Latin Aristotle outside university commentary practice for a long time. In fact, it took more than forty years after the *editio princeps* of Gaza's *De animalibus* to have university commentaries based on it.[6] Such perplexities would be broken only in 1521, on Sunday, November 10, when Pietro Pomponazzi, professor of natural philosophy at the University of Bologna, began a course on the *Parts of Animals,* and he did not comment on medieval translations (such as that from Arabic made by Michael Scot, or that from Greek made by William of Moerbeke), but on Gaza's elegant humanist Latin.[7] After the pioneering course of Pomponazzi, the production of university commentaries on Aristotle's zoological treatises had an extraordinary flowering in the first half of the century (with such names as Niccolò Leonico Tomeo, Agostino Nifo, Francesco Vimercato, and Julius Caesar Scaliger).[8] (See Table 6.1.)

Renaissance culture had no institutional space for the science of animals, apart from university courses on natural philosophy (which consisted in analytical readings of Aristotle's books, often critically discussed and compared with other traditions of thought, as, for instance, Galen's). Aristotle's treatises on animals were facultative readings in courses of natural philosophy at the Faculty of Arts (i.e., philosophical disciplines). This renewed focus on Aristotle's zoological books did not stem from pure interest in the animal world. After a long acquaintance with *Physics, On the Soul, Meteorology,* and *Generation and Corruption,* most of these commentators simply aimed at expanding their exploration of Aristotle's natural philosophy in order to

TABLE 6.1: Sixteenth-Century Commentaries

Place	Date	Author	Subject
Bologna	1521–1523	Pietro Pomponazzi	*PA* I–III
Padua (?)	1520s	Niccolò Leonico Tomeo	*PA* I
Salerno	1534 (compl.)	Agostino Nifo	*HA, PA, GA*
Naples (?)	1540s (?)	Simone Porzio (?)	*PA* I.1
Paris	>1546 <1561	Francesco Vimercato	*PA* I–III
Agen	1538–1550s	Giulio Cesare Scaligero	*HA*
Padua	1570	Arcangelo Mercenario	*PA* I.1
Padua	1574	Daniel Furlanus	*PA* I
Padua	1599	Antonio Scaino	*GA*
Padua	1599/1600 (?)	Cesare Cremonini	*PA* I, *GA* I
Prague/ Frankfurt	<1601	Cristoforo Guarinoni	*HA* I, 1–6

see physical principles at work in living beings.[9] This explains the peculiar blend of philosophical apriorism and bookish erudition one finds in these works, and, conversely, the very scarce recourse to eyewitness data and direct experience.

Having exhausted the polemics on the mortality of the soul triggered by his *Treatise on the Immortality of the Soul* (1516), Pietro Pomponazzi wrote his two major works (*On Fate* and *On Incantations,* both 1520) and soon after went on to explore the theoretical implications of biology both in a treatise *On Nutrition* (1521) and in his final courses (he died in 1525). In these lectures on *De partibus,* which are part of such exploration of Aristotle's natural philosophy, one finds no factual verification or description based on eyewitness accounts; rather, Pomponazzi comes across as an acute commentator, highly skilled at using the instruments of logical, conceptual, and semantic analysis to test the internal consistency of Aristotle's discourse. Thus Pomponazzi, in order to criticize Aristotle from within, often focuses on inconsistencies of the *Parts of Animals* and exposes several ambiguities in Aristotle's text. This attitude applies not only to logical and argumentative fallacies, but also to inconsistencies in physical and biological reasoning proper. For instance, when commenting on the twelfth chapter of the second book, in which Aristotle says that "birds have auditory passages only" and not ears "owing to the hardness of their skin and because they have feathers instead of hairs, which means that they have not the right material for forming ears,"[10] Pomponazzi objects that "This reason of Aristotle's is plainly worthless, because birds have eyes and eyelids. Just as nature produced eyelids, could it not produce ears with that flesh?"[11]

A few lines above, our commentator had sketched a dialogue with an imaginary opponent: "You will say: birds have skin. To this I reply that their skin, being not hard, is really unfit for such a task. But—you will say—barn owls seem to have ears. I don't know and I don't remember if they have."[12]

Quite often in this commentary Pomponazzi reveals a lack of interest in (and information on) zoological details, which is quite peculiar given his rationalistic way of dealing with animals. Nevertheless the strong feature in Pomponazzi's commentary on the *Parts of Animals* is its irreverent and paradoxical tone, where his dissatisfaction with conventional interpretations speaks a Latin that combines scholastic jargon and vernacular overtones, sometimes pushed to obscene language or anticlerical jokes. For instance, when commenting on a passage in II, 1 in which Aristotle deals with the relationship between heart and viscera, Pomponazzi observes:

> It is to be noticed here that, according to Aristotle's opinion, the heart is formed first in animals and it is the starting-point of blood-vessels and

nerves. Consequently, the heart is full of blood, because, according to Aristotle, blood generates in the heart. Now, since the heart is so full of blood, the heart keeps for itself the best and purer part of blood for its own nutrition; then, what remains of the blood is sent to the other limbs. Therefore the heart behaves like friars, who keep good things for themselves, then give the poor, for God's sake, what they don't need, i.e., watery soup [*"poi quel che non voglieno loro, çoè la broda, danno per l'amor di Dio pauperibus"*]; similarly, the heart sends to the other limbs that blood which it does not need.[13]

Indeed, Pomponazzi works on Aristotle's zoological discourse with several instruments. He tries to resort to all the bookish sources at his disposal (ancient, medieval, and contemporary). When discussing the tissues and organs of animals Pomponazzi employs not only Avicenna or Galen, but also a panoply of medical writings, from the late medieval Torrigiano de' Torregiani's *Plusquamcommentum* and Gentile da Foligno's commentary on Avicenna's *Canon* to his contemporaries Jacques Despars and Iacopo Berengario da Carpi. Another typical trait of Pomponazzi's is his recourse to information drawn from hunters, fishermen, and other "technicians." Here is a nice example:

> Although our physicians make up this prescription, i.e "take the bone from a deer heart," I asked truthful apothecaries about this bone from the deer heart. They said they never saw this bone from the deer heart, but what they put in that preparation is bull bone. But the apothecary added that they pretend it is bone from deer heart in order to earn more: since few deer are captured, we say "bone from the deer heart," so that it sounds of great value, but, in reality, it is a bone from the heart of a bull or of a horse.[14]

In conclusion, Pomponazzi's commentary (the first Renaissance commentary on Aristotle's zoology) is something of a program of reasoned skepticism, more than an exercise in progressive naturalism. This school of doubt does not spare even the reliability of Aristotle's knowledge of animals:

> Aristotle seems to suggest that in Africa one may find animals of bigger dimensions, so that some oviparous beast might exist that is bigger than a viviparous one, etc. First, it is to be stressed that Aristotle in this book did not have true science, but credulity and belief, since Aristotle did not see all these animals with his eyes (had he lived a thousand years, he would not have seen them); rather he trusted in those who saw these things. [...] Aristotle had about these things the same knowledge that we Christians

have about Christ: for we did not see Christ, but we believe those who wrote about him.[15]

While Pomponazzi analyzed Aristotle's zoology to display his own philosophical criticism, other professional Aristotelians conjoined scholasticism and encyclopedic erudition. The format itself of the scholastic *commentum*—its modularity—allowed the accumulation of many glosses, including not only erudite digressions and references to manifold authors (according to the humanistic taste), but also new data on exotic fauna. The most notable example is to be found in Agostino Nifo's *Expositiones* of Aristotle's zoological works (completed in 1534, published in 1546). After a brilliant academic career with well-paid positions at the universities of Padua, Rome, and Pisa, Nifo was a full professor of natural philosophy and medicine at the university of Salerno from 1522 to his death in 1538, and here he wrote his commentaries on all of Aristotle's major zoological works (*History, Parts,* and *Generation of Animals*). Nifo's aim was to keep together, within the medieval format of *commentum cum quaestionibus,* scholasticism (e.g., syllogistic formalizations of Aristotle's arguments), humanistic philology (e.g., references to the original Greek text), literary erudition, and naturalistic information.

One finds a telling passage in the preface, when Nifo discusses the relationship between the epistemic status of Aristotle's zoology and the new discoveries of animals. Of course, he says, it is not possible to know every detail of the natural world (*"notitia animalium omnium perfecte non potest haberi"*), since new exotic species are constantly discovered, for instance in Africa (*"semper aliquid novi fert Africa"*), and also because animals that live deep under the ground or at the bottom of the sea escape perception (*"non cadunt sub sensum"*). Nevertheless, Nifo continues, Aristotle developed the reliable theoretical structure of zoology, that is, a system of ultimate species and genera that allows the explanation of every possible single occurrence, including the new. For, whatever animal is born or discovered "can only be aquatic or terrestrial; if aquatic, it will be fish or crustacean or gastropod or cephalopod; and if fish, it will be oviparous or viviparous, like cetaceans." These classifying schemes enable us to gather any novel information within a structured natural system "through the ultimate genera and through their proper predicates and through the causes of those predicates."[16]

It is relevant that Nifo commented not only on *Parts* and *Generation* (i.e., the most theoretical treatises, where Aristotle analyzes the causes of parts and functions, referring them to the fully developed ὀυσία as their final cause), but also on the monumental nine books of *History of Animals,* which are filled with factual data and descriptions. Nifo approached them by surrounding Aristotle's data with reasoned lexical inserts and other pieces of information on animals drawn from every book at his disposal; the main sources are

Pliny and Albert the Great, but one also finds eclectic references to Homer, Aeschylus, Plautus, Caesar, Virgil, Lucretius, and Ovid (sometimes on the basis of weak analogies with Aristotle's text). As a matter of fact this led to an uncontrollable hypertrophism.[17] In Agostino Nifo's *Expositiones* each sentence of Aristotle's text is surrounded by an overflowing mass of annotations, which range from philosophical, philological, and naturalistic remarks to virtually everything noteworthy written by previous commentators and authors (Galen, John Philoponus, Michael of Ephesus, Averroes, Albert the Great, and so on). Such an accumulative tendency could only lead to an impasse.

It is now clear that, generally, university commentaries did not feed any knowledge on animals capable of going out of the bookish borders of university halls. Yet new animals were pushing at the doors of these halls, so to speak. For these were the years of Da Gama, Columbus, Cabot, Vespucci, Magellan, Pigafetta, when exploration spread in all directions: to Africa, India, the Pacific Ocean, and the Americas. In this context a rich travel literature was being written, which also recorded descriptions of novel animals (and sometimes even the animals themselves, in flesh and bones, were taken to European menageries).

Faced with all this new material, Aristotelian commentators at first tried to incorporate. But very soon it became clear that it was impossible to keep together—within the commentary format—several disparate intellectual practices: namely, *divisio textus, expositio litterae, sensus, quaestiones,* and also humanist philology, literary erudition, naturalistic descriptions, and new data from travel literature and contemporary medical literature. All this could only generate hypertrophic literary monsters.

ANIMALIUM HISTORIAE: MONOGRAPHS AND ENCYCLOPEDIAS ON ANIMALS

As a matter of fact, around the 1550s two interlinked phenomena took place. The production of overgrown commentaries on Aristotle's zoological treatises drastically decreased and gave way to short partial expositions, dedicated only to methodological sections, as the first book of the *De partibus animalium,* if not only its first lines, with no further concern for the zoological sections proper.[18] At the same time, while professional Aristotelians at the universities would lose their confidence in making science on animals by commenting on Aristotle's *De partibus animalium* line by line (and by adding erudite digressions),[19] other intellectuals devoted their energies to other formats. Put simply, zoological content left the commentary practice and *migrated* to different literary genres. Most of these new books on animals have the word *historia* in the title (*Historia animalium … Historia aquatilium …*). Here is an overall glance at the main representatives.

On one hand are the monumental encyclopedias (such as Conrad Gesner's *Historia animalium*):

> Conrad Gesner, *Historia animalium, liber primus. De quadrupedibus vi-viparis* (1551);
> *Historia animalium, liber secundus. De quadrupedibus oviparis* (1554);
> *Historia animalium, liber tertius, qui est de avium natura* (1555);
> *Historia animalium, liber quartus, qui est de piscium et aquatilium natura* (1558);

On the other hand are monographs, that is, books dealing with a particular section of the animal world:

> Pierre Belon, *L'histoire naturelle des estranges poissons marins* (Paris, 1551), *De aquatilibus* (Paris, 1553), *La nature et la diversité des poissons* (Paris, 1555), *L'histoire de la nature des oyseaux* (Paris, 1555);
> Guillaume Rondelet, *Libri de piscibus marinis* (Lyons, 1554) and *Universa aquatilium historia* (Lyons, 1555), *L'histoire entière des poissons* (Lyons, 1558);
> Ippolito Salviani, *Aquatilium animalium historia* (Rome, 1554–1558);

There is also a third group (halfway between the first two):

> Adam Lonitzer (Lonicerus), *Naturalis historiae opus novum* (Frankfurt, 1551);
> Edward Wotton, *De differentiis animalium libri decem* (Paris, 1552);
> Johannes Schmid (Ioannes Fabricius Montanus), *Differentiae animalium quadrupedum secundum locos communes*/ Otho Vuerdmüller, *Similitudinum ab omni animalium genere desumptarum libri VI* (Zurich, 1555).

As Brian Ogilvie explains, "Histories of nature entered the European consciousness more generally only in the 1540s" (with Gesner's *Historia plantarum et vires*, 1541, and Leonhart Fuchs's *De historia stirpiuum commentarii insignes,*1542); previously, in the fifteenth and early sixteenth century, natural history was discussed in "a disciplinary and literary structure inherited from the Middle Ages," that is, that of treatises "on the *properties*" or "on the *natures*" of things.[20] Somehow overcoming the scholastic notion of *historia* (as bare knowledge of facts without their causes), sixteenth-century naturalists gave this term a multilayered meaning, which also covers inquiry and knowledge based on sense perception, and description of particular cases.[21]

Although I distinguish between monograph and encyclopedia, these two terms do not refer to two structurally different literary genres: both were instances of the *historia*-genre, that is, a book made of sequential entries. The main distinction does not lie in the literary format, but in the range of reality covered and in the number of relevant contributions authored by the writer.

Both encyclopedias and monographs offered an alternative to the crisis of hypertrophy that was afflicting the traditional way of making natural science through commentaries. Both afforded a more agile reception of novel data.

The encyclopedia-style was a systematic organization of the erudition on animals as a comprehensive and alphabetized catalog, in which ancient and contemporary books on nature were deconstructed and filed into alphabetical entries. The most relevant case is Conrad Gesner's *Historia animalium,* which appeared in five volumes between 1551 and 1587.[22] Here the Swiss polymath supplies for each animal a file made of several sections. These include the onomatology in ancient and modern languages, geographical distribution, morphology, ethological aspects, edible usage, pharmacological usage, fictional information, and symbolic value. Each section is actually a compilation of quotations taken from classical authors (Biblical, Greek, and Latin), from medieval authors (such as Albert the Great and Thomas of Cantimpré) and, especially for the ichthyologic tome, from contemporary naturalists (such as the previously mentioned Belon and Rondelet).[23] As Gesner himself makes clear, his bulky *Historia animalium* is not conceived for an uninterrupted reading, but for being used as any dictionary, chiefly to investigate: "those who accused us of being too prolix in this work did not understand that."[24]

The encyclopedia à la Gesner answers the desire of having a book made of books, a sort of hyperbook that might replace the actual reading of many books by different authors. But compilations were also based on one single author, for instance, Edward Wotton's *On Differences of Animals* (1552).[25] Here we have in the title another keyword closely linked to the epistemic plan of Aristotle's and Theophrastus's ἱστορίαι, namely "difference" (διαφορά). For *historia,* in its wider literary and epistemic sense, has to be a system (or, at least, an exposition) of *differences.* Wotton's *De differentiis* is sometimes misremembered as an original contribution from an early modern naturalist. In fact, as the author himself admits, this work is a compilation made of literal excerpts taken from all of Aristotle's biological works (including *Parva naturalia*). Wotton's peculiar contribution is to order their exposition according to the epistemic principles of Aristotle's *History of Animals.* After establishing methodological criteria on parts and differences in the first two books, subsequently Wotton examines all the Aristotelian groupings of blooded and bloodless animals (man, viviparous and oviparous quadrupeds, serpents, birds, fishes, cephalopods, crustaceans, and insects) within the schemes expounded in the two opening books. With the exception of onomatological and erudite sections (printed in smaller characters), the main body of the text is almost entirely made of literal excerpts taken from Aristotle's biological works. So Wotton's *De differentiis* is a coherent and compact reorganization of excerpts from Aristotle. Or, even more to the point, we can recall a book published in 1563 and compiled by Cesare Odoni, a professor of medicine and a botanist in Bologna. The title speaks for itself: *Aristotelis sparsae de animalibus sententiae in continuatam seriem ad propria capita revocatae nominaque secundum literarum ordinem disposita*, that is, *Aristotle's scattered sentences on animals now rearranged in alphabetical order.* Here Odoni does with Aristotle what he had already done with Theophrastus's botany in 1561 by taking the *History of Animals* to pieces and rearranging it as alphabetical entries, from *acarus* to *xylophtorus*.[26] Although the alphabetical arrangement might seem reminiscent of medieval bestiaries and encyclopedias, such a book is peculiar to its own period, when the main function of classical naturalists was not to be commented on, but to provide pieces of information.

As for the other two representatives of the third group of works mentioned previously (those halfway between encyclopedia and monograph), there is not much to say. Adam Lonitzer's (Lonicerus) *Naturalis historiae opus novum* (Frankfurt, 1551) already from the title echoes the "practical" Pliny: in fact, this work is mainly aimed at the knowledge and use of herbs and other natural remedies. Here pieces of information on animals from ancient authors are just summarized and attached to the descriptions in the main text. Johannes Schmid's (Ioannes Fabricius Montanus) *Differentiae animalium quadrupedum* ... (Zurich, 1555) is a minimalist, compact book of *differentiae*, designed to be used as a tool, in correlation with Book 1 of Gesner's *Historia animalium* (it must be remembered that Montanus studied under Gesner).

But *historiae* were also written in which the personal contributions of the author were decidedly relevant (I mean contributions in terms of discoveries, novel findings, innovative description, and so on). These are what I call monographs. Such treatises, typically centered on a particular section of the natural world (e.g., aquatic fauna, or birds, or dogs), were produced in great number in the third quarter of the sixteenth century. Consider the traveler-writer Pierre Belon, who wrote illustrated books in French and in Latin, such as *L'histoire naturelle des estranges poissons marins* (1551), *De aquatilibus* (1553), *La nature et la diversité des poissons* (1555), and *L'histoire de la nature des oyseaux* (1555); or Guillaume Rondelet with his *Libri de piscibus marinis* (1554) and *Universa aquatilium historia* (1555), later translated into French as *L'histoire entière des poissons* (1558) (these are also illustrated); or Ippolito Salviani, who worked out an *Aquatilium animalium historia* (1554–1558) with magnificent copperplates.[27] Monographs gathered a large range of brand-new direct observations, due to the authors themselves or collected from other sources (e.g., from travel literature), and they often merged such direct observations with segments of information drawn from classical authors.

Both encyclopedias and monographs employed illustrations as an indispensable visual aid to identify species. And the presence of illustrations (woodcuts or copperplates) that are increasingly realistic and rich in detail is, indeed, one of the most typical traits of Renaissance natural-history books.

In a sort of virtuous circle, monographs were supported by the very availability of the encyclopedias (that legitimized and afforded a different use of the classics, no longer as texts to be commented upon in a *lectio continua*, but as sources of data susceptible to innovative textual arrangements), and encyclopedias too grew rich and were constantly updated thanks to many pieces of information drawn from contemporary monographs.

Besides being a remedy for the crisis of hypertrophy of university commentaries, this renewed naturalistic literature on the one side gave expression to the travelers' discoveries and to different ways of investigating nature (think of Georgius Agricola's monograph on the subterranean life of animals),[28] while on the other side it met the curiosity of new readers; not only intellectuals of the faculty of arts and physicians, but also cultivated readers of humanist courts and bourgeois readers could find attractive such monograph style, with the description of the local fauna, the account of personal experiences, the clear arrangement of themes, and the frequent double version—Latin and vernacular.

It is quite obvious that such significant transformations in zoological literature took the evolution in herbals as their model: we may think of the *Gart der Gesundenheit* or *Herbarium zu Teutsch* (1485), the *Ortus sanitatis* (1491), up to Otto Brunfels's *Herbarum vere eicones ad nature imitationem* (1530), and Leonhart Fuchs's *De historia stirpium* (1542).[29] Indeed, the urgency of renewed literary forms had been felt in botany even before it was in zoology. From the pharmacological *usefulness* of plants stemmed the importance of properly identifying botanical species. Thus, encyclopedic style, with entries structured according to a standard module and with life-like illustrations, was the inevitable instrument to set in order the forest of onomatology and data of ancient authors, and to contain novel pieces of information (most of which derived from the great geographical explorations or from ad hoc expeditions, organized by naturalists).[30]

GUILLAUME RONDELET: *AQUATILIUM HISTORIA*

I would like to discuss here, as a case history, Guillaume Rondelet's *Aquatilium historia,* issued in two volumes in 1554–1555, since this work is, perhaps, the best example of the *migration* of Aristotelian schemes and epistemic patterns into a new kind of natural history book. Rondelet was a professional physician and a professor of medicine in the noble university of Montpellier. He wrote highly acclaimed medical treatises and was even celebrated, under the nickname of *Rondibilis,* by Rabelais, in the third book of *Pantagruel* (Chapters 29–35).

The work of Rondelet was issued in two volumes with different titles:

1. Gulielmi Rondeletii *Libri de piscibus marinis* (Lugduni: Matthias Bonhomme, 1554);

2. Id., *Universae aquatilium historiae pars altera, cum veris ipsorum imaginibus* (Lugduni: Matthias Bonhomme, 1555). The title *De piscibus marinis* appears on the frontispiece of the first volume only (and is not entirely appropriate, since several freshwater fishes are also described). The proper title for the whole work is *Aquatilium historia.* Also, the French translation, published in 1558, is entitled *L'histoire entière des poissons.*

This *Aquatilium historia* is a big book, in two volumes in folio, more than 900 pages, with beautiful woodcuts, highly praised by Cuvier.[31] But the descriptions of 440 aquatic animals (we shall consider them later) are preceded by 112 pages where Rondelet develops a discourse on method, which is clearly patterned on the epistemological framework of the first book of Aristotle's *Historia animalium.* Rondelet first sets out a theory of general and specific attributes as markers of difference between animals; then he proceeds by indicating where these differences are to be found: habitat, parts, functions, activities. In fact, the first part of the *Aquatilium historia* (Books I–IV, Volume 1, pp. 1–112) deals with characters, parts, and functions of the various fishes *in respect of something common* (Aristotle would say κατά τι κοινόν), that is, grouping analogous traits of different species within the treatment of a common aspect or function.

The second chapter (*"Quae sint piscium differentiae"*) might be summarized as follows:

1. knowledge (*"cognitio"*) about fishes depends on the differences (*"differentiae"*) between them, and difference means "everything that makes something different from another thing" (*"omne id quod aliud ab alio quoquo modo differre facit"*);

2. two kinds of difference are recognized: "accidens" and "proprium" (these two terms—clearly mirroring Aristotle's συμβεβεκός and ίδιον—might be rendered as "attribute" and "property");

3. since "specific properties" (*"differentiae propriae"*) are very few and "extremely difficult to find" (*"inventu difficillimae"*), we must take refuge in the knowledge of the attributes;

4. Rondelet concludes that the differences among fishes are to be drawn
   "a vita vivendique consuetudine, a partibus, ab actionibus, a moribus,"
   that is, "from habitat, parts, activities (or vital functions) and customs."[32] (It must be noticed that such strict Aristotelian assumptions
   also legitimate the regionalistic interests of the new monographs.)

This program is immediately put into effect, starting from the remainder
of the first book, which is devoted to the various environments where aquatic
animals live and to the consequent modes of feeding. The second book deals
with bodily differences in general (bodily constitution, shape, size, location of
organs, and so on); the third book deals with the description of each single
part (head, eyes, ears, mouth, and so on); and the fourth book deals with the
activities, and especially reproduction.

It is clear that in these first four books Rondelet is at his best, combining the
epistemic plan of the *Historia animalium* (the analysis of differences between
animals) with that of *De partibus animalium* and *De generatione animalium*
(the causal explanation of parts and functions, and also of reproductive organs
and activities). Both these methodological lines are enriched with critical references to classical authors and novel observational data. Of course, we should
not forget that such a relocation of all levels of analysis of Aristotle's zoology
within an epistemology of *differentiae,* in the style of *Historia animalium,* had
a proximate antecedent in Edward Wotton with his *De differentiis animalium*
(mentioned previously).

Let us now pass to the descriptions of animals. Rondelet deals with the
aquatic fauna in its entirety: not just fishes, but all animals living in an aquatic
environment. We range from Octopus to Cockle, from Whale to Beaver. The
consistency of the subject matter is not grounded on anatomical or physiological affinity, but on an "ecological" criterion, that is, the common aquatic environment. It would be anachronistic to look for a systematic taxonomy, in the
mode of Linnaeus. Indeed, Rondelet is much closer to the fluid and multidi-
mensional taxonomies of Aristotle.[33]

Aquatic animals first are divided into blooded and bloodless (a trait obviously borrowed from Aristotle). Then cephalopods, crustaceans, testaceans,
and insects plus zoophytes are grouped as major genera under the heading of
"bloodless" (this too is patterned on Aristotle).

These general partitions are then filled with entries, each dedicated to a
single aquatic animal (and each animal has its own picture). Each entry contains several levels:

1. a *determination* that includes a critical collation of ancient sources;
2. a table of synonymy in ancient and modern languages;

3. a morphological description of the exterior;
4. the anatomy of interior parts;
5. ethological notes;
6. finally, the author provides "useful" suggestions, that is, recipes for cooking, recipes for drugs, or employment in pharmacology and techniques of fishing.

The outstanding value of Rondelet's descriptions can be appreciated by comparing them with those of a competitor and rival, namely Pierre Belon, who published his *De aquatilibus* in 1554 and leveled accusations of plagiarism against Rondelet.[34] In Belon—apart from the fact that the collation of classical sources, the anatomy, and the practical suggestions are absent—the morphological descriptions themselves are often shabby. A telling example is the morphological section of the entry "turbot" (*Rhombus aculeatus*, which Rondelet distinguishes from *Rhombus laevis* and *Rhomboides*):

[RONDELET:] This fish is flat and inhabits the sea-shore; in its dark-coloured lower part there are many stings, especially around the head, and from the head to the tail. In this same part a black line is drawn, and pinnae too are black there, white elsewhere. It has a big mouth, wide open, without teeth, but with jagged jaw-bones instead of them. From the lower jaw-bone two appendages hang down, like thin beards. Not far from them, the turbot has a vent. From here a big pinna begins, continuing down to the tail. Another similar pinna begins from the head. Both of them increase progressively from the beginning to the middle, then both proportionally decrease. These somehow frame the whole body and characterize the turbot's figure.[35]

[BELON:] It has a skin full of wrinkles, ash-coloured, with whitish spots, armed everywhere with sharp hooks [...]. A white curved line separates the skin on both sides [...]. The head of the turbot (like that of the gilt-head) is full of thorny bones so much different and various with each other, that common people think here one might find almost all mechanical tools.[36]

The description provided by Rondelet is decidedly more accurate and surely owes much to direct inspections and anatomical dissections he practiced on fishes.[37]

We must also consider that the *Aquatilium historia* of Rondelet is rich in eyewitness data. A nice example is when Rondelet explains that, notwithstanding the belief of some, the German (and English) stockfish—that is, a fish softened by being beaten with a stick—is not the *salpa* (a fish that, according to Pliny, is treated in the same way).[38] While Belon had limited himself to a bare denial of such identification,[39] Rondelet gives reasons and adds lively eyewitness testimony on the preparation of stockfish at the market of Antwerp:

> *Stock Fisch* according to the language of Germans means "stick fish," i.e., a fish beaten with a stick before being cooked. They call with such a name every kind of fish which is seasoned with salt and dried by being smoked or simply *en plein air* (for instance, skate, sole, plaice, turbot and many others). I saw a remarkable quantity of them in Antwerp, in some stalls of traders. And they explained this preparation: these fishes, being dry and very hard, first are crushed with a stick or a hammer; then, after being soaked in water for some time, they are boiled. They have plenty of such fishes—I mean flat and thin—which can be dried easily, and, after being dried, are carried to Germany. Therefore *Stock Fisch* is not a species of fish, as experts in the German language confirmed to me.[40]

The *Aquatilium historia* of Rondelet is an outstanding example of how innovation and *deep fidelity* to the ancient legacy can coexist in an early modern monograph on animals. An author like Belon actually offered a radical alternative to the tradition of commenting on Aristotle. His production shows tight links with the books of travelers and explorers. His aim was to collect a vast amount of reliable positive information in a form as compact as possible. On the contrary, the *Aquatilium historia* of Rondelet—with its first part on the common characters and functions and the second dealing with the single species—is not properly meant to overcome Aristotle's biological *episteme,* but to replace its section on the aquatic fauna with a work that is still Aristotelian both in method and contents (at least to a certain extent). One should be tempted to see in the work of Rondelet something like an aquatic *Historia, De partibus,* and *De generatione* in a single work. Again, Rondelet is pleasant to read, full of nice local stories, eyewitness descriptions, and hints for edible and pharmacological uses. Finally, gastronomy and pharmacology remind us that Rondelet was a professor of medicine and wrote not only for cultivated or curious readers, but also for physicians. Yet the point is that this work of Rondelet is truly the last attempt to do natural philosophy by holding together—and on the same level—three sources of knowledge: an epistemology of Aristotelian inspiration, information drawn from ancient authors, and new acquisitions stemming from oral or written secondhand information or from eyewitness experience. The interplay of these three levels in Rondelet is almost perfect, while in Belon, as in other authors of monographs, this ratio is always somehow out of balance.

AN ALTERNATIVE VIEW:
MONTAIGNE AND "THERIOPHILY"

In classical antiquity several authors, instead of looking at animals with a scientific attitude, preferred to extol the animal condition, by claiming that beasts are as rational as men (if not more than men) and surely better than men as regards their physical constitution, conduct of life according to nature, moral habits, and technical skills. This complex of ideas has been labeled as "theriophily" by George Boas.[41] In particular, according to Diogenes of Sinope, the Cynic philosopher (fifth to fourth century B.C.), beasts possess the perfect model of life according to nature, uncorrupted by laws and other human inventions. Subsequently Plutarch of Chaeronia (C.F. ca. 45–ca. 125) shifted emphasis on the thesis of animal rationality, for example, in his *Gryllus* and in *On the Cleverness of the Beasts*.[42] These works, which are diametrically opposed to anthropocentrism, were rediscovered in the humanistic period (we have already noted their presence in Theodore Gaza) and finally found a thorough exposition and housing in Michel de Montaigne (1533–1592), who can be considered the main representative of "theriophily" in the Renaissance.

The key text is the *Apology for Raimond Sebond*,[43] where Montaigne appropriates the defense of animal rationality advocated by Plutarch, Sextus Empiricus, and Porphyry against the Stoics. It was customary for Montaigne to develop his own positions through an impressive display of quotations from ancient and contemporary authors. For instance, in the thirty pages devoted to animals in the *Apologie pour Raimond Sebond* one finds some 120 references to literature, and, especially, long passages entirely (and often tacitly) modeled on Sextus Empiricus, Cornelius Agrippa, and Plutarch.[44] Although on a first reading the sequence of arguments gives the impression of a disorganized stream of consciousness, upon closer consideration the text reveals a solid structure.[45]

In order to support the theory of rationality in animals, Montaigne displays all the examples of animal intelligence and morality one finds in ancient authors, particularly in Plutarch and Pliny. He ranges from the government of the bees, to the architectural ability of the swallow, to the chastity of different animals. By resorting to Plutarch's *On the Cleverness of the Beasts* (*De sollertia animalium*, in *Moralia* XII), he argues that animal strategies reveal a tacit syllogistic reasoning; for instance, it is reported that in Thrace, when the foxes come to a frozen river, they put their ears close to the ice to evaluate its thickness. If they hear the water running beneath, they conclude that the ice is too thin to support their weight.[46] In the moral field, too, animals prove to be better than men, in the first place because they do not make war against others of their kind. And Montaigne goes on with traditional examples of animal piety, fidelity, gratitude, and magnanimity. Furthermore, beasts have learning skills, even for things that are not necessary for mere survival (as dancing to music or guiding the blind). Finally, we have learned from them several techniques, such as weaving from the spider and building from the swallow.[47]

As in every previous instance of "theriophily," these illustrations of the various forms of cleverness in animals do not stem from a genuine interest in the animal world itself, but rather from the will to undermine anthropocentrism. Accordingly, in Montaigne's skeptical strategy, too, this eulogy of animal skills is meant as a dialectical weapon against all pretense of human superiority. The ideas of Montaigne on animals would be subsequently spread thanks to the exposition of Pierre Charron (1541–1603) in his *Treatise on Wisdom* (*Traité de la sagesse*, 1601).

CHAPTER SEVEN

Meticulous Depiction

Animals in Art, 1400–1600

VICTORIA DICKENSON

In the preface to Part Two of *Lives of the Artists,* Giorgio Vasari (1511–1574) wrote that artists of the Italian Quattrocento

> tried to reproduce neither more nor less than they saw in nature, and as a result their work began to show more careful observation and understanding. ... They endeavoured to compose their pictures with greater regard for real appearances, attempting to make their landscapes more realistic, along with the trees, the grass, the flowers, the air, the clouds, and the other phenomena of nature.[1]

The "regard for real appearances" in painting and sculpture that began in the late Middle Ages continues to inform our aesthetic canon. More than half a millennium later, we still marvel at the "careful observation" of the Quattrocento artists, and their ability to depict with seemingly photographic accuracy the objects of the natural world. We praise for their realism the "life-like" butterflies that hover above the pages of a *Book of Hours* by the Master of Mary of Burgundy, or the illusionistic dragonfly that has alighted on a page of the Grimani *Breviary.*[2] This ability to render exactly leads us to assume a congruence between the way in which people in the Renaissance, or at least artists and their viewers, saw the natural world and its inhabitants and the way in which we regard the phenomena of nature today. We assume that naturalistic representation of living things—animals, plants, shells, fossils—must reflect a view of life not dissimilar to our own. For us, the specific is defined through the visual. Our post-Linnaean vision assumes that naturalistic realism not only makes the subject immediately recognizable as a portrait of itself, but also as a representative of a species. We read the works of earlier artists with our own vocabulary of genus, species and habitat, and our internalized database of animal representation. We look for accurate depiction of form, color, pattern, and scale, and the notion of specificity informs our judgment not only on the quality of the representation but also on the motives of the artist in seeking after "real appearances." By examining closely the animals that artists drew and painted during the period we define as the Renaissance, we can begin to renew our own vision, to distance ourselves from the classificatory universe we cannot help but inhabit and to understand better the ways in which the artists of early modern Europe sought "to reproduce neither more nor less than they saw in nature."

SAINT JEROME IN HIS STUDY

Let us start with a single small painting (see Figure 7.1). Sometime around 1475, when he was about forty-five years old, Antonello da Messina (ca. 1430–1479) painted Saint Jerome reading in his study. Saint Jerome (341–420) was one of the four Fathers of the Latin Church, responsible for the translation of the Scriptures from Greek and Hebrew into Latin, the Vulgate Bible. Jerome became one of the most frequently represented figures in European art from the fourteenth through sixteenth centuries,[3] a scholar-saint, renowned as much for his learning as his compassion for brute creation. Jerome's kindness toward an injured lion was the subject of one of the most popular of the "Golden Legends," the late thirteenth-century compilation of the lives and lore of the saints. From that point on, he was often pictured with a lion as attribute, or with other wildlife. Painting Jerome permitted Antonello to exercise his considerable technical skill, combining the precise delineation of the northern artists with the command of perspective favored by painters in Italy. He executed the painting on a small limewood panel using the relatively new technique of working in oil. Vasari credits him with having learned this technique from Jan van Eyck (ca.1395–ca. 1441) in Bruges and using his "secret" to acquire a great name for himself in Italy. Whether or not he did in fact visit Flanders, he was a deft user of the new medium that permitted great depth and permanence of color, high-resolution detail, and surface luster, and his precise style echoes that of the Flemish masters. Antonello has depicted Jerome, perhaps in imitation of a "lost" van Eyck,[4] reading in a well-appointed studiolo, open on three sides and placed within the interior of a church, a setting that allows Antonello to play not only with perspective but also with chiaroscuro.[5] The viewer looks through a brightly lit stone archway into a darker interior, then along shadowed corridors to windows

FIGURE 7.1: Antonello da Messina (ca. 1430–1479) *Saint Jerome in His Studio,* London: National Gallery (NG1418).

that frame blue sky and a sunlit landscape. The light falls through the archway on to Saint Jerome, illuminating the book he reads. Despite the formality of the setting, Antonello has included details that add a subtle domesticity to the scene: Jerome's shoes rest at the bottom of the steps leading up to his desk; on the floor of the studiolo, two plants, one perhaps a pink, are potted in majolica containers; a fringed linen towel hangs from the wall; and a small grey tabby cat dozes in the shade. Barely seen in the shadowy corridor, Jerome's spindly legged lion approaches the viewer, perhaps on his way to recline by his master, as he is so often shown in other paintings of Jerome at work. High above the saint's head, starlings sit on the ledges of the arched openings or take to the air. On the step of the framing archway are a partridge, perhaps a chukar (*Alectoris chukar*),[6] a peacock (*Pavo cristatus*), and a shiny brass bowl. Starlings and a cat are not unexpected in such a setting, and the lion, though not often found in churches, is found in the majority of paintings of Jerome. But a partridge and a peacock on the steps of a church? Are they pets? Does the brass bowl imply that Jerome is feeding them? Were these birds common inhabitants of cathedrals or cloisters? Why did Antonello, so precise and so seemingly dedicated to realistic depiction, choose to place these two birds in the foreground of his composition, almost in the same plane as the viewer? Understanding why Antonello chose to depict these two distinctive birds so prominently in his work reveals something of the way in which animals entered into the imagination of both artists and viewers in the Renaissance.

OF PEACOCKS AND PARTRIDGES

We have always lived closely with animals. At the end of the Middle Ages, after the devastation in the human population brought about by the Black Death, animals were in some areas more numerous than people. The depredations of plague at Florence between 1348 and 1427, which reduced the urban population by two-thirds, may also have opened up new spaces for birds and mammals close to the urban center.[7] Among these would have been the peacock and the partridge, hunted or raised as food since Roman times.[8] Roast peacock, brought to the table in its feathered glory, became an important dish not only at Roman tables, but also at lordly feasts throughout the Renaissance. Partridge too was a popular Renaissance dish, well-spiced and seasoned with grains of paradise, sugar, ginger, cinnamon, and cloves.[9] Antonello, then, would undoubtedly have been familiar with these birds, might even have eaten them, and would certainly have been able to obtain individuals as "sitters," enabling him to depict them with a fidelity to nature that permits us to identify them to the level of species. But why did Antonello include them in his painting, where they appear at best anomalous, and certainly out of place?

Antonello was not the only painter of his period to include an anomalous peacock in a scene. One of the most magnificent of these painted peacocks appears in a contemporaneous work by Sandro Botticelli. Here the bird perches on the ruins of a Roman building, watching over the Holy Family (see Figure 7.2). Peacocks would seem to be common inhabitants of stables along with ox and ass, at least in depictions of the Nativity or Adoration. A peacock perches above the Holy Family in Fra Angelico's *tondo* of the visit of the Magi from about 1445, and another is pictured in Domenico Ghirlandaio's fresco of the Adoration, painted between 1486 and 1490 in the chapel of Santa Maria Novella in Florence. Almost a century later, Tintoretto included the peacock in the stable along with a cock, in his large canvas of the *Adoration of the Shepherds,* painted for the Sala Grande of the Scuola di San Rocco in Venice between 1579 and 1581. The peacock is particularly associated with images of the Virgin. Several surround the panel *Madonna in the Rosary* by Stefano da Zevio,

FIGURE 7.2: Sandro Botticelli (1445–1510) *Adoration of the Magi*, London: National Gallery (NG1033).

executed around 1410. Peacocks appear as well in the enclosed garden visible through the open archway behind Mary and her child in van Eyck's 1435 painting, *The Virgin of Chancellor Rolin*. A peacock sits on the balustrade to the left of the Virgin and Child in the Barbarigo Altarpiece, painted in 1488, and another perches on a ledge above the Virgin, next to a caged bird and a dove in Crivelli's *Annunciation with Saint Emidius* (1486). One might infer from their inclusion in so many paintings that peacocks were common in the houses and gardens of Renaissance Europe; they are found perched in a window overlooking the *Last Supper* (Ghirlandaio, 1486), on a castle wall in the portrait of a young knight (see Figure 7.3), strutting beside two Venetian ladies (both by Carpaccio, 1510), and peering down through the *trompe l'oeil* oculus painted in 1475 by Andrea Mantegna on the ceiling of the Ducal palace in Mantua (see Figure 7.4). Peacocks also appear equally frequently and perhaps more aptly in paintings of the Garden of Eden or the Creation.[10] Partridges, at least in paint,

FIGURE 7.3: Vittore Carpaccio (1455–1525) *Portrait of a Young Knight,* Madrid: Fundación Colección Thyssen-Bornemisza. Photo credit: Erich Lessing/Art Resource, New York.

FIGURE 7.4: Andrea Mantegna (1431–1506) Ceiling oculus, Mantua: Palazzo ducale, Camera degli Sposi. Photo credit: Scala/Art Resource, New York.

are a somewhat rarer bird. Lucas Cranach the Elder had an evident affection for them, since they stand together in his *Paradise* (1530), rest beside an indolent nymph (*Nymph at the Fountain,* 1534), and huddle in the grass among the naked frolickers of the *Golden Age.* Saint Jerome also attracts partridges, either singletons (Catena, *Saint Jerome in his Study,* ca. 1510; Mansueti, *Saint Jerome in Penitence,* ca 1520; Cima da Conegliano, *Madonna dell'Arancato,* ca 1495), pairs (Cranach, *Saint Jerome in His Study,* 1526), or even families.

While we might well accept the inclusion of peacocks and partridges in scenes of animal creation or in the Garden of Eden, or even in more secular gardens, what can we infer by their representation in less likely places, such as the portico of a cathedral, or the study of a saint? An animal could be seen, of course, not only as a living creature but also as a sign of something else. These birds trailed behind them a long train of associations going back to antiquity and first recorded by Aristotle in his *Historia animalium,* still considered by Renaissance scholars as an authoritative source for natural history. Aristotle recorded detailed accounts of animal physiology and behavior, based on direct observation. He also speculated on the resemblances between animals and human beings:

In the great majority of animals there are traces of psychical qualities or attitudes, which qualities are more markedly differentiated in the case of human beings. For just as we pointed out resemblances in the physical organs, so in a number of animals we observe gentleness or fierceness, mildness or cross temper, courage, or timidity, fear or confidence, high spirit or low cunning, and, with regard to intelligence, something equivalent to sagacity. Some of these qualities in man, as compared with the corresponding qualities in animals, differ only quantitatively.[11]

Aristotle attributed a number of specific virtues or vices to particular animals: crows were chaste, partridges salacious, hares timid, lions courageous. (We still associate particular qualities with certain animals, and continue to describe people in everyday conversation as "eager beavers," "busy as a bee," "proud as a peacock.") These attributions of "psychical qualities" to certain animals were repeated in the works of subsequent authors like Pliny the Elder and Bartolemaeus Anglicus, and also entered the popular imagination through their inclusion in the medieval bestiaries.[12] In the twelfth century Alain de Lille echoed Aristotle: "Every creature of the world / Is like a book and a picture / To us, and a mirror."[13] Animals and people were linked together in a world in which the beast or bird could be a reflection of the human, in which the creature entered as participant into the moral and spiritual world of humankind. Animal tales, extracted from the rich stew of classical and Biblical sources, were also widely used as exempla in the sermons of thirteenth- and fourteenth-century preachers. Significantly for our inquiry, these tales were often illustrated. Carved on churches, woven into tapestries, illuminated in bestiaries, they became visual lessons. The author of the *Aberdeen Bestiary* noted: "In painting this picture I intend to improve the minds of ordinary people, in such a way that their soul will at least perceive physically things which it has difficulty in grasping mentally; that what they have difficulty comprehending with their ears, they will perceive with their eyes."[14] The stylized animals of the bestiaries may seem very distant from Antonello's wonderfully naturalistic partridge and peacock, his sleeping tabby, wheeling starlings, and stalking lion, but one still needs to understand how animals informed his world. Antonello was aware of them not only as coinhabitants of the natural world, but also as denizens of a mythic world in which they themselves were the protagonists in their own stories. The painted animal trailed associations after it as colorful and evocative as a peacock's tail, and Antonello could assume, I think, that his viewers could "read" the animals in the painting, just as they could understand his use of the conventions of perspective. By including such animals, Antonello could charge the serene surface of his painting with another level of meaning and emotion that allowed the viewers not only to take pleasure in virtuoso depiction, but also to read below the painting surface into the book of nature. Exploring the natural and cultural history of Antonello's two birds may permit us to begin to understand how we too might "read" them.

RARE BIRDS

Peacocks were introduced into the Mediterranean region from Asia in pre-classic times. Their name *pavo* appears to be of Asian origin, though a twelfth-century *Bestiary* suggests that the bird derives its name from its cry.[15] Peacocks were obviously attractive for their resplendent iridescent plumage, and particularly their long tail feathers, making them suitably impressive for a monarch's garden, and an object of commerce. I *Kings* 10:22 records that King Solomon received every three years by sea a cargo of "gold, and silver, ivory, and apes, and peacocks." The Egyptian pharaohs kept peacocks, and Alexander the Great was said to have brought them to Greece. In Rome, the bird became associated with Juno, the wife of Jupiter, and drew her chariot. (The peacock is later associated with another Queen of Heaven, the Virgin Mary.) Aristotle was certainly familiar with the peacock, and noted that "the bird moults when the earliest trees are shedding their leaves, and recovers its plumage when the same trees are recovering their foliage."[16] The annual molt would be interpreted by later bestiary authors as a symbol of conversion: "To throw off the old plumage is to abandon a long-standing attachment to a deceitful way of life. To assume new plumage is to hold to a way of life that is gentle and simple. For the plumage of the old way of life weighs you down, while that of the new growth raises you up."[17] Besides their superficial beauty, peacocks had another less obvious virtue, observed by Saint Augustine, who appreciated the peacock at table. In the *City of God* he testified to the incorruptibility of the bird's flesh:

For who but God the Creator of all things has given to the flesh of the peacock its antiseptic property? This property, when I first heard of it, seemed to me incredible; but it happened at Carthage that a bird of this kind was cooked and served up to me, and, taking a suitable slice of flesh from its breast, I ordered it to be kept, and when it had been kept as many days as make any other flesh stinking, it was produced and set before me, and emitted no offensive smell. And after it had been laid by for thirty days and more, it was still in the same state; and a year after, the same still, except that it was a little more shrivelled, and drier.[18]

This combination of beauty and incorruptibility, and the regrowth of its feathers each spring, made the peacock a potent symbol of immortality and resurrection, particularly associated with saintly or holy beings. In Konrad von Megenberg's *Book of Nature* (compiled in the mid-fourteenth century), the peacock represents a bishop and is linked as well with Saint Peter and Christ.[19] The peacock's iridescent feathers, particularly the magnificent tail feathers of the male with their eyespots, also made suitable plumage for

FIGURE 7.5: Benozzo Gozzoli (1420–1497) *Voyage of the Magi* (detail), Florence: Palazzo Medici-Riccardi. Photo credit: Scala/Art Resource, New York.

angels (as did that of pheasants). Chaucer described the "pecock, with his aungels fethres bryghte" in his poem *The Parlement of Foules*,[20] and Benozzo Gozzoli adorned the choir of angels with multicolored and eyespotted wings in his bird-filled fresco (see Figure 7.5) in the Medici-Riccardi palace in Florence, painted around 1460.[21] The author of the *Aberdeen Bestiary* also noted that the "diversity of the peacock's colouring ... signifies the diversity of the virtues."[22] But the peacock could also symbolize vices as well as virtues. Aristotle called the peacock "jealous and conceited" and in Cesare Ripa's late sixteenth-century *Iconologia*, it featured in the emblem for "Arrogance."[23] The male's strutting display with tail outspread was likened in the *Aberdeen Bestiary* (echoing Pliny) to unseemly pride, especially in a preacher:

> Note also that the peacock, when it is praised, raises its tail, in the same way that any churchman gets ideas above his station out of vainglory at the praise of flatterers. ... The peacock, therefore, should keep its tail down, just as what a teacher does, he should do with humility.[24]

Thus, the peacock, in the way of many animal exemplars during the Middle Ages and the Renaissance, could symbolize two things, both godliness and wickedness. The incorruptibility of its flesh and its beauty gave the peacock its place in numerous depictions of the Nativity, the Virgin, and the Last Supper. His ostentatious display and complaining call, however, made him a symbol for the sin of pride.

The partridge was a much more garden-variety type of bird than the resplendent peacock. There are several types of partridge in Italy, the Grey (*Perdix perdix,* often called the Hungarian in North America), native to western Eurasia; the Chukar (*Alectoris chukar*); and the Rock partridge (*Alectoris graeca*), the latter two practically indistinguishable. Certainly, as noted previously, partridge was very much on the menu in Renaissance homes. The partridge too was seen from two aspects, though more often in a negative light. Aristotle had called the partridge "salacious,"[25] and Pliny had little good to say of its habits:[26]

> Indeed, in no other animal is there any such susceptibility in the sexual feelings; if the female only stands opposite to the male, while the wind is blowing from that direction, she will become impregnated; and during this time she is in a state of the ... greatest excitement, the beak being wide open and the tongue thrust out. The female will conceive also from the action of the air, as the male flies above her, and very often from only hearing his voice.

Not only was the female given to unrestrained sexual ardor, but the male had homosexual tendencies: "The males, thus deprived of the females, fall to fighting among themselves; and it is said that the one that is conquered, is treated as a female by the other." Surely this was not a bird to be associated with a saintly scholar like Jerome! The partridge did, however, have its virtues. Aristotle noted that the female will draw the hunter away from its nest "until every one of her brood has had time to escape."[27] In the *Aberdeen Bestiary,* however, the mother partridge is "so deceitful that one will steal another's eggs. But the trick does not work. For when the young hear the cry of their real mother, their natural instinct is to leave the bird that is brooding them and return to the mother who produced them."[28] This latter habit inspired Leonardo da Vinci to make the partridge a sign of the "eventual triumph of truth" in his personal bestiary, since the young always return to their true mother.[29] The *Aberdeen Bestiary* has a similar gloss, associating the return of the stolen chicks with the return of the lost to Christ (conversion). The partridge, however, still retains its evil ways, cosseting men "with seductive pleasures of the flesh. But when they have heard the voice of Christ, growing spiritual wings, they wisely fly away and entrust themselves to Christ."[30]

What was Antonello presenting to his viewers when he placed the peacock and the partridge so prominently in his depiction of Saint Jerome? While both birds feature in works of other painters (Cranach, Cima, Bellini), they are uncommon; the lion is Jerome's attribute. Though Michael Baxandall reminds us of the "the eventual impalpability of the Quattrocento cognitive style,"[31] he does point out the importance attributed to sight as the most powerful and the most precise of the senses. The role of the picture (as also noted by the author of the *Aberdeen Bestiary*) was to tell the story in the most clear and memorable manner, using image to impress it in memory. While we cannot say exactly what Antonello wished to impress on the minds of his viewers, or what they themselves took from the painting, we can assume, I think, that they did share an imaginative vision that was shaped both by their natural environment and also by the allegorical universe of beast tales, fables, and classical learning. So here is Saint Jerome, seated at his desk, engaged in reading, or perhaps verifying a translation, his quill in an inkpot, his books marked with slips of paper. His lion has been off on business of its own, but his cat has kept him company. Let us also assume that cat, lion, and starlings are part of the domestic environment of Saint Jerome's studiolo. The peacock and partridge are not; they stand back to back, outside the frame in full illumination, waiting to be read. Perhaps Renaissance viewers saw their oppositional position as a representation of the learned teacher who turns his back on the Devil and the temptations of the flesh. The *Bestiary* reminds us that the peacock represents the learned teacher:

> The peacock has a fearful voice, as does a preacher when he threatens sinners with the unquenchable fire of Gehenna. It walks in an unaffected way, in the sense that the preacher does not overstep the bounds of humility in his behaviour. It has a serpent's head, as the preacher's mind is held in check by wise circumspection. But the sapphire colour of its breast signifies that the preacher longs in his mind for heaven. The red colour in the peacock's feathers signifies his love of contemplation. The length of the tail indicates the length of the life to come. The fact the peacock

seems to have eyes in its tail, is a reference to every teacher's capacity to foresee the danger that threatens each of us at the end.[32]

But the partridge seems so unassuming beside the gorgeous peacock. Perhaps this neat little bird is not the Devil, but rather represents the Church, which saves souls through adoption or conversion.[33] The brass bowl beside the birds is sometimes identified as a barber's bowl, associated with bloodletting,[34] and thus with the blood of Christ. Brass bowls similar to this were produced in northern Europe in the fifteenth century, used as alms bowls, or as washbasins,[35] and perhaps that is all this brass bowl is, a bowl that the learned teacher might use to wash his hands (his towel hangs on the wall). But perhaps this bowl might also feature in a baptism, like that used in the fresco of *The Baptism of the Neophytes* by Masaccio (1426–1427) in Florence. Perhaps these three items reminded viewers of all these things, of the Devil and the preacher, of salaciousness and pride, of conversion and resurrection, of Jerome's sanctity and his struggles against sin. It is certain that these incongruous inhabitants of the church step did not simply stand for themselves.

BESTIAL STAFFAGE

Antonello's Saint Jerome confronts us with the fact that naturalistic representation is not in itself naturalism. Antonello was evidently a skilled painter of animals (and of people) but he has not depicted a moment in the natural world, as we would understand it. Looking through the windows of the church, we can in fact see a "slice of life," a view of a river with people fishing from a boat, and riding on horseback. The peacock and the partridge do not belong to that world. Their incongruity in the space depicted in the painting (reinforced by their centrality and their hyperrealistic depiction) charges them with meaning beyond that of the starlings or the dozing cat. Though peacocks and partridges were familiar parts of the natural world of the period, perhaps more familiar to city dwellers than they are today, they were also saturated with meaning, now so faded that we can only summon up "proud as a peacock" to describe them as anything other than birds. Not all depictions of animals, however, carry so much symbolic weight (even if a particular animal might), and animals appear in many paintings as part of a natural scene, a kind of bestial staffage, appearing where we would expect to see them. Antonello's starlings flutter at the church windows; flocks of minute birds wing through the skies of Dürer's woodcuts and engravings;[36] cranes soar in V-formation high above Cranach's *Saint Jerome in Penitence* (1525); crows wheel and caw in the sky in Geertgen tot Sint Jans's depiction of *Saint John in the Wilderness* (1490–1495). Birds were in the Renaissance as they are now very visible inhabitants of the natural world. If anything, it may have been easier to see more and various birds in Europe in the fifteenth and sixteenth centuries than today, when urban growth has reduced habitat and city dwellers are certainly less likely to see a variety of birds close at hand.[37] Birds also formed an important part of the Renaissance diet, and were hunted or raised for the table, often in town. Most of the birds pictured by the artists of the period were familiar birds of town and countryside—starlings, doves, swallows, sparrows and finches, crows, jays and magpies, cranes, storks, geese, ducks, snipe, swans, gulls and herons. Owls frequented churchyards, and birds of prey were omnipresent, both in the wild and as animals trained for the hunt. The image of the hawk and heron locked in battle is everywhere present in the painted skies, and while this is a familiar motif in emblem books,[38] it was probably also a familiar sight, and certainly one associated in the minds of many viewers with the aristocratic sport of falconry. Similarly, while cranes and storks bear symbolic meanings (ranging from watchfulness and mutual protection to filial piety, as noted in the bestiaries), they were also common dwellers of ponds and housetops, where they are frequently pictured (as in Carpaccio's *Knight*, 1510; see Figure 7.3).

Sheep were also very much part of any pastoral scene. About the time that Antonello painted his *Saint Jerome*, for example, it is estimated that there were more than 2.5 million migratory sheep in Spain, and half a million in Italy.[39] It is not surprising then to see the hills dotted with sheep, especially in depictions of the Nativity and the Adoration of the Shepherds, where they might serve to recall to viewers Christ's role as the Good Shepherd and the Lamb of God.

Rabbits and hares are also amazingly common in paintings of this period. Hares have long been widespread in Europe, and unlike their congeners, they are solitary animals, with great capacity for running and jumping. They were considered animals of the chase, particularly suitable for coursing with grey-hounds. Wild rabbits are native to Spain and were introduced into Italy, where they became a favorite food of the Romans by the middle of the third century. The Romans started the practice of raising rabbits in warrens, but it was French monks who began to breed domestic rabbits between 500 and 1000. By the thirteenth century, domesticated rabbits had escaped their warrens and become feral through much of Europe, though they were not recorded in Germany until 1423.[40] Throughout the Middle Ages there was demand for both rabbit meat and fur, and rabbits were often raised in towns as a ready fresh meat supply, and a warren was an accoutrement of every proper villa. (It would seem that rabbits are on the menu for the New Year feast in the depiction of January in the *Très Riches Heures* of the Duc de Berry [see Figure 7.6].) While not as common a pictorial element as sheep, wild rabbits are found in many paintings of the period, often eating placidly or frolicking in a meadow. Neither rabbit nor hare is mentioned in the bestiary literature, but they are very present in popular animal lore and fables, and became part of the emblematic corpus. They are associated with both timidity and humility (a Christian meekness), and with sensuality

FIGURE 7.6: Limbourg Brothers (15th century), "January: The Feast of the Duc de Berry" from *Les très riches heures de Jean Duc de Berry*, Chantilly: Musée Condé. Photo credit: Réunion des musées nationaux/Art Resource, New York.

FIGURE 7.7: Andrea Mantegna (1431–1506) *Agony in the Garden,* London: National Gallery.

and fertility. They are used evidently as symbols of fertility in connection with the Virgin or Saint Anne, but also as indicators of the wild, for they often appear with Saint Jerome as cohabitors of the wilderness.[41] Some artists, Andrea Mantegna and Vittore Carpaccio among them, seem to delight in depicting animals for themselves, and sprinkle them liberally in their paintings, wherever the sense permits (even if the sense is somewhat strained). In Mantegna's *Agony in the Garden* (1495; see Figure 7.7), it is difficult to know what to make of the charming brown rabbits sitting in the road or hopping about, as Christ prays in solitude and Judas approaches with the soldiers. It is easy to see the two rabbits in Carpaccio's *Birth of the Virgin* (1504; see Figure 7.8) as symbols of fertility, but they are so much at home, nibbling a lettuce leaf in the bed chamber, that they seem to be more house pets than emblematic additions. Carpaccio also includes rabbits in two other canvases in this same series, the *Visitation* and the *Baptism of the Virgin,* where they likely signify fecundity, but the appearance of a black-and-white domestic variety in the latter, rather than a symbolic generic rabbit, is almost as anomalous as the peacock on the church step. Not everyone, however, found this casual inclusion of animals in sacred scenes to be charming or necessary. Saint Antonino, the Archbishop of Florence, criticized painters when they "paint curiosities into the stories of Saints and into churches, things

FIGURE 7.8. Vittore Carpaccio (1455–1525) *Birth of the Virgin*, Bergamo: Accademia Carrara. Photo credit: Scala/Art Resource, New York.

that do not serve to arouse devotion but laughter and vain thoughts—monkeys, and dogs chasing hares and so on … this I think unnecessary and vain."[42]

There were, nevertheless, certain contexts where animals were not only acceptable, but expected. Renaissance artists almost invariably placed the ox and the ass in the stable with the Christ Child, illustrating the prophecy of Isaiah 1:3: "The ox knoweth his owner, and the ass his master's crib," implying that even lowly animals such as these would recognize the son of God.[43] The Adoration of the Magi gave many artists the chance not only to paint cavalcades of richly caparisoned horses, but also to include the traditional "exotics" of the Renaissance—camels, cheetahs or leopards, and occasionally elephants and giraffes. These, with the lion, hyena, tiger, ape, and ostrich, were bestiary animals, and familiar at least in name if not in flesh, and could be seen at different times among the menagerie collections of the aristocracy. Frederick II (author of the celebrated *De arte venandi cum avibus* on falconry) appeared in Ravenna in

1231 with an entourage that included elephants, dromedaries, camels, cheetahs, gerfalcons, and hooded owls.[44] The Medici were renowned for their lions and leopards, and in 1486 the Sultan of Egypt sent Lorenzo de' Medici a giraffe, of whom Luca Landucci noted that she was a "very tall, very beautiful and pleasing giraffe; one can see what she looked like in the many places in Florence where she was painted."[45] The Ferrantes also owned a giraffe and a zebra, gifts from the Caliph of Baghdad. Pope Leo X received his famous elephant Hanno from Manuel of Portugal in 1514, to add to his already substantial collection that included among other wonders a chameleon. Artists took the opportunity to sketch these captive animals from life and to populate their frescos and canvases with what must have appeared at the time outlandish creatures. Gentile da Fabriano included a dromedary and two monkeys in the cavalcade of the Magi in 1423. Almost two generations later in 1459, Gozzoli populated his *Adoration* with hunting cheetahs and leopards (courtesy of the Medici), camels and dromedaries, as well as various hawks and hounds and their prey. Thirty years after Gozzoli, Ghirlandaio painted Lorenzo de' Medici's giraffe into a fresco of the Holy Family (1486–1490).

The depiction of exotic species and their inclusion in a painting were as much for the pleasure and prestige of the artist's client or patron, as for the verisimilitude of the scene. In 1469, Lodovico Gonzaga, the Marquis of Mantua, instructed Andrea Mantegna, who was in his employ, to draw "two guinea-fowl from the life, one cock and one hen, and send them to me here, since I want to have them woven by my tapesters: you can have a look at the guinea-fowl in the garden at Mantua."[46] The inclusion of an exotic animal, however, might equally serve the painter as a marker for a foreign setting. Was Carpaccio instructed by one of the governors of the confraternity of the Scuola di S. Orsola to include the guinea fowl and costumed monkey in *The Ambassadors Return to the English Court*, a canvas in the Saint Ursula cycle (1495–1500; see Figure 7.9), or was this Carpaccio's own attempt to create a pagan "English" setting for the legend (no matter how strange that may seem to us)? Carpaccio's guinea-fowl appears again in the *Disputation of St. Stephen* painted some ten years later, and would thus seem to be one of the means (along with exotic architecture and costume) by which the artist signified the "foreign." The guinea fowl was not, however, the only unusual animal Carpaccio employed in his narrative cycles. In 1502 he began a series of three paintings on the *Life of Saint Jerome*. Here, not only did he include the traditional lion, but he added to the courtyard of the monastery a mixed menagerie of creatures, both common and exotic, including a peacock, the guinea fowl again, a parrot, an otter, a rabbit, a stag, a roebuck, and a possible gazelle.[47] Carpaccio also drew an ichneumon (a bestiary substitute for otter) into another painting in the same series (*The Funeral of Saint Jerome*), as well as a long-eared Syrian goat, another inhabitant of Italian menageries.[48]

FIGURE 7.9: Vittore Carpaccio (1455–1525) *The Ambassadors Return to the English Court* (detail) Venice: Accademia. Photo credit: Scala/Art Resource, New York.

BIRDS AND BEASTS OF EVERY KIND

It is evident that Carpaccio enjoyed filling his canvases, where it did not create too much incongruity, with animals. In one sense, he was following the dictum of the day. The critic Leon Battisti Alberti praised the quality of copiousness in painting:

> That which first gives pleasure in the *istoria* comes from copiousness and variety of things. ... I say that *istoria* is most copious in which in their places are mixed old, young, maidens, women, youths, young boys, fowls, small dogs, birds, horses, sheep, buildings, landscapes and all similar things. I will praise any copiousness which belongs in that *istoria*.[49]

Similarly, when Ghirlandaio contracted in 1486 to provide a fresco in Santa Maria Novella in Florence, the client demanded that he paint "figures, buildings, castles, cities, mountains, hills, plains, rocks, costumes, animals, birds, and beasts of every kind."[50] There were evidently certain subjects, like the Adoration of the Magi, that lent themselves naturally to "copiousness" and to the inclusion of the exotic and the rare. For artists who delighted in the portrayal of animals, the Garden of Eden or the Creation (particularly the Naming of the Animals) and Noah's Ark proved irresistible. The works of Hieronymus Bosch redefined copiousness of all kinds. His *Garden of Earthly Delights,* painted between 1498 and 1500, spills over with strange and wonderful birds, beasts, insects and fish, some derived from observation, others from the artist's incredibly fertile, and some might say fervid, imagination. While some of the creatures defy description, others are more conventionally exotic. A giraffe and elephant apparently copied from illustrations to Cyriac of Ancona's (1391–1452) travel letters are company for a bear, lion, rabbits, monkey, a crested porcupine, a unicorn, and countless strange birds and creatures.[51] Nevertheless it is clear that Bosch was not only a creator of monsters but also an acute observer of animal behavior, as is evidenced in his flight of swifts spiralling upward from their roost (see Figure 7.10). Between 1515 and 1518, Raphael and his studio would appear to have taken full advantage of the animal "sitters" in the papal collections to produce a fresco of the *Creation* in the Apostolic Palace in Rome (see Figure 7.11). Lions, an

FIGURE 7.10 Hieronymus Bosch (ca. 1450–1516) *Garden of Earthly Delights* (detail), Madrid: Museo del Prado. Photo credit: Scala/Art Resource, New York.

elephant, a giraffe, a rhinoceros (another intended gift from Manuel in 1515), a bear, a badger, a monkey, as well as peacocks, an ostrich (?), cranes, storks, herons, horses, and countless other creeping and flying things emerge from the primeval ooze at God's command. By 1613, Jan Brueghel the Elder could populate his *Ark of Noah* with a whole new world of animals and birds (see Figure 7.12). Brueghel was fortunate in having at his disposal the menagerie assembled by the Archduke Albert and the Infanta Isabella at Brussels.[52] In addition to the usual exotics, he was also able to include from the Old World crested porcupines and a Preuss's monkey (*Cercopithecus preussi*), and from the New World, North American turkeys and chipmunks, as well as South American guinea pigs, an Amazon parrot, and macaws, resplendent in red, blue, and gold.

These and other works track the expansion of Europe eastward and westward from the Mediterranean heartland. In 1383, when Master Bertram painted the *Creation of the Animals* (see Figure 7.13), we are still among the creatures of the bestiary: owl, bat, rabbit, fox, bear, peacock, goldfinch, stag, ox, donkey, wolf, and various fish. Two centuries later, and particularly after the Columbus voyages, Europeans were coming into contact with new exotics, which they absorbed into their symbolic universe. That there was a brisk trade in animal novelties in the fifteenth and sixteenth centuries is obvious from the well-stocked menageries of dukes and princes. What is less evident is the scope of this trade,

FIGURE 7.11: School of Raphael (1483–1520), *Creation of the Animals*, Vatican State: Vatican Palace, Logge. Photo credit: Scala/Art Resource, New York.

FIGURE 7.12: Jan Brueghel the Elder (1568–1625) *Ark of Noah* (copy by Jan Snellinck), Milan: Castello Sforzesco. Photo credit: Giraudon/Art Resource, New York.

and the rapidity with which the natural novelty became incorporated into the painter's repertoire. Parrots (the English "popinjay") had long featured in the European imagination. Up until the sixteenth century the parrot familiar to most Europeans was the rose-ringed parakeet, *Psittacula krameri,* native to India. The *Aberdeen Bestiary* notes that "India alone produces the bird called the parrot, green in colour, with a deep-red neck and a large tongue, broader than those of other birds, with which it utters distinct words; so that if you did not see it, you would think it was a man talking."[53] In the large *Madonna with Canon van der Paele* (1436), Jan van Eyck has painted this common parakeet clutched firmly in the Christ Child's hand. It is almost certainly this parrot that Albrecht Dürer sketched in 1502, and the same bird that appears in *Our Lady of the Animals* (1503; see Figure 7.14) and in his engraving of *Adam and Eve* (1504).[54] Europeans also knew the African grey parrot (*Psittacus erithacus*) with its bright red tail, pictured by Cranach in a painting of Saint Jerome (Innsbruck 1525), and imported from Portuguese colonies in Africa. Red parrots, however, were seemingly unknown, at least until the discovery of America. Friedmann thus suggests that the all-red parrot that featured prominently in several paintings by Carpaccio, including *Saint Jerome Leading the Lion,* the *Baptism of the Selenites* (see Figure 7.15), the *Visitation,* and the *Meditation on the Dead Christ* is "pure invention."[55] Carpaccio was, however, a man who loved to paint animals, and as we have noted, the rarer the better. His all-red parrot deserves closer consideration. Is it simply a decorative addition, or is it a realistic rendering of a very

FIGURE 7.13: Master Bertram (d. 1415) *Creation of the Animals* (panel from the Grabow Altarpiece), Hamburg: St. Petri Church. Photo credit: Bildarchiv Preussischer Kulturbesitz/Art Resource, New York.

FIGURE 7.14: Albrecht Dürer (1471–1528) *Our Lady of the Animals*, Vienna: Graphische Sammlung Albertina. Photo credit: Erich Lessing/Art Resource, New York.

rare bird? There are in nature very few species of all-red parrots, and the likeliest candidate for Carpaccio's sitter is a Cardinal Lory (*Chalcopsitta cardinalis*) from the Bismarck Archipelago and Solomon Islands.[56] The Lory's presence is no less surprising than that of the white cockatoo (*Cacatua sulphurea*) in Mantegna's 1495 *Madonna of the Victory* (see Figure 7.16). Significantly, Friedmann also dismisses the cockatoo and the red parrot "with dusky wings" in the same painting as an example of artistic invention,[57] but the cockatoo is certainly an unlikely

FIGURE 7.15: Vittore Carpaccio (1455–1525) *Baptism of the Selenites*, Venice: Scuola di S. Giorgio degli Schiavoni. Photo credit: Scala/Art Resource, New York.

FIGURE 7.16: Andrea Mantegna (1431–1506) *Madonna della vittoria*, Paris: Louvre. Photo credit: Erich Lessing/Art Resource, New York.

invention, and Mantegna was an artist noted for his precise imitation of nature. A red parrot with darker wings may in fact be a Cardinal Lory, which is darker on the wings, or it might even be an Halmahera King Parrot (*Alisterus amboinensis hypophonius*). Strange and colorful birds were valued in the Renaissance and were relatively easily transported over long distances by sea or by land. Significantly, lories, cockatoos, and king parrots are the birds of the Spice Islands (Halmahera is the largest of the Moluccas). They could have been transhipped with cloves and rare Chinese porcelains via India through Malabar by the Italian merchants who ventured on the overland route from the Levant, decades before Vasco da Gama's 1498 expedition and the advent of the Portuguese spice trade.[58] Less problematic but still unusual is another rare red-and-blue bird that sits on a branch above Anna Cuspinian in Cranach's 1502 portrait. Again, Friedmann suggests it is a generalized "parrot," but it resembles more closely the scarlet macaw, which had appeared that same year on a map of South America commissioned from a Portuguese mapmaker by Alberto Cantino for Ercole d'Este. Like Carpaccio and Dürer, Cranach had an interest in odd animals, and perhaps the report of the large red-and-blue macaws found by Columbus was enough to encourage him to replace the by-then conventional green parrot with a New World exotic.

PETS AND EMBLEMS

It was not just rarities that gave pleasure and delight to artists and their patrons, or that featured in frescoes or portraits. With horses, dogs are probably the animal most often depicted in all paintings of the period. They are shown at the hunt, in city streets, on or under lordly tables, in palaces and farmhouses, in scholars' studies, in the stable at the Nativity, watching miracles, attending the crucifixion, and sitting with saints. The bestiaries distinguished many different breeds of dog,[59] from hunting to farm to herd to housedogs, almost all working dogs, and the fourteenth-century *Livre de chasse* of Gaston Phébus lovingly depicts dogs bred for different kinds of hunt (boar, bird, deer), as well as their care and feeding. Noble dogs, such as hounds (particularly greyhounds), setters and spaniels were welcomed into the house and are frequently pictured with their masters (Mantegna shows a devoted hound below the chair of Federigo of Mantua in a fresco painted for the ducal palace). But the dogs who most often appear, cradled in their owners' arms, or standing by their side, are the lapdogs. Dogs kept exclusively as pets were bred to be small, and were even carried about by both men and women as living heaters under a cloak. That they were indulged beyond the norm for their kind is evidenced by the appearance of two tiny dogs on the Duc de Berry's table in the miniature depicting the New Year feast (see Figure 7.6), and by the placement of a white griffin terrier in the foreground of van Eyck's Arnolfini wedding portrait

FIGURE 7.17: Vittore Carpaccio (1455–1525) *Saint Augustine's Vision,* Venice: Scuola di S. Giorgio degli Schiavoni. Photo credit: Erich Lessing/Art Resource, New York.

(1434). A small dog also appears in the foreground of Gozzoli's painting of Saint Augustine (1463–1467), and one very similar to the Arnolfini terrier gazes up at the saint in Carpaccio's *Saint Augustine's Vision* (ca. 1506, though in the original sketch, Carpaccio had drawn in a polecat, commonly used as a mouser; see Figure 7.17). Lorenzo Lotto places a tiny dog on a cushion in his drawing of a fashionable young prelate in his study, and Dürer famously engraves a sleeping dog next to the lion in Saint Jerome's study (1514). Dogs, large or small, are not, however, just household pets or cherished companions. The dog bears much symbolic weight, and has long been interpreted as a symbol of loyalty and fidelity, as the common canine name *Fido* suggests. As such the white terrier may symbolize the expectations of the Arnolfini marriage or the quality most cherished in a bride. The dog also symbolizes reasoning and wit, and the hound of Theory pursuing the hare of Practice (or the hound of Truth on the trail of the hare Problem) was a familiar allegory, and most suitable as inhabitant of the scholar's study.[60] But as with many animals in this period, the dog could embody vice as well as virtue. A sixteenth-century English writer complained of lapdogs that "The smaller they be, the more pleasure they provoke, as more meet fellows for mincing mistresses to bear in their bosoms, to keep company withal in their chambers, to succour with sleep in bed, and nourish with meat at board, to lay in their laps and lick their lips as they ride in wagons."[61] There is something rather unsavory in this description, and lapdogs bear an additional message beyond fidelity or reason; like the partridge, they

FIGURE 7.18: Titian (ca. 1488–1576) *Venus of Urbino,* Florence: Uffizzi. Photo credit: Erich Lessing/Art Resource, New York.

can indicate a seductive nature. Certainly the toy spaniel curled up on the bed of Titian's portrait of the naked and enticing Venus would seem to imply that at the very least, reason is asleep (1538; see Figure 7.18).

While the dog is the most common of the companion animals,[62] less common animals also appear in portraits. These may be pets, and certainly pet keeping by both men and women was not new. Salminbene degli Adami, a thirteenth-century chronicler, berated members of his own order, the Franciscans, for being overly devoted to animals, "which caused others to judge lightly of them. For they love to play with a cat or whelp or with some small fowl." Nuns as well were chastised for keeping "dogs, squirrels, and birds."[63] Franco Sacchetti, a fourteenth-century poet, complained of the extravagance of women, who "wear around their necks a little collar, to which are attached all sorts of little beasts that hang down onto their breasts."[64] Leonardo da Vinci painted Cecilia Gallerani with an ermine in her arms (1483–1490; see Figure 7.19), and Hans Holbein depicted a young woman gently holding a chained squirrel, with a starling perched by her shoulder (1527–1528). Holbein's delicate watercolor of the young Prince of Wales shows Edward holding a small monkey wearing a harness (1541–1542), and a contemporaneous portrait of a Medici child by Bronzino (ca. 1549) depicts a young boy holding a goldfinch. (Small birds were often given to children, and Dürer's 1515 drawing of Madonna and Child shows the infant Jesus holding a flying bird on a long

FIGURE 7.19: Leonardo da Vinci (1452–1519) *Lady with an Ermine*, Cracow: Czartorysky Museum. Photo credit: Erich Lessing/Art Resource, New York.

string.) Not every portrait in this period shows a sitter with an animal, and given the symbolic significance attached to specific creatures, it is evident that the inclusion of a beloved pet or other animal was a deliberate gesture on the part of both sitter and artist, a secular adaptation of the animal attribute more usually associated with a saint or holy figure.

The inclusion then of a specific animal ties the sitter to the train of meanings such creatures embody. Just as viewers could read Antonello's peacock and partridge, they could appreciate the rebus of the ermine in Leonardo's portrait of Cecilia Gallerani. The ermine was traditionally a symbol of chastity

FIGURE 7.20: Antonio Pisanello (ca. 1394–1455) *Princess of the House of Este*, Paris: Louvre. Photo credit: Erich Lessing/Art Resource, New York.

or purity, and as such was appropriate for Cecilia as a young maid. (A portrait in Hatfield House shows Queen Elizabeth I with an ermine running up her skirt, a reference to her virginity.) But in Leonardo's clever portrait, the ermine becomes almost a heraldic device, alluding both to the sitter— its name in Greek resembling the surname Gallerani—as well as to Cecilia's lover, Lodovico Sforza, whose emblem was L'Ermellino. In some portraits, the animals cannot be mistaken for pets, their inclusion being almost entirely symbolic. Pisanello depicted a princess of the House of Este in 1436, surrounding her with flowers and butterflies (*Vanessa atalanta*, the Red Admiral; *Iphiclides podalirius*, the Scarce Swallowtail; and probably *Colias croceus*, the Clouded Yellow).[65] Butterflies are symbols of both the evanescence of human life and the resurrection, and likely signify that this is a postmortem portrait (see Figure 7.20). Piero di Cosimo's portrait of Simonetta Vespucci (ca. 1480), the mistress of Giuliano de' Medici, shows the celebrated beauty with a snake encircling her neck, an allusion perhaps to the beautiful Cleopatra and her asp, and to the early death of Simonetta at the age of 23 in 1476. Finally, in the pair of portraits by Cranach of Dr. Johannes Cuspinian and his wife, the owl and the parrot (or macaw) are, according to Friedmann, emblematic of husband and wife, one representing the melancholic and one the sanguine temperament.[66]

A MULTITUDE OF ANIMALS

It is evident that when artists included animals in paintings, they were rarely an afterthought. Even when the animals filled a background or appeared as natural inhabitants of the scene, they bore a weight of meaning for the artist, patron, and viewer that is hard to imagine today. We look in paintings of the natural world for what seems appropriate, what is ecologically or situationally correct. An ox and an ass in the stable do not surprise us, but the peacock in the window or the macaw in the tree seems inappropriate or even out of place. What can we make then of these last three works: *The Vision of Saint Eustache*, painted by Pisanello around 1438–1443 (see Figure 7.21); *Our Lady of the Animals*, drawn in 1503–1504 by Albrecht Dürer (see Figure 7.14); and *Portrait of a Young Knight*, painted by Carpaccio in 1510 (see Figure 7.3)? Pisanello's *Saint Eustache* is a small panel painting of one the Golden Legends, in which the hunter becomes the hunted of Christ. It is populated by hounds and hares, stags and hinds, a bear, and birds of every description, including pelicans, hoopoes, swans, storks, and herons. This is not a landscape with animals, it is animals against a landscape, evocative of a tapestry where the animals are woven into a background, part of the picture but also part of the pattern. Vasari recorded that Pisanello "liked to depict animals,"[67] and he was much praised in his own lifetime for his ability to render deceptively

FIGURE 7.21: Antonio Pisanello (ca. 1394–1455) *Vision of Saint Eustache,* London: National Gallery (NG1436).

naturalistic images. Bartolome Facio, a contemporary, ascribes to Pisanello "almost a poet's talent for painting the forms of things and representing feelings. But in painting horses and other animals, he has, in the opinion of experts, surpassed all others." Facio notes particularly "a wilderness in which are many animals of different kinds that you would think alive,"[68] perhaps alluding to the Saint Eustache panel. Similarly, Albrecht Dürer's wonderful drawing of *Our Lady of the Animals* incorporates a wide variety of birds and beasts into the landscape surrounding the Virgin and Child. Mary sits outdoors, a dog at her feet, and a parrot perched companionably by her side, and around them peaceably arrayed are a tethered fox, two owls, a robin and swans, a woodpecker, a heron, a dragonfly, a snail, a stag beetle, and a crab! This is not a menagerie to be observed in nature, and as Eisler notes, Dürer was closer in this work to the "divine illogic of the Gothic than to the relentlessly rational perspective of the Renaissance."[69] Like Pisanello, Dürer has sought to fill his drawing with bestial copiousness, the expression of the bounty of the created earth. The subject of Carpaccio's panel painting recalls Pisanello's *Saint Eustache.* The chivalric young knight, painted in a Germanic style, stands before a castle with an entourage of animal figures that signify his virtues—an ermine for purity, a dog for loyalty, a peacock for beauty and immortality, a stork for filial devotion, a white rabbit for purity and Christian meekness, hawks for nobility, and a goose for watchfulness. Here the animals are emblematic, in the case of the ermine heraldic, appliquéd to the canvas in a quasi-naturalistic arrangement.

This combination of high realism and unnatural copiousness defines much of the work of this period. The animals in the paintings and drawings we have been examining are drawn and painted with the miniaturist's precision and attention to detail. This ability to render exactly, to fool the viewer, was highly prized in the Renaissance. Lynn White, Jr., traces the "passion for exact copying of nature" to Saint Thomas Aquinas's precept that "Art is imitation of nature. Works of art are successful to the extent that they achieve a likeness of nature."[70] Artists were routinely praised as "imitators of nature" and compared to Apelles, the classical Greek painter whose work fooled both man and beast. Beginning in the thirteenth century, they sketch animals "after life," as Villard de Honencourt famously noted about the rather stylized depiction of a lion in his sketchbook. Pisanello and Dürer left behind numerous drawings and watercolors that were prized and preserved by their contemporaries, and often copied or reused in other compositions. Dürer's *Hare* of 1502 is justly famous, as are Pisanello's studies of horses (ca. 1434–1438) and wild boar (ca. 1430–1435), and we have already noted Carpaccio's well-rendered guinea fowl and red parrot, which appear in a number of works. The fact that they and others used and reused their animal templates does not detract from the quality of the original realistic depiction, the "true-to-life" feeling these images evoke in the viewer. It is the tension, however, between the high realism of the individual object and the artificiality of the whole that disturbs modern sensibilities. We marvel at the skill with which Antonello painted his peacock, and then wonder what on earth it is doing on the church step.

It is in the disturbance, the moment of rupture, that we can begin to trace the outline of the "cognitive impalpability" of the Renaissance vision of the natural world. Eisler suggests that Dürer's *Our Lady of the Animals* is the "swan song" of the Gothic tradition.[71] Certainly by the middle of the sixteenth century the quality of brilliant depiction, what I have referred to as the hyperrealistic image appliquéd to the painting, is no longer so much in evidence. Animals are certainly still painted, and it can be argued that Jan Brueghel the Elder's visions of a prelapsarian world crowded with animals represent the pinnacle of animal portraiture in this period. And in the notion of portraiture lies the difference. For painters of the Quattrocento and the early fifteenth century, whether in Italy or the North, the animal represents more than just itself. Illustrations in medieval bestiaries were little more than caricatures, because the animal was little more than a symbol, a cryptogram to be solved to reveal divine purpose. The transformation of vision that occurred in the Renaissance demanded that animals, like people and buildings and draperies, be depicted with a fidelity to their appearance in the real world. Leonardo wrote that "painting ... compels the mind of the painter to transform itself into the mind of nature itself and to translate between nature and art."[72] Artists rejected the old workshop pattern book images, sketching a cat or a hare or a horse from every conceivable angle, but they could not as easily reject the old habits of thought. The "Gothic sensibility" that freighted the animal with such symbolic importance was used by the artists of this period to add another invisible level of meaning to their work. The animal could be read as animal, a cohabitor of home or stable or countryside, or it could be read as a charged image trailing multiple meanings for artist, patron, and viewer. Certainly animals continued to have significance beyond their physical presence, and the emblem books that had been first published in the fifteenth century became a popular form of dissemination of animal symbolism. Now, however, the animal symbolized a moral lesson or

FIGURE 7.22: Jacopo Ligozzi (ca. 1547–1632) *Macaw*, n. 1997, Florence: Uffizzi, Gabinetto dei Disegni e delle Stampe. Photo credit: Scala/Art Resource, New York.

alluded to a story more likely to be drawn from classical or contemporary literature than from the Bible or the beast fables. The animals of the emblem books were as caricatured as those in the bestiaries, but the animals in portraits and landscapes began to be depicted more naturally, and as Faber Kolb points out, more scientifically.[73] Jan Brueghel's paradise landscapes were a visual catalog of the natural world, and as the hyperrealistic charged animal image disappears from paintings, it reappears in the works of the great classifying artists of the end of the sixteenth century, like Georg (or Joris) Hoefnagel and Jacopo Ligozzi. In these extraordinarily virtuoso works, the interest is less in painting a recognizable animal in a naturalistic style than in painting a representative of a class. Hoefnagel appropriated Dürer's hare not to use as a symbol of fertility or wilderness, but to include in an assemblage of numbered specimens of "lepus" in his work *Animalia Quadrupedia et Reptilia* (ca.1575–1580). Jacopo Ligozzi, court painter to the Medici in the late sixteenth century, painted specimens for the celebrated Italian naturalist Ulisse Aldrovandi, who used Ligozzi's watercolors to prepare engraved illustrations for his encyclopaedic publications on the natural world. The Grand Duke of Tuscany commissioned and collected Ligozzi's watercolor illustrations of rare species as a documentary museum to accompany a collection of preserved specimens (see Figure 7.22). It is not that the skill of depicting animals has changed or improved during this period; it is that the motive for their depiction has shifted. In Brueghel's vision of *The Ark of Noah* (Figure 7.12), we can see that another way of imagining nature has begun to replace that of Antonello, a vision much closer to the classificatory universe that we inhabit today.[74]

NOTES

Introduction

1. See Dorothy Yamamoto, *The Boundaries of the Human in Medieval English Literature* (New York: Oxford University Press, 2000), especially pp. 12–33; Debra Hassig, *Medieval Bestiaries: Text, Image, Ideology* (Cambridge, UK: Cambridge University Press, 1995), passim; Willene B. Clark and Meradith T. McMunn, eds., *Beasts and Birds of the Middle Ages: The Bestiary and Its Legacy* (Philadelphia: University of Pennsylvania Press, 1989), pp. 2–7; Xenia Muratova, "Workshop Methods in English Late Twelfth-Century Illumination and the Production of Luxury Bestiaries," in Clark and McMunn, *Beasts and Birds*, pp. 53–68; Joan Bennett Lloyd, *African Animals in Renaissance Literature and Art* (Oxford, UK: Clarendon, 1971), pp. 1–18; Wilma George, *Animals and Maps* (Berkeley: University of California Press, 1969), pp. 26–56; Richard Barber, trans., *Bestiary, being an English Version of the Bodleian Library, Oxford M.S. Bodley 764* (Woodbridge, UK: Boydell, 1993), pp. 7–15; T. H. White, trans., *The Book of Beasts, being a Translation from a Latin Bestiary of the Twelfth Century* (1954; repr., New York: Dover, 1984), pp. 230–270; Bruce Boehrer, *Parrot Culture: Our 2500-Year-Long Fascination with the World's Most Talkative Bird* (Philadelphia: University of Pennsylvania Press, 2004), pp. 22–32.

2. See Jan M. Ziolkowski, *Talking Animals: Medieval Latin Beast Poetry, 750–1150* (Philadelphia: University of Pennsylvania Press, 1993), passim; A. Lytton Sells, *Animal Poetry in French and English Literature and the Greek Tradition* (Bloomington: Indiana University Press, 1955), pp. 37–55; Carmen Brown, "Bestiary Lessons on Pride and Lust," in Debra Hassig, ed., *The Mark of the Beast: The Medieval Bestiary in Art, Life, and Literature* (New York: Garland, 1999), pp. 53–70; Valerie Jones, "The Phoenix and the Resurrection," in Hassig, *Mark of the Beast*, pp. 99–115; Jeanette Beer, "Duel of Bestiaries," in Clark and McMunn, *Beasts and Birds*, pp. 96–105; Meradith T. McMunn, "Bestiary Influences in Two Thirteenth-Century Romances," in Clark and McMunn, *Beasts and Birds*, pp. 134–150.

3. See Gustave Loisel, *Histoire des ménageries de l'antiquité à nos jours*, 3 vols. (Paris: Henri Laurens, 1912), vol. 1, pp. 140–182.

4. For horse breeding in the Middle Ages, see R. H. C. Davis, "The Medieval War-horse," in F. M. L. Thompson, *Horses in European Economic History: A Preliminary Canter* (Reading, UK: The British Agricultural Society, 1983), pp. 5–7; R. H. C. Davis, *The Medieval Warhorse* (London: Thames and Hudson, 1989), pp. 31–48; Peter Edwards, *The Horse Trade of Tudor and Stuart England* (Cambridge, UK: Cambridge University Press, 1988), p. 22. For livestock in medieval England, see H. P. R. Finberg, gen. ed., *The Agrarian History of England and Wales*, 8 vols. (Cambridge, UK: Cambridge University Press, 1967–91), vol. 3, pp. 377–394; for the early modern period, see Joan Thirsk, *Economic Policy and Projects: The Development of a Consumer Society in Early Modern England* (Oxford, UK: Clarendon, 1978), pp. 164–166.

5. For medieval hunting, see Anne Rooney, *Hunting in Middle English Literature* (Cambridge, UK: Boydell, 1993), pp. 7–55; Gabriel Bise, *Medieval Hunting Scenes* (Fribourg, Switzerland: Editions Minerva, 1978), passim. For the culture of the warhorse, see Davis, "The Medieval Warhorse" and *The Medieval Warhorse*, passim; also Ann Hyland, *The Medieval Warhorse from Byzantium to the Crusades* (Conshohocken, PA: Combined Books, 1994), passim. For the horse in literature, see Begona Aguiriano, "Le cheval et le depart en aventure dans les romans de Chretien de Troyes," in *Le cheval dans le monde medieval* (Aix-en-Provence, France: Centre Universitaire d'Etudes at de Recherches Médiévales d'Aix, 1992), pp. 11–27 and "Gauvain, les femmes et le cheval," in *Le cheval dans le monde médiéval*, pp. 28–41; Regine Colliot, "Les chevaux symboliques d'*Amadas et Ydoine*," in *Le cheval dans le monde médiéval*, pp. 93–113.

6. References to cat torture are indebted to Teresa Grant's doctoral dissertation, "The Uses of Animals in Early Modern English Drama, 1558–1642."

7. Also see Juliana Schiesari, "'Bitches and Queens': Pets and Perversion at the Court of France's Henri III," in Erica Fudge, ed., *Renaissance Beasts: Of Animals, Humans, and Other Wonderful Creatures* (Champaign: University of Illinois Press, 2004), pp. 37–49.

8. Geoffrey Chaucer, *The Canterbury Tales*, General Prologue 146–149, in *The Riverside Chaucer*, gen. ed. Larry D. Benson (Boston: Houghton Mifflin, 1987).

9. Keith Thomas, *Man and the Natural World: Changing Attitudes in England 1500–1800* (London: Allen Lane, 1983), p. 95.

10. Peter Martyr, *De Orbe Novo: The Eight Decades of Peter Martyr D'Anghera*, trans. Francis Augustus MacNutt, 2 vols. (1912; repr., New York: Burt Franklin, 1970), vol. 1, pp. 65, 72.

11. Correspondence of Bartolomeo Marchioni, in Pedro Cabral, *The Voyage of Pedro Alvares Cabral to Brazil and India*, ed. and trans. William Brooks Greenlee (London: Hakluyt Society, 1938), p. 148.

12. Letter of Alberto Cantino to Hercules d'Este, Duke of Ferrara, in David B. Quinn, ed., *America from Concept to Discovery: Early Exploration of North America*, 6 vols. (New York: Arno P and Hector Bye Co., 1979), vol. 1, p. 149.

13. Household book of Henry VII, ibid., vol. 1, pp. 116, 119.

14. Cantino to Hercules d'Este, Duke of Ferrara, ibid., vol. 1, p. 149.

15. [Bartolome de las Casas,] *The Log of Christopher Columbus*, trans. Robert H. Fuson (Camden, ME: International Marine Publishing, 1992), p. 77.

16. Qtd. in Quinn, *America*, vol. 1, p. 157.

17. "Of Cannibals," in *The Complete Essays of Montaigne*, trans. Donald M. Frame (Stanford, CA: Stanford University Press, 1943), p. 158.

18. Stephen Greenblatt, *Marvelous Possessions: The Wonder of the New World* (Oxford, UK: Clarendon, 1991), p. 72.

19. Thomas, *Natural World,* p. 48.

20. For anthropocentrism and political hegemony, see Erica Fudge, *Perceiving Animals: Humans and Beasts in Early Modern English Culture* (New York: St. Martin's, 2000), especially pp. 20–24; Bruce Boehrer, *Shakespeare among the Animals: Nature and Society in the Drama of Early Modern England* (New York: Palgrave, 2002), especially pp. 17–27.

21. [Las Casas], *Log,* p. 84.

22. Amerigo Vespucci, *Letters from a New World: Amerigo Vespucci's Discovery of America,* trans. David Jacobson (New York: Marsilio, 1992), p. 31.

23. Antonio Pigafetta, "First Voyage around the World," in *Magellan's Voyage around the World: Three Contemporary Accounts,* ed. and trans. Charles E. Nowell (Evanston, IL: Northwestern University Press, 1962), p. 101.

24. Ibid., pp. 147, 156, 226.

25. Gomes Eannes de Azurara, *The Chronicle of the Discovery and Conquest of Guinea,* trans. Charles Raymond Beazley and Edgar Prestage (London: Hakluyt Society, 1896), p. 37.

26. Gonzalo Fernandez de Oviedo, *Natural History of the West Indies [Sumario],* trans. Sterling A. Stoudemire (Chapel Hill: University of North Carolina Press, 1959), pp. 45–46, 48–49, 53–54.

27. Antonello Gerbi, *Nature in the New World, from Christopher Columbus to Gonzalo Fernandez de Oviedo,* trans. Jeremy Moyle (Pittsburgh: University of Pittsburgh Press, 1985), p. 131.

28. Francisco Hernandez, *Rerum Medicarum Novae Hispaniae Thesaurus* (Rome, 1651), 9.13, 9.8; 323, 319. Translations by the author.

29. Victoria Dickenson, *Drawn from Life: Science and Art in the Portrayal of the New World* (Toronto: University of Toronto Press, 1998), p. 35.

30. Andrewe Thevet, *The Newe Found World or Antarctike [Les singularitez de la France Antarcticque]* (1568; facs., Amsterdam: Da Capo, 1971), pp. 21, 28.

31. Janet Whatley, "Introduction," in Jean de Léry, *History of a Voyage to the Land of Brazil,* trans. Janet Whatley (Berkeley: University of California Press, 1990), p. xxvi.

32. Thomas Harriot, *A Brief and True Report of the New Found Land of Virginia* (1588; facs., Ann Arbor: Edwards Brothers, 1931), sigs. D2r, D2v.

33. Qtd. in Michel Foucault, *The Order of Things* (New York: Vintage, 1973), p. xv.

34. Ibid., p. 39.

35. Whatley, "Introduction," p. xxii.

36. Michael Camille, "Bestiary or Biology? Aristotle's Animals in Oxford, Merton College, MS 271," in Carlos Steel, Guy Guldentops, and Pieter Beullens, eds., *Aristotle's Animals in the Middle Ages and Renaissance* (Leuven, Belgium: Leuven University Press, 1999), pp. 355–396, 356.

37. Stefano Perfetti, "Three Different Ways of Interpreting Aristotle's *De Partibus Animalium*: Pietro Pomponazzi, Niccolo Leonico Tomeo and Agostino Nifo," ibid., pp. 297–316, 309.

38. Ibid., p. 310. Translation by the author.

39. Lloyd, *African Animals,* pp. 81, 80.

40. Conrad Gesner in Edward Topsell, *The Historie of Foure-Footed Beastes* (London, 1607), n.p.

41. Aelian, *Ex Aeliani historia per P. Gyllium Latini facti … libri XVI. De vi & natura animalium* (Paris, 1533), p. 456; Ulysse Aldrovandi, *Ornithologiae hoc est, de avibus historiae*, Part II (XIII) (Bologna, 1599), p. 41.

42. Sir Francis Bacon, *The Proficience and Advancement of Learning*, in *Francis Bacon: A Selection of His Works*, ed. Sidney Warhaft (New York: Odyssey, 1965), p. 228.

43. Qtd. in Foucault, *Order*, p. 39.

44. Oviedo, *Natural History*, p. 60.

45. Qtd. in Silvio Bedini, *The Pope's Elephant* (Nashville: J. S. Sanders and Co., 1998), p. 161.

46. José de Acosta, *Natural and Moral History of the Indies*, trans. Frances M. Lopez-Morillas (Durham, NC: Duke University Press, 2002), p. 230.

47. Martyr, vol. 2, p. 305.

48. Bernal Díaz, *The Conquest of New Spain*, trans. J. M. Cohen (London: Penguin, 1963), p. 76.

49. Ibid., pp. 79–80.

50. Ibid., p. 79.

51. Martyr, vol. 2, pp. 60–61.

52. Alvise da Cadamosto, *The Voyages of Cadamosto and Other Documents on Western Africa in the Second Half of the Fifteenth Century*, trans. G. R. Crone (London: The Hakluyt Society, 1937), p. 17.

53. Lisa Jardine, *Worldly Goods: A New History of the Renaissance* (New York: W. W. Norton, 1996), pp. 74–75.

54. Ibid., p. 311.

55. Edwards, *Horse Trade*, p. 16.

56. Ibid., p. 41.

57. William Harrison, *The Description of England*, ed. George Edelin (Washington, DC, and New York: Folger Shakespeare Library and Dover Publications, 1994), p. 308.

58. For sheep in sixteenth-century England, see Finberg, *Agrarian History*, vol. 3, pp. 188–191.

59. Raphael Holinshed, *History of England* (London, 1587), under "1466"; qtd. in Harrison, *Description*, p. 309, n. 7.

60. Harrison, *Description*, p. 309.

61. Ibid.

62. Acosta, *History*, p. 230.

63. Ibid., p. 231.

64. See Cadamosto, *Voyages*, p. 69; João de Barros, *Asia*, ibid., p. 108.

65. Thévet, *Newe Found World*, p. 75; Hernán Cortés, *Fernando Cortés: His Five Letters of Relation to the Emperor Charles V*, trans. Francis Augustus MacNutt, 2 vols. (Cleveland: Arthur H. Clark Co., 1908), vol. 1, p. 254; "Jacques Cartier's First Account of the New Land, Called New France, Discovered in the Year 1534," in Quinn, *America*, vol. 1. pp. 321, 327.

66. See Léry, *History*, pp. 89, 210, 213; H. C. Heaton, ed., *The Discovery of the Amazon According to the Account of Friar Gaspar de Carvajal and Other Documents*, trans. Bertram Lee (New York: American Geographical Society, 1934), pp. 180, 210, 415; Richard Hakluyt, *The Principal Navigations, Voyages, Traffiques and Discoveries of the English Nation*, 12 vols. (New York: Macmillan, 1904), vol. 9,

p. 408. For parrot eating in the New World, see Bruce Boehrer, "The Parrot-Eaters: Psittacophagy in the Renaissance and Beyond," *Gastronomica* 4, no. 3 (Summer 2004): 46–59.

67. Cadamosto, *Voyages,* pp. 72, 17.

68. Ken Albala, *Eating Right in the Renaissance* (Berkeley: University of California Press, 2002), p. 233, n. 53.

69. Cadamosto, *Voyages,* p. 48; Albala, *Eating,* p. 233.

70. Martyr, *Decades,* vol. 1, p. 254; Oviedo, *History,* p. 63.

71. A. W. Schorger, *The Wild Turkey: Its History and Domestication* (Norman: University of Oklahoma Press, 1966), pp. 464–465, 471.

72. Charles Mosley, ed., *Burke's Peerage,* 2 vols. (Chicago: Fitzroy Dearborn, 1999), vol. 2, p. 2739.

73. Ibid.

74. John Leland, *Joannis Lelandi antiquarii. De rebus Britannicis collectanea,* 6 vols. (London, 1770), vol. 6, p. 38.

75. Antonio Zanon, *Dell' agricoltura, dell'arti, e del commercio … lettere* (Venice, 1763), vol. 3, pp. 32–33.

76. Pierre J. B. Le Grand d'Aussy, *Histoire de la vie prive des français* (Paris: SenS, 1999), p. 270.

77. Edwards, *Horse Trade,* pp. 40, 28, 39, 27.

78. Baldesar Castiglione, *The Book of the Courtier,* trans. George Bull (Harmondsworth, UK: Penguin, 1967), p. 62.

79. Ibid., p. 63.

80. John Astley, *The Art of Riding* (1584; facs., Amsterdam: Da Capo, 1968), p. 1.

81. Thomas Blundeville, *The Arte of Ryding and Breakinge Greate Horses* (1560; facs., Amsterdam: Da Capo, 1969), sigs. B2r-B4v.

82. Gervase Markham, *Country Contentments* (1615; facs., Amsterdam: Da Capo, 1973), p. 3.

83. Edwards, *Horse Trade,* p. 43.

84. [Dame Juliana Berners], *The Boke of Saint Albans* (1486; facs., Amsterdam: Da Capo, 1969), sigs. a2r, [2]a1r.

85. John Caius, *Of Englishe Dogges* [trans. Abraham Fleming] (1576; facs., Amsterdam: Da Capo, 1969), p. 2.

86. Ibid., pp. 23, 29, 35.

87. Ibid., p. 34.

88. Ibid., p. 20.

89. *The Two Gentlemen of Verona* 4.4.40, in Stephen Greenblatt et al., eds., *The Norton Shakespeare* (New York: W. W. Norton, 1997).

90. Ibid. 4.4.16–19.

91. *The Merchant of Venice* 1.3.114, in Greenblatt, *Norton Shakespeare.*

92. William Cavendish, *A New Method and Extraordinary Invention to Dress Horses* (London, 1667), p. 65.

93. Ralph Berry, *Shakespeare and the Awareness of the Audience* (London: Macmillan, 1985), p. 109.

94. *Henry V* 3.7.11–12, in Greenblatt, *Norton Shakespeare.*

95. *1 Henry IV* 2.5.92–93, in Greenblatt, *Norton Shakespeare.*

96. Stephen Greenblatt, *Will in the World: How Shakespeare Became Shakespeare* (New York: W. W. Norton, 2004), pp. 151–152. For broader discussion, see Edward

I. Berry, *Shakespeare and the Hunt: A Cultural and Social Study* (Cambridge, UK: Cambridge University Press, 2001), passim.

97. Roger B. Manning, *Hunters and Poachers: A Cultural and Social History of Unlawful Hunting in England, 1485–1640* (Oxford, UK: Clarendon, 1993), pp. 47, 209.

98. Pigafetta, "Voyage," p. 222.

99. See Boehrer, *Parrot Culture*, pp. 29–32.

100. Pierre Belon, *L'histoire de la nature des oyseaux* (Paris, 1555), p. 8.

101. Barbara Mearns and Richard Mearns, *The Bird Collectors* (San Diego: Academic Press, 1998), p. 43.

102. Patrick Mauries, *Cabinets of Curiosities* (London: Thames and Hudson, 2002), p. 25.

103. Lorraine Daston and Katharine Park, *Wonders and the Order of Nature, 1150–1750* (New York: Zone, 1998), p. 21.

104. Mauries, *Cabinets*, p. 35.

105. Jakob Burckhardt, *The Civilization of the Renaissance in Italy*, trans. S. G. C. Middlemore, 2 vols. (New York: Harper Brothers, 1958), vol. 2, p. 290.

106. Bedini, *Elephant*, p. 82.

107. Ibid., p. 83.

108. Burckhardt, *Renaissance*, vol. 2, p. 290; Bedini, *Elephant*, passim.

109. Bedini, *Elephant*, p. 84.

110. Burckhardt, *Renaissance*, vol. 2, p. 290, n. 1.

111. Paulus Jovius, *De Vita Leonis* (Florence, 1548), bk. 1, p. 17.

112. Giovanni Pontano, *De Magnificentia* 19, in *I trattati delle virtu sociali*, ed. Francesco Tatteo (Rome: Edizioni dell'Ateneo, 1965), p. 118.

113. Daniel Hahn, *The Tower Menagerie* (New York: Jeremy P. Tarcher/Penguin, 2003), p. 76.

114. A. E. Popham, "Elephantographia," *Life and Letters* 5, no. 27 (August 1930): 186–189; Loisel, *Histoire*, vol. 1, pp. 234–235.

115. Cortés, *Letters*, vol. 1, pp. 265–266.

116. Hahn, *Menagerie*, p. 75.

117. Nigel Rothfels, *Savages and Beasts: The Birth of the Modern Zoo* (Baltimore: Johns Hopkins University Press, 2002), p. 19.

118. Thomas, *Natural World*, p. 110.

119. See Marc Shell, "The Family Pet," *Representations* 15 (Summer, 1986), pp. 121–153; Thomas, *Natural World*, pp. 110–120.

120. For the parallel, see Yi-fu Tuan, *Dominance and Affection: The Making of Pets* (New Haven, CT: Yale University Press, 1984), pp. 69–161.

121. Chaucer, General Prologue ll. 146, 147, 148–149.

122. Agrippa d'Aubigné, *Histoire universelle*, ed. Le Baron Alphonse du Ruble (Paris: Remouard, 1893), vol. 7, p. 102.

123. See Alan Stewart, "Government by Beagle: The Impersonal Rule of James VI and I," in Fudge, *Renaissance Beasts*, pp. 101–115.

124. Ben Jonson, *Every Man Out of His Humour* 2.3.248, in *Ben Jonson*, ed. C. H. Herford, Percy Simpson, and Evelyn Simpson, 11 vols. (Oxford, UK: Clarendon, 1925–1952).

125. Ibid. 5.5.16–17.

126. Chaucer, General Prologue ll. 143–145.

127. Schiesari, "Bitches," p. 38.

128. See Stewart, "Beagle," p. 101.

129. Qtd. in Thomas, *Natural World,* p. 102.

130. E. P. Evans, *The Criminal Prosecution and Capital Punishment of Animals: The Lost History of Europe's Animal Trials* (1906; repr., London: Faber and Faber, 1987), p. 17, and passim.

131. Ibid., p. 162.

132. Ibid., p. 169.

133. *Two Gentlemen of Verona* 4.4.19.

134. Bedini, *Elephant,* pp. 51–52.

135. Ben Jonson, *Bartholomew Fair,* Induction.17–20, in Herford, Simpson, and Simpson, *Ben Jonson.*

136. See John Dando, *Maroccus Exstaticus, or Bankes Bay Horse in a Trance* (London, 1595), passim.

137. Caius, *Dogges,* p. 35.

138. *Much Ado about Nothing* 1.1.210–211.

139. Miguel de Cervantes, *Don Quixote,* trans. Peter Motteux (New York: Airmont, 1967), p. 639.

140. Qtd. in E. K. Chambers, *The Elizabethan Stage,* 4 vols. (Oxford, UK: Clarendon, 1923), vol. 2, p. 453.

141. Burckhardt, *Renaissance,* vol. 2, p. 288, n. 2.

142. Bedini, *Elephant,* pp. 117–119.

143. Hahn, *Menagerie,* pp. 92–93.

144. Robert Crowley, *One and Thyrtye Epigrams* (London, 1550), sig. I4r.

145. Thomas Beard, *The Theatre of Gods Iudgements* (London, 1597), p. 197.

146. Philip Stubbes, *The Anatomie of Abuses* (1583; facs., New York: Garland, 1973), sig. P2r.

Chapter 1

1. Geoffrey Whitney, *A Choice of Emblemes and Other Devises* (Leiden, 1586), sig. G2v.

2. This is seen most famously in Alfred Hitchcock's 1963 film version of the Daphne Du Maurier story, "The Birds." Also see Christine Robinson, "Seagulls Are Keeping Me a Prisoner," *Celebs on Sunday,* July 18, 2004, pp. 32–33.

3. Michel Desfayes, *A Thesaurus of Bird Names: Etymology of European Lexis through Paradigms,* 2 vols (Sion, UK: Museum of Natural History, 1998), vol. I, pp. 321–326, especially p. 321.

4. Whitney, *Emblemes,* sig. L4r.

5. See Michael Allaby, ed., *Oxford Dictionary of Natural History* (Oxford, UK: Oxford University Press, 1985), p. 466; Paul A. Johnsgard, *Cormorants, Darters, and Pelicans of the World* (Washington, DC: Smithsonian Institution Press, 1993), passim.

6. Whitney, *Emblemes,* sig. L4r.

7. See http://www.royalparks.gov.uk/parks/st_james_park/flora_fauna/pelicans.cfm.

8. See Susan Doran, ed., *Elizabeth: The Exhibition at the National Maritime Museum* (London: Chatto and Windus, 2003), pp. 191–193.

9. John Lyly, *Euphues and His England Containing His Voyage and His Aduentures* (London, 1580), sig. R1r.

10. George Wither, *Fidelia* (London, 1615), sig. D6r.

11. Thomas Paynell, *The Moste Excellent and Pleasaunt Booke, Entituled: The Treasurie of Amadis of Fraunce* (London, 1572), sigs. Ii2r–v.

12. Ibid., sig. Ii2v.

13. See Michael Ferber, *A Dictionary of Literary Symbols* (Cambridge, UK: Cambridge University Press, 1999), p. 152.

14. Hugh of Fouilloy, *The Medieval Book of Birds: Hugh of Fouilloy's Aviarum*, ed. and trans. Willene B. Clark (Binghamton, UK: Medieval and Renaissance Texts and Studies, 1992), p. 169.

15. Ibid., p. 171.

16. Ibid.

17. *The First Part of the Nature of a Woman Fitly Described in a Florentine Historie* (London, 1596), sig. B3v.

18. William Drummond, *Flowres of Sion* (London, 1623), sig. A4v.

19. Neither bird is mentioned in Shakespeare's non-Folio plays, but there is a mention of the Pelican legend at *Edward III* 3.4.122–6. See *King Edward III*, ed. Giorgio Melchiori (Cambridge, UK: Cambridge University Press, 1998), pp. 133–134.

20. *Richard II*, in *Mr William Shakespeares Comedies, Histories, & Tragedies* (London, 1623), sig. C3r. Unless stated otherwise, all Shakespeare references are to the Folio.

21. *Hamlet*, in *Comedies, Histories, & Tragedies*, sig. Pp3v.

22. William Shakespeare, *The Tragicall Historie of Hamlet, Prince of Denmarke* (London, 1604), sig. L1v.

23. *Hamlet*, in *Comedies, Histories, & Tragedies*, sig. Pp3v.

24. *King Lear*, in *Comedies, Histories, & Tragedies*, sig. Rr3r.

25. *The Holy Bible* ["Bishops'" version] (London, 1585), sigs. Kkk6v and Cccc6r; *The Bible in Englyshe* ["Great Bible" version] (Rouen, 1566), sigs. Hh5r and Ss8r; and *The Bible* ["Geneva" version] (London, 1616), sigs. Aaa2r and Ooo1v.

26. *The Holy Bible* ["Authorized" version] (London, 1611), sigs. Ii2v and Ss1r. The suppressed pelican is cited only in a marginal note.

27. *Love's Labour's Lost*, in *Comedies, Histories, & Tragedies*, sig. L1v.

28. *Richard II*, in *Comedies, Histories, & Tragedies*, sig. Cc2v.

29. *Troilus and Cressida*, in *Comedies, Histories, & Tragedies*, sig. Yy3r.

30. *Coriolanus*, in *Comedies, Histories, & Tragedies*, sig. Aa1v.

31. *Rede Me and Be Nott Wrothe for I Say No Thynge but Trothe* (Strasbourg, 1528), sig. G6r.

32. Pierre Boaistuau, *Certaine Secrete Wonders of Nature* (London, 1569), sig. U2v.

33. Thomas Churchyard, *Churchyards Challenge* (London, 1593), sig. Z3v.

34. Thomas Lupton, *A Moral and Pitiefvl Comedie, Intituled, All for Money* (London, 1578), sig. E2r.

35. Angell Day, *The English Secretorie* (London, 1586), sig. M2v.

36. Thomas Bell, *The Speculation of Vsurie* (London, 1596), sig. D3r.

37. Ibid.

38. Thomas Adams, *The Blacke Devil or the Apostate* (London, 1615), sig. D2v.

39. Ibid., sig. D3r.

40. Ibid.

41. Ibid.

42. Thomas Adams, *Five Sermons Preached Vpon Sundry Especiall Occasions* (London, 1626), sig. C3r.

43. John Taylor, *The Water-Cormorant His Complaint* (London, 1622), prefatory matter.

44. Taylor's self-conscious commercialism reappears in the last lines of the work (sig. F4r).

45. Taylor, *Water-Cormorant*, prefatory matter.

46. Ibid., sig. A3r.

47. Ibid.

48. Ibid., sig. A4v.

49. Ibid., sig. B1v.

50. Ibid., sig. B4r.

51. Ibid., sig. C1v.

52. Ibid., sig. F2r.

53. Richard Younge, *Philarguromastix, or The Arraignment of Covetousnesse, and Ambition, in Our Great and Greedy Cormorants* (London, 1653), sig. B2v.

54. Ibid., sig. A2r.

55. Ibid.

56. G[eorge]. F[idge], *The Great Eater of Grayes Inne, or The Life of Mr. Marriot the Cormorant* (London, 1652), sig. A3r.

57. Ibid., sig. E2r.

58. Ibid., sig. B4r-v.

59. Ibid., sig. A3r.

60. Ibid., sig. A3v.

61. *A Letter to Mr. Marriot from a Friend of His: Wherein His Name Is Redeemed* (London, 1652), prefatory material.

62. Ibid., sig. A3v.

63. R. W., *A Necessary Family-Book ... for Taking and Killing All Manner of Vermin* (London, 1688), sig. E6r.

64. Ibid., sig. E1r.

65. *The Wonder of All Nations!! Or the English Cormorants Anatomized* (Norwich, 1831), p. 21.

66. Ibid., p. 9.

67. Ibid.

68. Ibid., p. 3.

69. James Roberts, *The Cormorant of Threadneedle Street* (London, 1875), p. 35.

70. Ibid., p. 126.

71. Gage Earle Freeman and Francis Henry Salvin, *Falconry: Its Claims, History, and Practice* (London, 1859), p. 330.

72. See Oliver T. Coomes, "Cormorant Fishing in Southwestern China: A Traditional Fishery under Siege," *Geographical Review*, 92 (2002), pp. 597–603; Berthold Laufer, *The Domestication of the Cormorant in China and Japan* (Chicago: Field Museum of Natural History, 1931); Brian Patten, *The Sly Cormorant and the Fishes* (Harmondsworth, UK: Penguin, 1977).

73. James Edmund Harting, *The Ornithology of Shakespeare* (London, 1871), p. 260.

74. Freeman and Salvin, *Falconry*, pp. 330, 331, and 334.

75. Ibid., pp. 335, 337, and 341.

76. Ibid., prefatory material.

77. W. H. Hudson, *British Birds* (London: J. M. Dent, 1923), p. 303.

78. Liam O'Flaherty, *The Short Stories of Liam O'Flaherty* (London: Jonathan Cape, 1948), p. 226.

79. Stephen Gregory, *The Cormorant* (London: Heinemann, 1986), p. 11.

80. Ibid., p. 13.

81. Eílís Ní Dhuibne, *The Uncommon Cormorant* (Swords, Ireland: Poolbeg Press, 1990), p. 10.

82. See Paul Brown, "Cull 'Will Wipe Out Cormorants,'" *The Guardian,* September 17, 2004, http://www.guardian.co.uk/conservation/story/0,13369,1306774,00.html.

83. http://www.cormorantbusters.co.uk.

84. http://www.pisces.demon.co.uk/corm.html.

85. See http://www.socialistviewpoint.org/dec_02/dec_02_30.html; http://www.pwsrcac. org/about/history.html; and http://www.mcsuk.org/marineworld/species/seabirds.

86. See Jonathan Elphick, *Birds: The Art of Ornithology* (London: Scriptum Editions, 2004), p. 259.

87. Edward Topsell, *The Fowles of Heauen, or History of Birdes,* ed. Thomas P. Harrison and F. David Hoeniger (Austin: University of Texas Press, 1972), p. 158.

88. Ibid., p. 161.

89. I am grateful to Sarah Hatchuel and Lucy Munro for their help with this chapter.

Chapter 2

1. John Nichols, *The Progresses and Public Processions of Queen Elizabeth,* 3 vols. (London, 1832; repr., New York: Burt Franklin, n.d.), vol. 1, pp. 435–436.

2. Ibid., p. 438.

3. See D. H. Madden, *The Diary of Master William Silence: A Study of Shakespeare and Elizabethan Sport* (New York: Longmans, Green, 1903); D. H. Madden, *A Chapter of Medieval History: The Fathers of Field Sport and Horses* (Port Washington, NY: Kennikat Press, 1924); Marcia Vale, *The Gentleman's Recreations: Accomplishments and Pastimes of the English Gentleman 1580–1630* (Cambridge, UK: D. S. Brewer, 1977); John Cummins, *The Hound and the Hawk: The Art of Medieval Hunting* (New York: St. Martin's, 1988); and G. Kenneth Whitehead, *Hunting and Stalking Deer in Britain through the Ages* (London: B. T. Batsford, 1980). For specific hunting manuals, see Edward, Second Duke of York, *The Master of Game,* ed. William A. Baillie-Grohman and F. Baillie-Grohman (London: Chatto and Windus, 1909); Rachel Hands, *English Hawking and Hunting in "The Boke of St. Albans"* (Oxford, UK: Oxford University Press, 1975).

4. See Roger B. Manning, *Hunters and Poachers: A Cultural and Social History of Unlawful Hunting in England 1485–1640* (Oxford, UK: Clarendon, 1993); and Keith Thomas, *Man and the Natural World: A History of the Modern Sensibility* (New York: Pantheon, 1983).

5. See Ann Rooney, *Hunting in Middle English Literature* (Cambridge, UK: Boydell, 1993), p. 45 and elsewhere; Marcelle Thiébaux, *The Stage of Love: The Chase in Medieval Literature* (Ithaca, NY: Cornell University Press, 1974); Don Cameron Allen, *Image and Meaning: Metaphoric Traditions in Renaissance Poetry* (Baltimore: Johns Hopkins Press, 1968), pp. 42–57; Richard Marienstras, *New Perspectives on the Shakespearean World,* trans. Janet Lloyd (Cambridge, UK: Cambridge University Press, 1985), pp. 11–47; and Charles Bergman, *Orion's Legacy: A Cultural History of Man as Hunter* (New York: Dutton, 1996).

6. See Claus Uhlig, "The Sobbing Deer: *As You Like It,* II.i.21–66 and the Historical Context," *Renaissance Drama* 3 (1970), pp. 79–109; Matt Cartmill, *A View to a Death in the Morning: Hunting and Nature through History* (Cambridge, MA: Harvard University Press, 1993), pp. 76–91; Edward Berry, *Shakespeare and the Hunt: A Cultural and Social Study* (Cambridge, UK: Cambridge University Press, 2001).

7. Berry, *Shakespeare,* p. 37.

8. Manning, *Hunters and Poachers,* p. 33.

9. José Ortega y Gasset, *Meditations on Hunting,* trans. Howard B. Wescott (New York: Charles Scribner's Sons, 1985).

10. Thomas, *Natural World,* p. 21.

11. [George Gascoigne], *The Noble Arte [sic] of Venerie or Hunting* (1611; facs., Oxford, UK: Oxford University Press, 1908).

12. Ibid., n. p.

13. Thomas, *Natural World,* p. 145.

14. Manning, *Hunters and Poachers,* p. 35.

15. Berry, *Shakespeare,* p. 3.

16. Vale, *Recreations,* pp. 27–28.

17. Manning, *Hunters and Poachers,* pp. 198, 112.

18. Whitehead, *Hunting and Stalking,* p. 19.

19. Qtd. in J. William Hebel and Hoyt H. Hudson, *Poetry of the English Renaissance 1509–1660* (New York: Appelton-Century-Crofts, 1957), p. 8.

20. Nichols, *Progresses,* vol. 1, p. 17.

21. Ibid., vol. 3, p. 91.

22. John Manwood, *A Treatise of the Lawes of the Forest* (London, 1615; facs., Amsterdam: Theatrum Orbis Terrarum, 1976), pp. 8–9.

23. Derek Yalden, *The History of British Mammals* (London: Academic Press, 1999), pp. 152–153.

24. Ibid., pp. 158–159.

25. Manning, *Hunters and Poachers,* p. 58; Yalden, *British Mammals,* p. 53.

26. Manning, *Hunters and Poachers,* p. 57.

27. Manwood, *Lawes,* pp. 91–96.

28. Hands, *Hawking and Hunting,* p. 57.

29. James Edmund Harting, *British Animals Extinct within Historic Times* (Boston, 1880), p. 151.

30. Ibid., p. 100; Yalden, *British Mammals,* p. 157.

31. Marienstras, *New Perspectives,* p. 28.

32. Thomas, *Natural World,* p. 60.

33. James I, *Basilikon Doron,* ed. C. H. McIlwain, *The Political Works of James I* (Cambridge, MA: Harvard University Press, 1918), pp. 48–49.

34. William Harrison, *The Description of England,* ed. Georges Edelin (Ithaca, NY: Cornell University Press, 1968), p. 344.

35. Manning, *Hunters and Poachers,* pp. 54–55.

36. Thomas Elyot, *The Book Named The Governor,* ed. S. E. Lehmberg (New York: Dutton, 1970), p. 68.

37. Hebel and Hudson, *Poetry of the English Renaissance,* p. 11.

38. Berry, *Shakespeare,* p. 39.

39. Thomas, *Natural World,* p. 25.

40. Gervase Markham, *Countrey Contentments* (London, 1615; facs., Amsterdam: Theatrum Orbis Terrarum, 1973), p. 2.

41. Ortega y Gasset, *Meditations,* p. 49.

42. Ibid., p. 48.

43. Elyot, *Governor,* p. 65, p. 64.

44. Nichols, *Progresses,* vol. 3., p. 599n.

45. Berry, *Shakespeare,* p. 11.

46. [Gascoigne], *Noble Arte,* pp. 127–135.

47. Marienstras, *New Perspectives,* p. 34.

48. Berry, *Shakespeare,* p. 75.

49. Ortega y Gasset, *Meditations,* pp. 77–78.

50. Markham, *Countrey Contentments,* p. 9.

51. William Shakespeare, *A Midsummer Night's Dream* 4.1.114–18, in G. Blakemore Evans et al., eds., *The Riverside Shakespeare* (Boston: Houghton-Mifflin, 1997).

52. Thomas, *Natural World,* p. 29; Berry, *Shakespeare,* pp. 40–41.

53. Markham, *Countrey Contentments,* p. 3.

54. [Gascoigne], *Noble Arte,* p. 32.

55. Ibid., p. 35.

56. Madden, *Diary,* p. 76.

57. Shakespeare, *The Taming of the Shrew,* Induction 1.12–6.

58. Ortega y Gasset, *Meditations,* p. 82.

59. Ibid., p. 81.

60. Vicki Hearne, *Adam's Task: Calling Animals by Name* (New York: HarperCollins, 1994), p. 79.

61. Qtd. in Manning, *Hunters and Poachers,* p. 196.

62. Uhlig, "Sobbing Deer," p. 97.

63. Cartmill, *A View,* p. 76.

64. Berry, *Shakespeare,* pp. 24ff.

65. See Charles Prouty and Ruth Prouty, "George Gascoigne, *The Noble Arte of Venerie,* and Queen Elizabeth at Kenilworth," in James G. McManaway, Giles E. Dawson, and Edwin E. Willoughby, eds., *Joseph Quincy Adams Memorial Studies* (Washington, DC: Folger Shakespeare Library, 1948), p. 648.

66. [Gascoigne], *Noble Arte,* p. 125.

67. Ibid.

68. Ibid.

69. Ibid.

70. Ibid.

71. Prouty and Prouty, "George Gascoigne," p. 646.

72. Manning, *Hunters and Poachers,* p. 24.

73. Cartmill, *A View,* p. 66.

74. William A. Baillie-Grohman, *Sport in Art: An Iconography of Sport during Four Hundred Years from the Beginning of the Fifteenth to the End of the Eighteenth Centuries* (New York: Benjamin Blom, 1925), p. 98.

75. Ortega y Gasset, *Meditations,* p. 89.

76. Ibid., p. 88.

77. Ibid., p. 89.

78. [Gascoigne], *Noble Arte,* p. 137.

79. Ibid.

80. Ibid., p. 140.

81. Ibid., p. 177.

82. Ibid., p. 179.

83. Ibid., p. 199.

84. Ibid., p. 202.

85. Cartmill, *A View,* p. 83.

86. Prouty and Prouty, "George Gascoigne," p. 646.

87. Berry, *Shakespeare,* p. 11.

88. Michel de Montaigne, "Of Cruelty," *The Essayes of Montaigne,* trans. John Florio (New York: The Modern Library, n.d.), p. 382.

89. Ibid.

90. Ibid., p. 383.

91. Ibid., pp. 384–385.

92. Ibid., p. 385.

Chapter 3

1. R. Dubos, *Beast or Angel? Choices That Make Us Human* (New York: Charles Scribner's Sons, 1974), p. 25.

2. G. E. R. Lloyd, *Aristotle: The Growth and Structure of His Thought* (Cambridge, UK: Cambridge University Press, 1968), pp. 191–192, 239–240.

3. Keith Thomas, *Man and the Natural World: Changing Attitudes in England 1500–1800* (London: Allen Lane, 1983), pp. 17, 30; Genesis 9:2–3.

4. Thomas, *Natural World,* p. 41.

5. J. Cottingham, *Descartes* (Oxford, UK: Oxford University Press, 1998), pp. 225–233.

6. Thomas Blundeville, *The Fower Chiefyst Offices Belongyng to Horsemanshippe* (London, 1565), fol. 2r.

7. Thomas, *Natural World,* pp. 144, 145.

8. Peter Edwards, *Horse and Man in Early Modern England: A Special Relationship* (London: Hambledon, forthcoming); see Thomas Blundeville, *The Arte of Rydynge* (London, ca.1560), fols. 4v–7v.

9. Michel de Montaigne, *The Complete Essays of Montaigne,* trans. D. A. Frame (Stanford, CA: Stanford University Press, 1965), p. 331.

10. Thomas, *Natural World,* p. 154.

11. F. Braudel, *Civilization and Capitalism 15th.–18th. Century, I, The Structures of Everyday Life* (London: Collins, 1981), p. 33; C. M. Cipolla, *Before the Industrial Revolution: European Society and Economy, 1000–1700* (London: Methuen, 1976), p. 200.

12. W. Abel, *Agrarkrisen und Agrakunjunktur in Mitteleuropa vom 13. bis zum 19. Jahrhundert* (Berlin: Paul Pary, 1935), pp. 32–33; J. L. van Zanden, *The Rise and Decline of Holland's Economy: Merchant Capitalism and the Labour Market* (Manchester, UK: Manchester University Press, 1993), p. 30.

13. G. E. Fussell, *The Classical Tradition in West European Farming* (Newton Abbott, UK: David & Charles, 1972), pp. 88, 91; Abel, *Agrarkrisen,* p. 54; Braudel, *Civilization,* vol. 1, p. 195; C. Dyer, *Standards of Living in the Later Middle Ages: Social Change in England c. 1200–1520* (Cambridge, UK: Cambridge University Press, 1989), p. 159.

14. Hughes Neveux et al., *Histoire de la France rurale, II, l'age classique 1340–1789* (Paris: Seuil, 1975), pp. 89, 111, 115; A. De Maddalena, "Rural Europe 1500–1700," in C. Cipolla, *The Fontana Economic History of Europe, II, The Sixteenth and Seventeenth Centuries* (Hassocks, UK: Harvester, 1977), pp. 308–309, 322–322, 330; J. Thirsk, "The Farming Regions of England," in *The Agrarian History of England and Wales, IV 1500–1640,* ed. J. Thirsk (Cambridge, UK: Cambridge University Press, 1967), pp. 2–3, 44, 51–52, 53, 56–57, 66–67, 90–91; De Maddalena, "Rural Europe," p. 330.

15. De Maddalena, "Rural Europe," pp. 304, 329.

16. Conrad von Heresbach, *Foure Bookes of Husbandry*, trans. Barnaby Googe (London, 1577), fols. 111r–111v.

17. R. L. Hopcroft, *Regions, Institutions, and Agrarian Change in European History* (Ann Arbor: University of Michigan Press, 1999), p. 170.

18. J. A. Van Houtte, *An Economic History of the Low Countries 800–1800* (London: Weidenfeld and Nicolson, 1977), p. 170; De Maddalena, "Rural Europe," p. 324.

19. J. Jacquart, "French Agriculture in the Seventeenth Century," in *Essays in European Economic History 1500–1800*, ed. P. Earle (Oxford, UK: Oxford University Press, 1974), p. 173; Thirsk, "Farming Regions," *Agrarian History*, vol. 4, pp. 41, 56.

20. H. Kamen, *European Society 1500–1700* (London: Unwin Hyman, 1984), p. 149; Braudel, *Civilization*, vol. 1, p. 117.

21. Van Houtte, *Low Countries*, p. 69; Hopcroft, *Regions*, p. 98; Kamen, *European Socety*, p. 149.

22. Charles Estienne and Jean Liébault, *L'Agriculture et Maison Rustique* (Paris, 1598), fol. 53r.

23. Peter Edwards, *The Horse Trade of Tudor and Stuart England* (Cambridge, UK: Cambridge University Press, 1988), pp. 4–5; R. Meens, "Eating Animals in the Early Middle Ages: Classifying the Animal World and Building Group Identities," in *The Animal-Human Boundary*, ed. A. N. H. Creager and W. C. Jordan (Rochester, NY: University of Rochester Press, 2002), pp. 3–28.

24. John Fitzherbert, *Boke of Husbandrye* (London, 1523), fol. 4v; Estienne and Liébault, fols. 53v, 297r.

25. Edwards, *Horse Trade*, pp. 4–5.

26. J. Langdon, *Horses, Oxen and Technological Innovation: The Use of Draught Animals in English Farming from 1066–1500* (Cambridge, UK: Cambridge University Press, 1986), pp. 212–213, 252–253.

27. Van Houtte, *Low Countries*, p. 149; B. H. Slicher van Bath, *The Agrarian History of Western Europe A.D. 500–1850* (London: Edward Arnold, 1963), p. 292.

28. J.-R. Trochet, "Les véhicules de transport utilitaires dans la France rurale traditionnelle," in *Voitures, chevaux et attelages du XVIe au XIXe Siècle*, ed. D. Reytier (Paris: Association pour Académie d'Art Equestre de Versailles, 2000), p. 130; Braudel, *Civilization*, vol. 1, pp. 343–434; Slicher van Bath, *Agrarian History*, p. 289; P. Jones, "Medieval Agrarian Society in Its Prime," in *The Cambridge Economic History of Europe, I, The Agrarian Life of the Middle Ages*, ed. M. M. Postan (Cambridge, UK: Cambridge University Press, 1971 ed.), pp. 374, 379.

29. Hopcroft, *Regions*, p. 206.

30. Edwards, *Horse and Man*; G. Carbourdin, *Terre et Hommes en Lorraine [1550–1635]: Toulouse et Comté de Vaudément* (Nancy, France: University of Nancy Press, 1977), pp. 642–644.

31. Jacquart, "French Agriculture," p. 169.

32. Estienne and Liébault, *L'Agriculture*, fols. 83v–84r; Braudel, *Civilization*, vol. 1, p. 350.

33. Estienne and Liébault, *L'Agriculture*, fol. 53r; Jones, "Agrarian Society," p. 374; Jacquart, "French Agriculture," p. 169; Braudel, *Civilization*, vol. 1, p. 344.

34. Leonard Mascall, *The Second Booke, intreating the gouernment of Horses* (London, 1587), pp. 117–118.

35. Heresbach, *Foure Bookes*, fol. 114r.

36. Michael Baret, *An Hipponomie or the Vineyard of Horsemanship* (London, 1618), p. 6.

37. Ibid.
38. Blundeville, *Offices*, fol. 11r.
39. *Inventory of King Henry VIII*, 1547, Society of Antiquaries, MS 129, fols. 444r–448r.
40. Edwards, *Horse Trade*, pp. 24–31.
41. Braudel, *Civilization*, vol. 1, p. 345.
42. Estienne and Liébault, *L'Agriculture*, fols. 83v, 297r; Edward Topsell, *The Historie of Foure-Footed Beastes* (London, 1607), pp. 22–23.
43. J. Clutton-Brock, *A Natural History of Domesticated Animals* (Cambridge, UK: Cambridge University Press, 1999), p. 119.
44. Braudel, *Civilization*, vol. 1, p. 350.
45. *Letters & Papers of Henry VIII*, 17, 1542, p. 436.
46. D. Gerhold, "Packhorses and Wheeled Vehicles in England, 1550–1800," *Journal of Transport History*, 3rd ser., 14 (1993): 11–12; For Kendal ca.1692, Cumbria R. O. (Kendal), WQ/01 Order Book 1669–1696.
47. D. Gerhold, *Carriers and Coachmasters: Trade and Travel before the Turnpikes* (Chichester, UK: Phillimore, 2005), p. 4.
48. *L & P Henry VIII*, 3, ii, 1522–1523, pp. 935–936.
49. Mascall, *Horses*, pp. 117–118.
50. Peter Keen, *Description of England* (London, 1599), fol. 128.
51. John Cheny, *A Historical List of All Horse-Matches Run* (London, 1739), passim; D. Wilkinson, *Early Horse Racing in Yorkshire and the Origins of the Thoroughbred* (York, UK: Old Bald Peg Publications, 2003), pp. 6–7; J. P. Hore, *The History of Newmarket and the Annals of the Turf, III* (London, 1886), p. 248; Gervase Markham, *Cavelarice* (London, 1607), bk. 6, p. 2.
52. Blundeville, *Offices*, fols. 10v–11r.
53. Markham, *Cavelarice*, bk. 6, p. 2; K. Raber & T. Tucker, "Introduction," in *The Culture of the Horse: Status, Discipline and Identity in the Early Modern World*, ed. K. Raber and T. Tucker (Basingstoke, UK: Palgrave Macmillan, 2005), pp. 70–71.
54. *Cal. State Papers Venetian*, 3, 1520–1526, pp. 37–38, 67; *L & P Henry VIII*, 17, 1542, p. 437.
55. Society of Antiquaries, MS 129, fol. 444v.
56. Van Houtte, *Low Countries*, p. 69.
57. Blundeville, *Offices*, fols. 9r–10v.
58. Andrew Borde, *The First Boke of the Introduction of Knowledge* (London, 1542), 8th chapter, n. p.; Blundeville, *Offices*, fols. 9v–10r.
59. Braudel, *Civilization*, vol. 1, p. 349.
60. E. Coczian-Szentpeteri, "L'évolution du coche ou l'histoire d'une invention hongroise," in *Voitures, chevaux et attelages du XVIe au XIXe Siècle*, ed. D. Reytier (Paris: Association pour Académie d'Art Equestre de Versailles, 2000), pp. 85–87.
61. Edwards, *Horse and Man*.
62. Raber and Tucker, "Introduction," p. 29.
63. Edwards, *Horse Trade*, p. 40.
64. A Young, *Tudor and Jacobean Tournaments* (London: Sheridan House, 1986), p. 68; W. Jerdan, ed., *Rutland Papers* (London: Camden Society, 1842), p. 28.
65. A. Hyland, *The Medieval Warhorse* (Far Thrupp, Stroud, UK: Sutton, 1994), pp. 55–57; S. Loch, *The Royal Horse of Europe* (London: J. A. Allen, 1986),

p. 75; D. M. Goodall, *A History of Horse Breeding* (London: Robert Hale, 1977), pp. 157, 161, 163; *C.S.P.V.*, 2, 1509–1519, p. 198.

66. E. Tobey, "The Palio Horse in Renaissance and Early Modern Italy," in Raber and Tucker, pp. 71–75.

67. *C.S.P.V.*, 2, 1509–1519, pp. 174–175, 179, 183, 198, 379, 389; 3, 1520–1526, pp. 319, 321; *L & P Henry VIII*, 1, ii, 1513–1514, p. 1451.

68. Gervase Markham, *Cheape and Good Husbandry* (London, 1614), pp. 41, 43.

69. Leonard Mascall, *The First Booke of Cattell* (London, 1587), p. 49.

70. Topsell, *Beastes*, p. 62.

71. Markham, *Husbandry*, p. 43.

72. Ibid., pp. 44–45.

73. Mascall, *Cattell*, p. 4.

74. Topsell, *Beastes*, p. 66; Heresbach, *Foure Bookes*, fol. 128r.

75. Markham, *Husbandry*, pp. 41–42; W. Folkingham, *Feudigraphia* (London, 1610), p. 9; J. Thirsk, "Farming Techniques," in Thirsk, *Agrarian History*, vol. 4, pp. 186–187.

76. Van Houtte, *Low Countries*, pp. 69–70, 152.

77. Mascall, *Cattell*, p. 1; Topsell, *Beastes*, pp. 66–68.

78. A. F. Pollard and M. Blatcher, eds., "Henry Townshend's Journal," *Bulletin of the Institute of Historical Research* 12 (1934–1935): 16; Thirsk, "Farming Regions," *Agrarian History*, vol. 4, pp. 31–32, 47, 80, 83–84, 94.

79. Van Houtte, *Low Countries*, p. 152; De Maddalena, "Rural Europe," p. 315; Braudel, *Civilization*, vol. 1, p. 210.

80. Hopcroft, *Regions*, p. 175; Braudel, *Civilization*, vol. 1, p. 201.

81. Jones, "Agrarian Society," pp. 381–382; Braudel, *Civilization*, vol. 1, p. 210.

82. De Maddalena, "Rural Europe," p. 323.

83. Markham, *Husbandry*, p. 44.

84. Slicher van Bath, *Agrarian History*, pp. 285; P. Braunstein, "Resaux Familiaux, Resaux D'Affaires en Pays D'Empire: Les Facteurs de Societés," in *Le Négoce International XIIIe–XXe siècle*, ed. F. M. Crouzet (Paris: Economica, 1989), p. 31; A. M. Everitt, "The Marketing of Agricultural Produce," in Thirsk, *Agrarian History*, vol. 4, pp. 540–542; H. Wiese and J. Bölts, *Rinderhandel und Rinderhaltung in nordwest-europäischen Küstengebiet vom 15. bis zum 19. Jahrhundert* (Stuttgart, Germany: Gustav Fischer, 1966), pp. 5–9; B. H. Slicher van Bath, "Agriculture in the Vital Revolution," in *The Cambridge Economic History of Europe, V, The Economic Organization of Early Modern Europe*, ed. E. E. Rich and C. H. Wilson (Cambridge, UK: Cambridge University Press, 1977), p. 91.

85. P. J. Bowden, "Agricultural Prices, Farm Profits, and Rents," in Thirsk, *Agrarian History*, vol. 4, p. 643.

86. Slicher van Bath, *Agrarian History*, pp. 286; Wiese and Bölts, *Rinderhandel*, p. 10; Bowden, "Agricultural Prices," pp. 643–644.

87. Bowden, "Agricultural Prices," p. 643; Jones, "Agrarian Society," p. 382; Jacquart, "French Agriculture," p. 173.

88. Thirsk, "Farming Regions," *Agrarian History*, vol. 4, pp. 43, 60; Bowden, "Agricultural Prices," p. 644; J. Thirsk, "Enclosure and Engrossing," in Thirsk, *Agrarian History*, vol. 4, p. 226.

89. P. R. Edwards, "The Farming Economy of North-East Shropshire in the Seventeenth Century" (PhD diss., Oxford University, 1976), p. 102; Wiese and Bölts, *Rinderhandel*, p. 10.

90. Slicher van Bath, *Agrarian History*, p. 285; De Maddalena, "Rural Europe," p. 306; Wiese and Bölts, *Rinderhandel*, pp. 5–10.

91. Slicher van Bath, *Agrarian History*, p. 286; Wiese and Bölts, *Rinderhandel*, p. 10.

92. Markham, *Husbandry*, p. 81; Leonard Mascall, *The Third Booke intreating the Ordering of Sheep and Goates, Hogs and Dogs* (London, 1587), p. 253.

93. C. Dyer, "Alternative Agriculture: Goats in Medieval England," in *People, Landscape and Alternative Agriculture*, ed. R. W. Hoyle (Reading, UK: British Agricultural History Society, 2004), p. 35.

94. Mascall, *Sheep and Goates, Hogs and Dogs*, p. 189.

95. Together with some cattle.

96. D. Hay, *Europe in the Fourteenth and Fifteenth Centuries* (London: Longman, 1966), p. 28.

97. See J. Klein, *The Mesta: A Study in Spanish Economic History, 1273–1836* (Cambridge, MA: Harvard University Press, 1920), pp. 18–20.

98. Jacquart, "French Agriculture," p. 173; Jones, "Agrarian Society," p. 380.

99. P. J. Bowden, *The Wool Trade of Tudor and Stuart England* (London: Frank Cass, 1971), p. 25.

100. Bowden, *Wool Trade*, pp. 26ff; Heresbach, *Foure Bookes*, fol. 137v.

101. J. Munro, "Spanish Merino Wools and the Nouvelles Draperies: An Industrial Transformation in the Late Medieval Low Countries," *Economic History Review* 58, no. 3 (2005): 431ff; M .L. Ryder, "Medieval Sheep and Wool Types," *Agricultural History Review* 32, no. 1 (1984): 24; Bowden, *Wool Trade*, pp. 30–31.

102. Markham, *Husbandry*, pp. 64–65; Bowden, *Wool Trade*, pp. 30–31.

103. Munro, "Merino Wools," p. 439.

104. Cited in Munro, "Merino Wools," p. 470; Bowden, *Wool Trade*, pp. 26–27.

105. Bowden, *Wool Trade*, p. 25; Jones, "Agrarian Society," p. 382.

106. B. Pullan, *Crisis and Change in the Venetian Economy in the Sixteenth and Seventeenth Centuries* (London: Methuen, 1968), pp. 113, 116.

107. Bowden, *Wool Trade*, p. 13; M. Mate, "Pastoral Farming in South-East England in the Fifteenth Century," *Economic History Review*, 2nd ser., 40 (1967): 528.

108. Jones, "Agrarian Society," p. 382.

109. Heresbach, *Foure Bookes*, fol. 146r; Estienne and Liébault, *L'Agriculture*, fol. 69r.

110. Markham, *Husbandry*, p. 82; Estienne and Liébault, *L'Agriculture*, fol. 69r.

111. Markham, *Husbandry*, p. 65.

112. Mascall, *Sheep and Goates, Hogs and Dogs*, p. 251; R. W. Malcolmson, *The English Pig: A History* (London: Hambledon, 1998), p. 34.

113. Leonard Mascall, *The Husbandrie Ordering and Gouernment of Poultrie* (London, 1581), cap. 41; Markham, *Husbandry*, p. 127; Mascall, *Sheep and Goates, Hogs and Dogs*, pp. 259–260; Markham, *Husbandry*, p. 89.

114. Fitzherbert, *Husbandrye*, fol. 37r.

115. Bowden, "Agricultural Prices," p. 673.

116. R. Baehrel, *Une Croissance: La Basse-Provence Rurale: fin XVIe siècle–1789* (Paris: S.E.V.P.E.N., 1961), p. 171; Markham, *Husbandry*, p. 87, repeating Mascall, *Sheep and Goates, Hogs and Dogs*, p. 259.

117. Mascall, *Poultrie*, cap. 33, cap. 41; Markham, *Husbandry*, p. 127.

118. Mascall, *Poultrie*, cap. 44; Markham, *Husbandry*, p. 132.

119. Heresbach, fol.173v; Markham, *Husbandry*, p. 151.

120. Mascall, *Poultrie*, cap. 44; Markham, *Husbandry*, p. 125.

121. Heresbach, *Foure Bookes*, fol. 148r; Folkingham, *Feudigraphia*, p. 8.

122. Braudel, *Civilization*, vol. 1, p. 213; Mascall, *Poultrie*, cap. 40; Estienne and Liébault, *L'Agriculture*, fol. 45r.
123. Heresbach, *Foure Bookes*, fol. 173v.
124. Thomas, *Natural World*, p. 109.
125. Thomas, *Natural World*, p. 102; Heresbach, *Foure Bookes*, fols. 153v–154r.
126. Topsell, *Beastes*, p. 159.
127. John Caius, *Of English Dogs*, trans. Abraham Fleming (Alton, UK: Beech, 1993), p. 28.
128. Caius, *Dogs*, p. 30; Topsell, *Beastes*, p. 160; Mascall, *Poultrie*, cap. 33; Herse-bach, *Foure Bookes*, fol. 166r.
129. Also called *raches*.
130. J. Cummins, *The Hound and the Hawk: The Art of Medieval Hunting* (London: Phoenix, 2001), p. 15.
131. Cummins, *Hunting*, p. 15; Edward of Norwich, *The Master of Game*, ed. W. A. Baillie-Grohman and F. N. Baillie-Grohman (Philadelphia: University of Pennsylvania Press, 2005), pp. 106–107.
132. Cummins, *Hunting*, pp. 22–23; Caius, *Dogs*, p. 15; Topsell, *Beastes*, p. 148.
133. Cummins, *Hunting*, pp. 23, 47; *Cal. State Papers Dom. 1547–1580*, p. 672.
134. Cummins, *Hunting*, p. 14; Topsell, *Beastes*, p. 148; Edward of Norwich, *Master of Game*, pp. 116–117.
135. Edward of Norwich, *Master of Game*, pp. xii, 118.
136. Edward of Norwich, *Master of Game*, pp. 113–115; Cummins, *Hunting*, p. 14; *L & P Henry VIII, 19, 1544*, p. 343; Sir Thomas Elyot, *The Boke Named the Governour* (London, 1531), fol. 72v.
137. Caius, *Dogs*, p. 10.
138. Ibid.
139. Thomas, *Man and the Natural World*, pp. 112–114.
140. Ibid., p. 110.
141. Caius, *Dogs*, pp. 23–24.
142. Thomas, *Natural World*, p. 107; R. Hutchinson, *The Last Days of Henry VIII* (London: Weidenfeld and Nicolson, 2005), p. 166.
143. Thomas, *Natural World*, p. 109.
144. Topsell, *Beastes*, p. 106.
145. Ibid.
146. H. Naïs, *Les animaux dans la poésie française de la Renaissance* (Paris: n.p., 1961), p. 594. I am grateful to Kathleen Walker-Meikle for this reference.
147. Clutton-Brock, *Domesticated Animals*, p. 133; Topsell, *Beastes*, p. 105.
148. Topsell, *Beastes*, p. 141.
149. Naïs, *Poésie*, p. 605.
150. Thomas, *Natural World*, p. 105.

Chapter 4

1. William Lambarde, *A Perambulation of Kent* (London, 1576), pp. 187–188.
2. Bruce Boehrer, *Shakespeare among the Animals* (New York: Palgrave, 2002), pp. 137–145; Barbara Ravelhofer, "'Beasts of Recreacion': Henslowe's White Bears," *English Literary Renaissance* 32, no. 2 (Spring 2002): 287–293; S. P. "The

Master of the Bears in Art and Enterprise," *Medieval and Renaissance Drama in England* 5 (1991): 195–209.

3. John Norden, *Speculum Britanniae* (London, 1593), pp. 26–27. See http://vrcoll. fa.pitt.edu/medart/image/England/london/Maps-of-London/London-Maps.html for Norden's and Visscher's maps.

4. Andrew Gurr, *The Shakespearean Stage 1574–1642* (Cambridge, UK: Cambridge University Press, 1997), pp. 117–118.

5. Teresa Grant, "White Bears in *Mucedorus, The Winter's Tale,* and *Oberon, the Fairy Prince,*" *Notes and Queries,* n.s. 48, no. 3 (September 2001): 311–313; Ravelhofer, "'Beasts,'" passim.

6. John Stow, *The Survey of London* (London, 1598), p. 67.

7. Stephen Mullaney, "Shakespeare and the Liberties," *Encyclopaedia Britannica's Guide to Shakespeare,* 12 pars., April 23, 2006, http://www.britannia.com/shake speare/article-9396031, par. 4.

8. Stow, *Survey,* pp. 69–73.

9. See Francois Laroque, *Shakespeare's Festive World,* trans. J. Lloyd (Cambridge, UK: Cambridge University Press, 1991), passim.

10. Stow, *Survey,* pp. 331–333.

11. Mullaney, "Shakespeare," par. 5.

12. Of course, some people, especially Puritans and those in civil authority, saw the "merrie and sportfull" as unsavory by association.

13. Ben Jonson, *Bartholomew Fair,* ed. G. R. Hibbard (London: Ernest Benn, 1977), Induction.18–19.

14. E. Griffith, "Banks, William (*fl.* 1591–1637)," in *Oxford Dictionary of National Biography,* ed. H. C. G. Matthew and B. Harrison (Oxford, UK: Oxford University Press, 2004), http://www.oxforddnb.com/view/article/1292.

15. For dating see K. Schlueter, "Introduction," in William Shakespeare, *The Two Gentlemen of Verona,* ed. K. Schlueter (Cambridge, UK: Cambridge University Press, 1990).

16. Richard Beadle, "Crab's Pedigree," in *English Comedy,* ed. M. Cordner, P. Holland, and J. Kerrigan (Cambridge, UK: Cambridge University Press, 1994), pp. 12–35; Boehrer, *Shakespeare,* pp. 133–168.

17. Boehrer, *Shakespeare,* p. 152.

18. James I, *The Kings Majesties Declaration to His Subjects, concerning Lawfull Sports to be Used* (London, 1618).

19. William Shakespeare, *Macbeth* 3.1.91–98, in *The Riverside Shakespeare,* ed. G. Blakemore Evans et al. (Boston: Houghton Mifflin, 1997). All references to Shakespeare are to this edition.

20. Ben Jonson, *Every Man Out of His Humour,* ed. Helen Ostovich (Manchester, UK: Manchester University Press, 2001), 5.3.225–226.

21. Ibid., 5.3.432–433.

22. Ibid., 5.3.572–573.

23. Beadle, "Pedigree," p. 24.

24. Keith Thomas, *Man and the Natural World: Changing Attitudes in England 1500–1800* (London: Allen Lane, 1983), p. 108.

25. Ibid., p. 106.

26. John Caius, *Of Englishe Dogges,* trans. Abraham Fleming (London, 1576), p. 40.

27. Edward Topsell, *The Historie of Foure-Footed Beastes* (London, 1607), p. 147.
28. Caius, *Dogges*, p. 2; Thomas, *Natural World*, p. 106.
29. Ian MacInnes, "Mastiffs and Spaniels: Gender and Nation in the English Dog," *Textual Practice* 17, no. 1 (2003): 21–40.
30. Thomas, *Natural World*, pp. 105, 106.
31. Jonson, *Every Man Out*, 2.1.345–346.
32. Ibid., 3.1.163.
33. Ibid., 3.1.487–488.
34. Ibid., 3.1.491–492.
35. Ibid., 3.1.77–78.
36. MacInnes, "Mastiffs," pp. 32ff.
37. Jonson, *Every Man Out*, 5.3.177.
38. Ibid., 3.1.76.
39. Boehrer, *Shakespeare*, p. 146.
40. Jonson, *Every Man Out*, 5.3.221–226.
41. Boehrer, *Shakespeare*, pp. 146–148.
42. George Chapman, John Marston, and Ben Jonson, *Eastward Ho!* (London, 1605), sig. H2r.
43. Boehrer, *Shakespeare*, p. 143.
44. D. A. Scheve, "Jonson's *Volpone* and Traditional Fox Lore," *Review of English Studies* (1950): 242–244.
45. Topsell, *Historie*, p. 226; Oppian, *Halieutica* in *Oppian, Colluthus and Tryphiodorus*, trans. A. W. Mair (London: William Heinemann, 1928), pp. 291–292.
46. Wilma George and B. Yapp, *The Naming of the Beasts: Natural History in the Medieval Bestiary* (London: Duckworth, 1991), p. 10.
47. Beadle, "Pedigree," passim.
48. Beadle, "Pedigree," p. 13; Boehrer, *Shakespeare*, p. 167.
49. Boehrer, *Shakespeare*, p. 167.
50. Jonson, *Every Man Out*, 5.2.194.
51. Ibid., 5.1.85.
52. Plutarch, *The Philosophie, commonlie called, the Morals*, trans. Philemon Holland (London, 1603), p. 967.
53. The Islip quarto (1600) and the Short quarto (1601) print "Kickes him out."; the Ling quarto dated (wrongly) 1600 has "Kickes him." The 1616 Folio has no stage direction.
54. Beadle, "Pedigree," p. 22.
55. Boehrer, *Shakespeare*, p. 167.
56. Ibid.
57. Ibid.
58. William Rowley, Thomas Dekker, and John Ford, *The Witch of Edmonton*, in *Three Jacobean Witchcraft Plays*, ed. P. Corbin and D. Sedge (Manchester, UK: Manchester University Press, 1986), 4.1.235–237.
59. W. J. Lawrence, "Shakespeare's Use of Animals," *The Dublin Magazine* 7 (January–March, 1937): 18.
60. John Marston, *Histrio-mastix* (London, 1610), sig. C2r.
61. Ibid.
62. Ibid.
63. Thomas Middleton and Thomas Dekker, *The Roaring Girl*, ed. P. Mulholland (Manchester, UK: Manchester University Press, 1987), 2.1.399–end.

64. L. B. Wright, "Animal Actors on the English Stage before 1642," *Publications of the Modern Language Association of America (PMLA)* 42 (1927): 665.

65. Middleton and Dekker, *The Roaring Girl,* 2.1.413–415.

66. Ibid., 4.2.37–39.

67. Ibid., 1.2.212.

68. MacInnes, "Mastiffs," p. 33.

69. Cyrus Hoy, "Introductions," "Notes," and "Commentaries to Texts" in *The Dramatic Works of Thomas Dekker,* 4 vols., ed. F. Bowers (Cambridge, UK: Cambridge University Press, 1980), vol. 3, p. 29.

70. William Davenant, *The Works of Sir William Davenant* (London, 1673), p. 289.

71. Ibid., pp. 290–291.

72. Ibid., p. 291.

73. Middleton and Dekker, *The Roaring Girl,* p. 127.

74. Rowley, Dekker, and Ford, *The Witch of Edmonton,* 4.1.237.

75. Middleton and Dekker, *The Roaring Girl,* 2.1.401, 2.411 s.d.

76. Wright, "Animal Actors," p. 665. He has confused their names.

77. Qtd. in Middleton and Dekker, *The Roaring Girl,* p. 121.

78. Ibid.

79. Hoy, "Introductions," vol. 3, p. 28.

80. John Marston, *The Malcontent,* ed. B. Harris (London: Ernest Benn, 1967), III.i.136–140.

81. Samuel Daniel, *The Queenes Arcadia* in *Certaine Small Workes* (London, 1607), sig. B2v. I am grateful to Lucy Munro for this reference.

82. Rowley, Dekker, and Ford, *The Witch of Edmonton,* 4.1.260–261.

83. See W. Abbott, *A Bibliography of Oliver Cromwell* (Cambridge, MA: Harvard University Press, 1929), p. 408.

84. See Harry Levin, *Shakespeare and the Revolution of the Times* (New York: Oxford University Press, 1976), pp. 121–130; H. Maclean, "Time and Horsemanship in Shakespeare's Histories," *University of Toronto Quarterly* 35 (1965–1966): 229–245; Robert. N. Watson, "Horsemanship in Shakespeare's Second Tetralogy," *English Literary Renaissance* 13, no. 3 (1983): 274–300.

85. *Woodstock,* ed. P. Corbin and D. Sedge (Manchester, UK: Manchester University Press, 2002), 3.2.

86. Levin, *Shakespeare,* pp. 121–130; Lawrence, "Animals," p. 271.

87. William Shakespeare, *Henry V,* Prologue.26–28.

88. Levin, *Shakespeare,* p. 123.

89. *Woodstock,* 3.2.114–125.

90. *Look about You* (London, 1600), sig. A2r.

91. *Woodstock,* 3.2.126.

92. Ibid., 3.2.218–219

93. Lawrence, "Animals," p. 272.

94. B. Wendell, *William Shakespeare* (London, 1894), p. 308.

95. Lawrence, "Animals," pp. 272–273.

96. *Woodstock,* 3.2.156–158.

97. Ibid., 1.3.104–106.

98. Ibid., 1.1.203–205.

99. Ibid., 1.1.208.

100. Ibid., 1.1.213–214.

101. Ibid., 1.1.212.

102. Ibid., 1.3.103.
103. Ibid., 1.3.78–79.
104. Ibid., 1.3.115–116.
105. Ibid., 3.2.111–112.
106. Ibid., 3.2.161–164.
107. Ibid., 3.2.168–169.
108. Ibid., 3.2.169–170.
109. E. Phipson, *The Animal Lore of Shakespeare's Time* (London, 1883), p. 107.
110. *Woodstock,* 3.2.165–166.
111. Ibid., 3.2.84.
112. Ibid., 1.3.179.
113. Ibid., 1.3.60–61.
114. Ibid., 1.3.70–71.
115. Moelwyn Merchant, *The Critical Idiom: Comedy* (London: Methuen, 1972), p. 27.
116. John Dando, *Maroccus Exstaticus, or Bankes Bay Horse in a Trance* (London, 1595), sig. A3r.
117. Ibid., sigs. C2v, C1r.
118. Ibid., title page.
119. E. Griffith, "Banks, William (*fl.* 1591–1637)," in *Oxford Dictionary of National Biography,* ed. H. C. G. Matthew and B. Harrison (Oxford, UK: Oxford University Press, 2004).
120. Dando, *Maroccus,* sig. C2v.
121. Peter Ure, "Introduction," in William Shakespeare, *King Richard II,* ed. P. Ure (London: Methuen, 1956), p. lix.
122. See Grant, "White Bears."
123. Gurr, *Stage,* p. 19.

Chapter 5

1. *Dizionario biografico degli Italiani,* Rome: Instituto della Enciclopedia italiana, 1960– , vol. 56, 2001, s.v. Paolo Giovio.
2. C. Gesner, *Historiae animalium, liber IV, qui est de piscium et aquatilium animantium natura* (C. Froschouerus, 1558), fol. B4v°.
3. References in bibliography.
4. W. B. Ashworth, "The Persistent Beast: Recurring Images in Early Zoological Illustration," in *The Natural Sciences and the Arts* (Stockholm: Almqvist and Wiksell International, 1985), pp. 46–66.
5. G. Rondelet (1554–1555), *Libri de Piscibus Marinis ...* (Lyon, 1554), vol. 1, fol. A5r°.
6. See D. M. Balme, "The Place of Biology in Aristotle's Philosophy," in *Philosophical Issues in Aristotle's Biology,* ed. A. Gotthelf and J. G. Lennox (Cambridge, UK: Cambridge University Press, 2000), pp. 9–20; R. Bolton, "Definition and Scientific Method in Aristotle's *Posterior Analytics* and *Generation of Animals,*" ibid., pp. 120–166; P. Pellegrin, *La classification des animaux chez Aristote. Statut de la biologie et unité de l'aristotélisme* (Paris: Les Belles Lettres, 1982), passim; P. Mack, "La fonction descriptive de l'*Histoire des animaux* d'Aristote," *Phronesis* 31 (1986): 148–166 ; V. Pratt, "Aristotle and the Essence of Natural History," *History and Philosophy of Life Sciences* 4 (1982): 203–223.

7. L. Fuchs, *L'Histoire des plantes* (Lyon, 1550), p. 447; *De historia stirpium commentarii insignes …* (Lyon, 1549), p. 62.

8. P. Belon, *L'histoire de la nature des oyseaux avec leurs descriptions, et naifs portraicts retirez du naturel* (Guillaume Cavellat, 1555), p. 106.

9. C. Singer, *A Short History of Scientific Ideas to 1900* (Oxford, UK: Oxford University Press, 1959), p. 207.

10. P. Belon, *L'histoire naturelle des estranges poissons marins* (Paris, 1551), fols. A2r–v.

11. P. Louis, "Le mot ιστορια chez Aristote," *Revue de philologie, de littérature et d'histoire anciennes* 29 (1955): 39–44.

12. Ibid., p. 43.

13. C. Gesner, *De stirpium maxime earum quae in Germania nostra nascuntur,* in H. Bock, *De stirpium maxime earum quae in Germania nostra nascuntur* (Strasbourg, 1552), fol. Bir.

14. See Romans 1:20, *The Holy Bible* (London, 1625).

15. P. Belon, *De aquatilibus Libri duo* (Paris, 1553), pp. 129–130.

16. See M. Cogan, "Rodolphus Agricola and the Semantic Revolutions of the History of Invention," *Rhetorica* 2 (1984): 163–194; P. Joachimsen, "*Loci communes.* Eine Untersuchung zur Geistesgeschichte des Humanismus und der Reformation," *Luther-Jahrbuch* 8 (1926): 27–97; E. Kessler, "Humanismus und Naturwissenschaft. Zur Legitimation neuzeitlicher Naturwissenschaft durch den Humanismus," *Zeitschrift für Philosophische Forschung* 33 (1979): 23–40; M. C. Leff, "The Topics of Argumentative Invention in Latin Rhetorical Theory from Cicero to Boethius," *Rhetorica* 1 (1983): 23–44; P. Mack, *Renaissance Argument: Valla and Agricola in the Traditions of Rhetoric and Dialectic* (Leiden: E. J. Brill, 1993); W. Schmidt-Biggemann, *Topica universalis. Eine Modellgeschichte humanistischer und barocker Wissenschaft* (Hamburg, Germany: Felix Meiner, 1983); C. Vasoli, "La retorica e la cultura del Rinascimento," *Rhetorica* 2 (1984): 121–137 ; C. Vasoli, "L'humanisme rhétorique en Italie au XVe siècle," in *Histoire de la rhétorique dans l'Europe moderne, 1450–1950,* ed. M. Fumaroli (Paris: Presses Universitaires de France, 1999), pp. 45–129.

17. G. Castor, *Pléiade Poetics: A Study in the Sixteenth-Century Thought and Terminology* (Cambridge, UK: Cambridge University Press, 1964).

18. Belon, *L'histoire de la nature des oyseaux,* p. 3.

19. Ibid., pp. 329–331.

20. Aristotle, *De Rhetorica,* trans. J. H. Freese (Cambridge, MA: Harvard University Press, 1975), pp. 151–159.

21. P. A. Mattioli, *Commentaires de M. Pierre André Matthiole sur les six livres de Pedacius Dioscoride* (Lyon, 1572), fol. ††5r).

22. Ibid.

23. Ibid.

24. Compare Rondelet, *Libri de piscibus* I, p. 115, *Histoire entiere des poissons* I, p. 108.

25. U. Aldrovandi, *Ornithologiae. Hoc est de avibus historiae libri XII* (Bologna, 1681), p. 508.

26. Belon, *L'histoire de la nature des oyseaux,* p. 66.

27. Rondelet, *Libri de piscibus,* vol. 2, p. 121.

28. P. Belon, *La nature et diversité des poissons avec leurs pourtraicts* (Paris, 1555), p. 375.

29. Aldrovandi, *Ornithologiae*, p. 472.

30. Gesner, *Historiae animalium, liber IV*, p. 119.

31. See M. Lowry, *The World of Aldus Manutius: Business and Scholarship in Renaissance Venice* (Oxford, UK: Blackwell, 1979).

32. Belon, *La nature et diversité des poissons*, p. 414.

33. Ibid., p. 125.

34. Ibid., p. 415.

35. P. Belon, *Les observations de plusieurs singularitez et choses memorables* ... (Paris, 1553), fol. 165r, p. 308.

36. Belon, *La nature et diversité des poissons*, p. 28.

37. Ibid., p. 25.

38. Thus the verbs *pinguere, depinguere,* and *delineare*.

39. Fuchs, *De historia stirpium*, p. 69.

40. Ibid.

41. Gesner, *Historiae animalium I*, fol. B1v.

42. Ibid., p. 70.

43. W. Turner, *Avium praecipuarum [...] brevis et succincta historia* ... (Köln, 1544), fol. D4v.

44. Rondelet, *Libri de piscibus*, vol. 1, p. 401.

45. See Fuchs, *Histoire des plantes*, p. 51, and *Commentaires tres excellens de l'hystoire des plantes* (Lyon, 1549), chap. XXII, n.p.

46. See M.-L. Demonet, *Les voix du signe. Nature et origine du langage a la Renaissance (1480–1580)* (Paris: Champion, 1992); P. Findlen, "Jokes of Nature and Jokes of Knowledge: The Playfulness of Scientific Discourse in Early Modern Europe," *Renaissance Quarterly* 43 (1990): 292–331; I. Maclean, *Logic, Signs and Nature in the Renaissance: The Case of Learned Medicine* (Cambridge, UK: Cambridge University Press, 2002).

47. P. Glardon, *L'histoire naturelle au XVIe siècle: regards, lectures et discours sur la nature* ... (Lausanne, Switzerland: University of Lausanne, 2005), pp. 289–352.

48. P. Belon, *Les observations de plusieurs singularitez* ... (Anvers, 1555), fol. 233v. This passage is absent from the first edition.

49. Castor, *Pléiade Poetics*.

50. E. Garin, *L'homme de la Renaissance* (Paris: Seuil, 1990), p. 174.

51. P. A. Mattioli, *Les Commentaires de M. P. André Matthiolus* (Lyon, 1605), fol. A2r.

52. Castor, *Pléiade Poetics*.

53. Ibid. See T. Cave, *The Cornucopian Text: Problems of Writing in the French Renaissance* (Oxford, UK: Clarendon, 1979).

54. *L'énigme de la chronique de Pierre Belon*, ed. M. Barsi (Milan: Edizioni Universitarie di Lettere Economia Diritto, 2001), fol. 107v.

55. Belon, *La nature et diversité des poissons*, p. 262.

56. Belon, *L'histoire de la nature des poissons*, p. 130.

57. Ibid., fol.   iiijr.

58. C. Gesner, *Nomenclator Aquatilium animalium animantium* (Zurich, 1560), fol. AA4v.

59. See J. de Acosta, *Historia natural y moral de las Indias* (Barcelona, 1591); J. de Léry, *Histoire d'un voyage fait en la terre de Bresil, autrement dit Amerique* (Paris, 1578); A. Thévet, *Les Singularitez de la France Antarctique, autrement nommée Amerique* (Paris, 1558).

60. Aldrovandi, *Ornithologiae,* p. 879.
61. C. Balavoine, "Le statut de l'image dans les livres emblématiques en France de 1580–1630," in *L'automne de la Renaissance,* ed. J. Lafond and A. Stegmann (Paris: Vrin, 1981), pp. 163–178; F. Lecercle, "Arts et littérature," in *Précis de littérature française du XVIe siècle. La Renaissance,* ed. R. Aulotte (Paris: Presses Universitaires de France, 1991).

Chapter 6

1. *Editio princeps* Venice, 1469. See C. G. Nauert, Jr., "Humanists, Scientists, and Pliny: Changing Approaches to a Classical Author," *American Historical Review* 84 (1979): 72–85 and "Caius Plinius Secundus," in *Catalogus translationum et commentariorum: Medieval and Renaissance Latin Translations and Commentaries,* ed. F. E. Cranz and P. O. Kristeller (Washington: The Catholic University of America Press, 1980), vol. 4, pp. 297–422; M. Davies, "Making Sense of Pliny in the Quattrocento," *Renaissance Studies* 9 (1995): 240–257. Also see L. Thorndike, *A History of Magic and Experimental Science* (New York: Columbia University Press, 1941), vol. 4, pp. 593–610; V. Nutton, "The Rise of Medical Humanism: Ferrara, 1464–1555," *Renaissance Studies* 11 (1997): 2–19.
2. The *editio princeps* of Gaza's translation (Venice, 1476) was followed by many further editions: see F. E. Cranz, *A Bibliography of Aristotle's Editions, 1501–1600,* rev. C. B. Schmitt (Baden-Baden: Körner, 1984); J. Monfasani, "The Pseudo-Aristotelian *Problemata* and Aristotle's *De animalibus* in the Renaissance," in *Natural Particulars: Nature and the Disciplines in Renaissance Europe,* ed. A. Grafton and N. G. Siraisi (Cambridge, MA: MIT Press, 1999), pp. 205–247; S. Perfetti, "Cultius atque integrius. Teodoro Gaza traduttore umanistico del *De partibus animalium,*" *Rinascimento,* 2nd ser., 35 (1995): 253–286, and *Aristotle's Zoology and Its Renaissance Commentators (1521–1601)* (Leuven, Belgium: Leuven University Press, 2000), pp. 11–28; L. Repici, "Teodoro Gaza traduttore e interprete di Teofrasto: la ricezione della botanica antica tra Quattro e Cinquecento," *Rinascimento,* 2nd ser., 43 (2004): 417–505.
3. Theodorus Gaza, *In libros Aristotelis de animalibus* [. . .] *praefatio,* in *Aristotelis Libri omnes ad animalium cognitionem spectantes* (1562; facs., Frankfurt: Minerva, 1962), fols. 3v–4r.
4. Ibid., fol. 4r.
5. Ibid.
6. On Gaza's first *fortuna* see Monfasani, "*Problemata,*" pp. 241–217; Perfetti, "Cultius," pp. 256–258 and *Aristotle's Zoology,* pp. 26–27.
7. See Pomponazzi, *Expositio super primo et secundo De partibus animalium,* ed. S. Perfetti (Florence: Olschki, 2004).
8. See Perfetti, *Aristotle's Zoology* and "Three Different Ways of Interpreting Aristotle's *De Partibus Animalium:* Pietro Pomponazzi, Niccolò Leonico Tomeo and Agostino Nifo," in *Aristotle's Animals in the Middle Ages and Renaissance,* ed. C. Steel, P. Beullens, and G. Guldentops (Leuven, Flanders: Leuven University Press, 1999), pp. 289–308.
9. See I. Maclean, "White Crows, Graying Hair, and Eyelashes: Problems for Natural Historians in the Reception of Aristotelian Logic and Biology from Pomponazzi to Bacon," in *Historia: Empiricism and Erudition in Early Modern Europe,* ed. G. Pomata and N. G. Siraisi (Cambridge, MA: MIT Press, 2005), pp. 147–179.

10. Aristotle, *Parts of Animals,* trans. A. L. Peck (London: Heinemannn, 1961), II, 12, 657 a 17–20.

11. Pomponazzi, *Expositio,* pp. 301, 146–148.

12. Ibid., pp. 301, 142–145.

13. Ibid., pp. 145, 164–172.

14. Ibid., pp. 273, 79–85.

15. Ibid., pp. 227, 182–196.

16. Augustinus Niphus, *Expositiones in omnes Aristotelis libros* (Venice, 1546), fol. 4r.

17. See L. Bianchi, "Una caduta senza declino? Considerazioni sulla crisi dell'aristotelismo fra Rinascimento ed età moderna," in *Studi sull'Aristotelismo del Rinascimento,* ed. F. Dominguez et al. (Padua: Il Poligrafo, 2003), pp. 133–172; S. Perfetti, "Metamorfosi di una traduzione: Agostino Nifo revisore dei *De animalibus* gaziani," *Medioevo. Rivista di Storia della Filosofia Medievale* 22 (1996): 298–301 and "How and When the Medieval Commentary Died Out: The Case of Aristotle's Zoological Writings," in *Il commento filosofico nell'Occidente latino (secoli XIII-XV),* ed. G. Fioravanti, C. Leonardi, and S. Perfetti (Turnhout, Belgium: Brepols, 2002), pp. 429–443.

18. For example, Daniel Furlanus Cretensis, *In libros Aristotelis De partibus animalium commentarius primus* (Venice, 1574) and Cesare Cremonini's commentary on *Parts of Animals* I, 1 and *Generation of Animals* I (mss. Padova B. Civica 494, fols. 1r–98r and Venezia B. Marciana Lat. VI 179, fols1r–142v).

19. See Perfetti, *Aristotle's Zoology,* pp. 185–232.

20. B. Ogilvie, "Natural History, Ethics, and Physico-Theology," in Pomata and Siraisi, *Historia,* pp. 75–103, 78 and 80.

21. See G. Pomata, "*Praxis Historialis:* The Uses of Historia in Early Modern Medicine," in Pomata and Siraisi, *Historia,* pp. 105–146.

22. Conrad Gesner, *Historiae animalium liber primus. De quadrupedibus viviparis,* (Zurich, 1551); *Liber secundus. De quadrupedibus oviparis* (1554); *Liber tertius, qui est de avium natura* (1555); *Liber quartus, qui est de piscium et aquatilium natura* (1558); *Liber V. Historiae insectorum libellus* (1587).

23. See L. Pinon, "Conrad Gesner and the Historical Depth of Renaissance Natural History," in Pomata and Siraisi, *Historia,* pp. 241–267; G. Cuvier, *Histoire des sciences naturelles depuis leur origine jusqu'a nos jours, deuxième partie, comprenant les 16e et 17e siècles,* tome deuxieme (facs.; Bruxelles: Culture et Civilization, 1969), pp. 83–91; Ä. Bäumer-Schleinkofer, "Die Enzyklopädien als Etablierung des Forschungsgebiets Zoologie in der Renaissance," in *Gattungen wissenschaftlicher Literatur in der Antike,* ed. W. Kullmann, J. Althoff, and M. Asper (Tübingen, Germany: Gunter Narr, 1998), pp. 141–159.

24. Conrad Gesner, *De libris a se editis epistola ad Guilielmum Turnerum, theologum et medicum excellentissimum in Anglia* (Zurich, 1551), qtd. in Pinon, "Conrad Gesner," p. 247.

25. Edward Wotton, *De differentiis animalium libri decem* (Paris, 1552).

26. *Aristotelis sparsae de animalibus sententiae* (Bologna, 1651); see Perfetti, *Aristotle's Zoology,* pp. 189–192.

27. See Cuvier, *Histoire des sciences,* pp. 74–80; G. Sarton, *Appreciation of Ancient and Medieval Science during the Renaissance (1450–1600)* (Philadelphia: University of Pennsylvania Press, 1955), pp. 55–63; L. Pinon, *Livres de zoologie de la Renaissance: une anthologie* (Paris: Kincksieck, 1995); P. Glardon, "Introduction," in

Pierre Belon du Mans, *L'histoire de la nature des oyseaux. Fac-similé de l'edition de 1555* (Geneva: Librairie Droz, 1997), pp. xiii-lxxi; F. Meunier and J.-L. d'Hondt, "Introduction," in Guillaume Rondelet, *L'histoire entière des poissons* (Paris: Éditions du CTHS, 2002), pp. 7–26138. Georgius Agricola, *De animantibus subterraneis liber* ([Basel], 1549).

28. Georgius Agricola, *De animantibus subterraneis liber* ([Basel], 1549).

29. See A. Arber, *Herbals, Their Origin and Evolution: A Chapter in the History of Botany (1470–1670)* (Cambridge, UK: Cambridge University Press, 1986); J. Stannard, *Herbs and Herbalism in the Middle Ages and Renaissance*, ed. K. E. Stannard and R. Kay (Aldershot, UK: Ashgate, 1999); I. Beretta, *Illustration and Representation: Botany in the Renaissance*, in *Immagini per conoscere. Dal Rinascimento alla Rivoluzione scientifica*, ed. F. Meroi and C. Pogliano (Florence: Olschki, 2001), pp. 43–60; Repici, "Teodoro Gaza," pp. 467–490.

30. See C. B. Schmitt, "Science in the Italian Universities in the Sixteenth and Early Seventeenth Centuries," in *The Emergence of Science in Western Europe*, ed. M. P. Crosland (London: Macmillan, 1975), pp. 35–56, 39–44 and "Philosophy and Science in Sixteenth-Century Italian Universities," in *The Renaissance: Essays in Interpretation to Eugenio Garin* (London: Methuen, 1982), pp. 297–336, 308; S. Perfetti, "Giulio Cesare Scaligero commentatore e filosofo naturale tra Padova e Francia," in *La presenza dell'Aristotelismo padovano nella filosofia della prima modernità*, ed. G. Piaia (Rome: Antenore, 2002), pp. 3–31, 16–17.

31. Cuvier, *Histoire des sciences*, pp. 78–79.

32. Rondelet, *Histoire entière*, vol. 1, p. 3.

33. See D. M. Balme, "Aristotle's Use of Division and Differentiae," in *Philosophical Issues in Aristotle's Biology*, ed. A. Gotthelf and J. Lennox (Cambridge, UK: Cambridge University Press, 1987), pp. 69–89; D. Charles, "Natural Kinds and Natural History," in *Biologie, logique et métaphysique chez Aristote*, ed. D. Devereux and P. Pellegrin (Paris: Editions du CNRS, 1990), pp. 145–167; G. E. R. Lloyd, "The Development of Aristotle's Theory of the Classification of Animals," *Phronesis* 1 (1961): 59–81; P. Pellegrin, *Aristotle's Classification of Animals* (Berkeley: University of California Press, 1986); M. Vegetti, "Origini e metodi della zoologia aristotelica," in Aristotele, *Opere biologiche*, ed. D. Lanza and M. Vegetti (Turin: Utet, 1971), pp. 102–120.

34. Petri Bellonii Cenomani, *De aquatilibus, Libri duo* (Paris, 1553).

35. Rondelet, *Histoire entière*, vol. 1, pp. 310–311.

36. Belon, *De aquatilibus*, p. 139.

37. Cf. Rondelet, *Histoire entière*, vol. 1, fols. a 5v–6r.

38. Pliny, *Naturalis Historia*, bk. 9, chap. 68.

39. Belon, *De aquatilibus*, p. 187.

40. Rondelet, *Histoire entière*, vol. 1, p. 155.

41. See G. Boas, "Theriophily," in *Dictionary of the History of Ideas: Studies of Selected Pivotal Ideas*, ed. P. P. Wiener (New York: Charles Scribner's Sons, 1973), vol. 4, pp. 384–389; A. O. Lovejoy and G. Boas, *Primitivism and Related Ideas in Antiquity* (Baltimore: Johns Hopkins University Press, 1935; repr., 1997), chaps. 4 and 13; G. Boas, *The Happy Beast in French Literature in the Seventeenth Century* (Baltimore: Johns Hopkins University Press, 1933).

42. *Editio princeps:* Plutarchus, *Opuscula LXXXXII* (Venice, 1509).

43. Michel de Montaigne, *Essais* (Paris: Éditions Garnier Frères, 1962), vol. 1, pp. 479–681.

44. T. Gontier, *De l'homme à l'animal. Montaigne et Descartes ou les paradoxes de la philosophie moderne sur la nature des animaux* (Paris: Vrin, 1998), p. 41.

45. Ibid., pp. 42–44.

46. Boas, "Theriophily," p. 387.

47. Ibid.

Chapter 7

1. Giorgio Vasari, *Lives of the Artists* (Harmondsworth, UK: Penguin, 1965), p. 93.

2. Otto Pächt, *The Master of Mary of Burgundy* (London: Faber and Faber, 1948), pl. D; Gian Lorenzo Mellini, Giorgio E. Ferrari, and Mario Salmi, *The Grimani Breviary* (London: Thames and Hudson, 1972), pl. 100.

3. Herbert Friedmann, *A Bestiary for Saint Jerome: Animal Symbolism in European Religious Art* (Washington, DC: Smithsonian Institution, 1980), p. 22.

4. Ibid., p. 159.

5. See Pächt, *Master*, pp. 32–33.

6. Friedmann (*Bestiary*, p. 282) identifies the partridge as the Chukar (*Alectoris chukar*), but it might equally be the Rock partridge (*Alectoris graeca*).

7. Sheldon Watts, *Epidemics and History: Disease, Power and Imperialism* (New Haven, CT: Yale University Press, 1999), p. 2.

8. See Pliny the Elder, *The Natural History*, trans. J. Bostock (London: Taylor and Francis, 1855), bk. 10, pp. 23–79.

9. Taillevent, *Le cuisinier Taillevent* (Lyon, ca. 1495; facs., Martin Harvard, http://visualiseur.bnf.fr/CadresFenetre?O=NUMM-106141&M=notice&Y=Image), p. 9.

10. See Mellini, Ferrari, and Salmi, *Grimani*, pl. 45; Raffaello 1518–1519; Cranach 1530; Tintoretto 1550; Bassano 1570–1573; Brueghel 1610.

11. Aristotle, *Historia Animalium*, trans. D'Arcy Wentworth Thompson (Oxford, UK: Clarendon, 1910; facs., http://etext.lib.virginia.edu/toc/modeng/public/AriHian.html), bk. 8, par. 1.

12. Joyce Salisbury, *The Beast Within: Animals in the Middle Ages* (New York: Routledge, 1994), p. 115.

13. Qtd in N. C. Flores, ed. *Animals in the Middle Ages: A Book of Essays* (New York: Garland, 1996), p. ix.

14. *Aberdeen Bestiary*, Aberdeen University Library MS 24 (facs., http://www.abdn.ac.uk/bestiary/index.hti), fol. 25v.

15. *The Book of Beasts being a Translation from a Latin Bestiary of the Twelfth Century*, trans. T. H. White (1954; repr., New York: Dover, 1984), p. 149.

16. Aristotle, *Historia*, bk. 6, par. 9.

17. *Aberdeen Bestiary*, fol. 30v.

18. Saint Augustine, *The City of God*, trans. Rev. March Dods (Edinburgh, 1886; facs., http://etext.lib.virginia.edu/toc/modeng/public/AugCity.html), bk. 21, chap. 4.

19. Regina Scheibe, "The Major Professional Skills of the Dove in *The Buke of the Howlat*," in *Animals and the Symbolic in Medieval Art and Literature*, ed. L. A. J. R. Houwen (Groningen, Netherlands: Egbert Forstein, 1997), p. 117.

20. Qtd. in Francis Klingender, *Animals in Art and Thought to the End of the Middle Ages*, ed. E. Antal and J. Harthan (Cambridge, MA: MIT Press, 1971), p. 375.

21. Colin Eisler notes that Dürer's *Wing of a Roller* was the model for many of Dürer's angel wings (*Dürer's Animals* [Washington, DC: Smithsonian Institution, 1991], p. 332).

22. *Aberdeen Bestiary*, fol. 61r.

23. Aristotle, *Historia,* bk. 1, par. 1.
24. *Aberdeen Bestiary,* fol. 61r.
25. Aristotle, *Historia,* bk. 1, par. 1.
26. Pliny, *Natural History,* bk. 10, pp. 51, 55.
27. Aristotle, *Historia,* bk. 9, par. 8.
28. *Aberdeen Bestiary,* fol. 54r.
29. Friedmann, *Bestiary,* p. 284.
30. *Aberdeen Bestiary,* fol. 54r.
31. Michael Baxandall, *Painting and Experience in Fifteenth-Century Italy: A Primer in the Social History of Pictorial Style* (Oxford, UK: Oxford University Press, 1988), p. 108.
32. *Aberdeen Bestiary,* fols. 60v–61r.
33. Friedmann, *Bestiary,* p. 282.
34. Mellini, Ferrari, and Salmi, *Grimani,* pl. 18.
35. Ibid., pls. 70, 44.
36. Eisler, *Animals,* p. 66.
37. See Malcolm Andrews, *Landscape and Western Art* (Oxford, UK: Oxford University Press, 1999), pp. 53–67.
38. See Friedmann, *Bestiary,* p. 213.
39. Salisbury, *Beast Within,* p. 25.
40. John E. C. Flux, "World Distribution," in *The European Rabbit: History and Biology of a Successful Colonizer,* ed. H. V. Thompson and C. M. King (Oxford, UK: Oxford University Press, 2003), p. 9.
41. Friedmann, *Bestiary,* pp. 286–287.
42. Qtd. in Baxandall, *Painting,* p. 43.
43. Klingender, *Animals,* p. 444.
44. Ibid., p. 480.
45. Joan Bennett Lloyd, *African Animals in Renaissance Literature and Art* (Oxford, UK: Clarendon, 1971), p. 49.
46. Baxandall, *Painting,* p. 12.
47. For gazelles, see Lloyd, *African Animals,* pp. 55–56.
48. W. N. Howe, *Animal Life in Italian Painting* (London: George Allen and Company, 1912), p. 88 n.
49. Leon Battista Alberti, *On Painting,* trans. J. R. Spencer (New Haven, CT: Yale University Press, 1970); facs., http://www.noteaccess.com/Texts/Alberti/index.htm, pp. 52–53.
50. Baxandall, *Painting,* pp. 17–18.
51. Hans Belting, *Hieronymus Bosch "Garden of Earthly Delights"* (Munich: Prestel, 2002), p. 26.
52. Arianne Faber Kolb, *Jan Brueghel the Elder: The Entry of the Animals into Noah's Ark* (Los Angeles: The J. Paul Getty Museum, 2005), p. 1.
53. *Aberdeen Bestiary,* fol. 46v.
54. Dürer's wife was given a small green parrot (Eisler, *Animals,* p. 268).
55. Friedmann, *Bestiary,* p. 281.
56. Personal communication, Professor J. Rising, Department of Zoology, University of Toronto. February 6, 2006.
57. Friedmann, *Bestiary,* p. 281.
58. Jack Turner, *Spice, the History of a Temptation* (London: HarperPerennial, 2004), p. 18.

59. White, *Beasts,* p. 60.

60. Patrik Reuterswärd, *The Visible and Invisible in Art: Essays in the History of Art* (Vienna: IRSA, 1991), p. 211.

61. Qtd. in Keith Thomas, *Man and the Natural World* (London: Allen Lane, 1983), pp. 107–108.

62. Cats were considered of "base nature" (Thomas, *Natural World,* p. 58); see Friedmann, *Bestiary,* p. 162.

63. Howe, *Animal Life,* p. 6, n. 6.

64. Ibid., p. 91.

65. *Vanessa atalanta,* the Red Admiral, is misidentified as the peacock butterfly by Luke Syson and Dillian Gordon (*Pisanello: Painter to the Renaissance Court* [London: National Gallery Company, 2001], illus. 3.21); personal communication, Peter Hall. January 15, 2006.

66. Friedmann, *Bestiary,* p. 277.

67. Syson and Gordon, *Pisanello,* p. 22.

68. Ibid., p. 188.

69. Eisler, *Animals,* p. 43.

70. Lynn White Jr., "Natural Science and Naturalistic Art in the Middle Ages," *American Historical Review* 52, no. 3 (1947): 428.

71. Eisler, *Animals,* p. 244.

72. Baxandall, *Painting,* p. 119.

73. Kolb, *Breughel,* p. 2.

74. The research for this essay was made possible by the Web Gallery of Art (www. wga.hu). I am deeply grateful to its creators, Dr. Emil Krén and Dániel Marx.

BIBLIOGRAPHY

Abbott, W. *A Bibliography of Oliver Cromwell*. Cambridge, MA: Harvard University Press, 1929.

Abel, W. *Agrarkrisen und Agrakunjunktur in Mitteleuropa vom 13. bis zum 19. Jahrhundert*. Berlin: Paul Pary, 1935.

Aberdeen Bestiary, Aberdeen University Library MS 24. Facs., http://www.abdn.ac.uk/bestiary/index.hti.

Ackerman, J. S. "The Involvement of Artists in Renaissance Science." In *Science and the Arts in the Renaissance*, edited by J. W. Shirley and F. D. Hoeniger, pp. 92–129. Washington, DC: The Folger Shakespeare Library, 1985.

Ackerman, J. S. "Early Renaissance 'Naturalism' and Scientific Illustration." In *The Natural Sciences and the Arts: Aspects of Interaction from Renaissance to the 20th Century*, pp. 1–17. Stockholm: Almqvist and Wiksell International, 1985.

Acosta, J. de. *Historia natural y moral de las Indias*. Barcelona, 1591.

Acosta, J. de. *Natural and Moral History of the Indies*. Translated by F. M. Lopez-Morillas. Durham, NC: Duke University Press, 2002.

Adams, T. *The Blacke Devil or the Apostate*. London, 1615.

Adams, T. *Five Sermons Preached Vpon Sundry Especiall Occasions*. London, 1626.

Aelian. *Ex Aeliani historia per P. Gyllium latini facti ... libri XVI. De vi & natura animalium*. Paris, 1533.

Agricola, G. *De animantibus subterraneis liber* [Basel], 1549.

Aguiriano, B. "Le cheval et le depart en aventure dans les romans de Chretien de Troyes." In *Le cheval dans le monde mediéval*, pp. 11–27.

Aguiriano, B. "Gauvain, les femmes et le cheval." In *Le cheval dans le monde mediéval*, pp. 28–41.

Albala, K. *Eating Right in the Renaissance*. Berkeley: University of California Press, 2002.

Alberti, L. B., *On Painting*. Translated by J. R. Spencer. New Haven, CT: Yale University Press, 1970. Facs., http://www.noteaccess.com/Texts/Alberti/index.htm.

Aldrovandi, U. *Ornithologiae, hoc est de avibus historiae libri XII*. Bologna, 1599.

Aldrovandi, U. *Ornithologiae, hoc est de avibus historiae libri XII*. Bologna, 1681.

Allaby, M., ed. *Oxford Dictionary of Natural History*. Oxford, UK: Oxford University Press, 1985.

Allen, D. C. *Image and Meaning: Metaphoric Traditions in Renaissance Poetry*. Baltimore: Johns Hopkins Press, 1968.

Andrews, M. *Landscape and Western Art*. Oxford, UK: Oxford University Press, 1999.

Arber, A. *Herbals, Their Origin and Evolution: A Chapter in the History of Botany (1470–1670)*. Cambridge, UK: Cambridge University Press, 1986.

Aristotle. *De animalibus [...] interprete Theodoro Gaza*. Venice, 1476.

Aristotle. *Parts of Animals*. Translated by A. L. Peck. London: Heinemann, 1961.

Aristotle. *Historia Animalium*. Translated by D'Arcy Wentworth Thompson. Oxford, UK: Clarendon, 1910. Facs., http://etext.lib.virginia.edu/toc/modeng/public/AriHian.html.

Ashworth, W. B. "The Persistent Beast: Recurring Images in Early Zoological Illustration." In *The Natural Sciences and the Arts: Aspects of Interaction from Renaissance to the 20th Century*, pp. 46–66. Stockholm: Almqvist and Wiksell International, 1985.

Astley, J. *The Art of Riding*, 1584. Facs., Amsterdam: Da Capo, 1968.

Aubigné, A. d'. *Histoire universelle*. Edited by A. du Ruble. Paris: Remouard, 1893.

Augustine, St. *The City of God*. Translated by Rev. March Dods. Edinburgh: T&T Clark, Wm. B. Eerdmans, 1886. Facs., http://etext.lib.virginia.edu/toc/modeng/public/AugCity.html.

Aussy, P. J. B. Le Grand d'. *Histoire de la vie privé des français*. Paris: SenS, 1999.

Azurara, G. E. de. *The Chronicle of the Discovery and Conquest of Guinea*. Translated by C. R. Beazley and E. Prestage. London: Hakluyt Society, 1896.

Bacon, F. *Francis Bacon: A Selection of His Works*. Edited by S. Warhaft. New York: Odyssey, 1965.

Baehrel, R. *Une Croissance: La Basse-Provence Rurale: fin XVIe siècle–1789*. Paris: S.E.V.P.E.N, 1961.

Baillie-Grohman, W. A. *Sport in Art: An Iconography of Sport during Four Hundred Years from the Beginning of the Fifteenth to the End of the Eighteenth Centuries*. New York: Benjamin Blom, 1925.

Balavoine, C. "Le statut de l'image dans les livres emblématiques en France de 1580 à 1630." In *L'automne de la Renaissance*, edited by J. Lafond and A. Stegmann, pp. 163–178. Paris: Vrin, 1981.

Balme, D. M. "Aristotle's Use of Division and Differentiae." In *Philosophical Issues in Aristotle's Biology*, edited by A. Gotthelf and J. Lennox, pp. 69–89. Cambridge, UK: Cambridge University Press, 1987.

Balme, D. M. "The Place of Biology in Aristotle's Philosophy." In Gotthelf and Lennox, *Philosophical Issues in Aristotle's Biology*, pp. 9–20. Cambridge, UK: Cambridge University Press, 1987.

Barbera, G. *Antonello da Messina, Sicily's Renaissance Master*. New York: The Metropolitan Museum of Art / New Haven, CT: Yale University Press, 2005.

Baret, M. *An Hipponomie or the Vineyard of Horsemanship*. London, 1618.

Bäumer-Schleinkofer, Ä. "Die Enzyklopädien als Etablierung des Forschungsgebiets Zoologie in der Renaissance." In *Gattungen wissenschaftlicher Literatur in der Antike*, edited by W. Kullmann, J. Althoff, and M. Asper, pp. 141–159. Tübingen: Gunter Narr, 1998.

Baxandall, M. *Painting and Experience in Fifteenth-Century Italy: A Primer in the Social History of Pictorial Style*. Oxford, UK: Oxford University Press, 1988.

Beadle, R. "Crab's Pedigree." In *English Comedy,* edited by M. Cordner, P. Holland, and J. Kerrigan, pp. 12–35. Cambridge, UK: Cambridge University Press, 1994.

Beard, T. *The Theatre of Gods Iudgements.* London, 1597.

Bedini, S. *The Pope's Elephant.* Nashville: J. S. Sanders and Co., 1998.

Beer, J. "Duel of Bestiaries." In *Beasts and Birds of the Middle Ages: The Bestiary and Its Legacy,* edited by W. B. Clark and M. T. McMunn, pp. 96–105. Philadelphia: University of Pennsylvania Press, 1989.

Bell, T. *The Speculation of Vsurie.* London, 1596.

Belon, P. *L'histoire naturelle des estranges poissons marins, avec la vraie peincture et description du Daulphin, et de plusieurs autres de son espece.* Paris, 1551.

Belon, P. *Les observations de plusieurs singularitez et choses memorables, trouvées en Grece, Asie, Judée, Egypte, Arabie, et autres pays estranges, redigées en trois livres.* Paris, 1553.

Belon, P. *De aquatilibus Libri duo, cum eiconibus* [sic] *ad vivam ipsorum effigiem, quoad ejus fieri potuit, expressis.* Paris, 1553.

Belon, P. *La nature et diversité des poissons avec leurs pourtraicts, representez au plus pres du naturel.* Paris, 1555.

Belon, P. *L'histoire de la nature des oyseaux avec leurs descriptions, et naïfs portraicts retirez du naturel.* Paris, 1555.

Belon, P. *Les observations de plusieurs singularitez et choses memorables, trouvées en Grece, Asie, Judée, Egypte, Arabie, et autres pays estranges.* Anvers, 1555.

Belon, P. *L'histoire de la nature des oyseaux avec leurs descriptions, et naïfs portraicts retirez du naturel.* Edited by P. Glardon. Genève: Droz, 1997.

Belon, P. *L'énigme de la chronique de Pierre Belon. Avec édition critique du manuscrit Arsenal 4651.* Edited by M. Barsi. Milan: Edizioni Universitarie di Lettere Economia Diritto, 2001.

Belting, H. *Hieronymus Bosch "Garden of Earthly Delights."* Munich: Prestel, 2002.

Beretta, I. *Illustration and Representation: Botany in the Renaissance.* In *Immagini per conoscere. Dal Rinascimento alla Rivoluzione scientifica,* edited by F. Meroi and C. Pogliano, pp. 43–60. Florence: Olschki, 2001.

Bergman, C. *Orion's Legacy: A Cultural History of Man as Hunter.* New York: Dutton, 1996.

[Berners, J.] *The Boke of Saint Albans.* 1486. Facs., Amsterdam: Da Capo, 1969.

Berry, E. I. *Shakespeare and the Hunt: A Cultural and Social Study.* Cambridge, UK: Cambridge University Press, 2001.

Berry, R. *Shakespeare and the Awareness of the Audience.* London: Macmillan, 1985.

Bestiary, being an English Version of the Bodleian Library, Oxford M.S. Bodley 764. Translated by R. Barber. Woodbridge, UK: Boydell, 1993.

Bianchi, L. "Una caduta senza declino? Considerazioni sulla crisi dell'aristotelismo fra Rinascimento ed età moderna." In *Studi sull'Aristotelismo del Rinascimento,* edited by F. Dominguez, R. Imbach, T. Pindl, and P. Walter, pp. 133–172. Padua: Il Poligrafo, 2003.

The Bible in Englyshe [the "Great Bible"], Rouen, 1566.

The Bible ["Geneva" version], London, 1616.

Bise, G. *Medieval Hunting Scenes.* Fribourg: Editions Minerva, 1978.

Blundeville, T. *The Arte of Rydynge.* London, ca. 1560.

Blundeville, T. *The Fower Chiefyst Offices belongyng to Horsemanshippe.* London, 1565.

Blundeville, T. *The Arte of Ryding and Breakinge Great Horses.* 1560. Facs., Amsterdam: Da Capo, 1969.

Boaistuau, P. *Certaine Secrete Wonders of Nature.* London, 1569.

Boas, G. *The Happy Beast in French Literature in the Seventeenth Century.* Baltimore: Johns Hopkins University Press, 1933.

Boas, G. "Theriophily." In *Dictionary of the History of Ideas: Studies of Selected Pivotal Ideas,* edited by P. P. Wiener, vol. 4, pp. 384–389. New York: Charles Scribner's Sons, 1973.

Bock, H. *De stirpium maxime earum quae in Germania nostra nascuntur, usitatis nomenclaturis [...] ac facultatibus, commentariorum libri tres, germanica primum lingua conscripti, nunc in Latinam conversi.* Translated by D. Kyber. Strasbourg, 1552.

Boehrer, B. *Shakespeare among the Animals: Nature and Society in the Drama of Early Modern England.* New York: Palgrave, 2002.

Boehrer, B. *Parrot Culture: Our 2500-Year-Long Fascination with the World's Most Talkative Bird.* Philadelphia: University of Pennsylvania Press, 2004.

Boehrer, B. "The Parrot-Eaters: Psittacophagy in the Renaissance and Beyond." *Gastronomica* 4, no. 3 (Summer 2004): 46–59.

Bolton, R. "Definition and Scientific Method in Aristotle's *Posterior Analytics* and *Generation of Animals.*" In Gotthelf and Lennox, *Philosophical Issues,* pp. 120–166.

The Book of Beasts, being a Translation from a Latin Bestiary of the Twelfth Century. Translated by T. H. White. 1954. Reprint, New York: Dover, 1984.

Borde, A. *The First Boke of the Introduction of Knowledge.* London, 1542.

Bowden, P. J. "Agricultural Prices, Farm Profits, and Rents." In *The Agrarian History of England and Wales, IV, 1500–1640,* edited by J. Thirsk, pp. 593–695. Cambridge, UK: Cambridge University Press, 1967.

Bowden, P. J. *The Wool Trade of Tudor and Stuart England.* London: Frank Cass, 1971.

Braudel, F. *Civilization & Capitalism 15th.–18th. Century, I, The Structures of Everyday Life.* London: Collins, 1981.

Braunstein, P. "Resaux Familiaux, Resaux D'Affaires en Pays D'Empire: Les Facteurs de Societés." In *Le Négoce International XIIIe–XXe siècle,* edited by F. M. Crouzet, pp. 23–34. Paris: Economica, 1989.

Brown, C. "Bestiary Lessons on Pride and Lust." In Hassig, *Mark of the Beast,* pp. 53–70.

Brown, P. "Cull 'Will Wipe Out Cormorants,'" *The Guardian,* September 17, 2004. http://www.guardian.co.uk/conservation/story/0,13369,1306774,00.html.

Brunfels, O. *Herbarum vivae eicones ad naturam imitationem, summa cum diligentia et artificio effigiatae, una cum effectibus earundem, in gratiam veteris illius, et jamjam renascentis Herbariae Medicinae.* Strasburg, 1530–1536.

Burckhardt, J. *The Civilization of the Renaissance in Italy.* Translated by S. G. C. Middlemore. 2 vols. New York: Harper Brothers, 1958.

Cabral, P. *The Voyage of Pedro Alvares Cabral to Brazil and India.* Edited and translated by W. B. Greenlee. London: Hakluyt Society, 1938.

Cadamosto, A. da. *The Voyages of Cadamosto and Other Documents on Western Africa in the Second Half of the Fifteenth Century.* Translated by G. R. Crone. London: The Hakluyt Society, 1937.

Caius, J. *Of Englishe Dogges.* Translated by A. Fleming. London, 1576.

Caius, J. *Of Englishe Dogges* [Translated by A. Fleming.] 1576. Facs., Amsterdam: Da Capo, 1969.

Caius, J. *Of English Dogs.* Translated by A. Fleming. Alton, UK: Beech, 1993.

Calendar of State Papers Domestic, 1547–1580.

Calendar of State Papers Venetian, 2, 1509–1519.

Calendar of State Papers Venetian, 3, 1520–1526.

Camille, M. "Bestiary or Biology? Aristotle's Animals in Oxford, Merton College, MS 271." In *Aristotle's Animals in the Middle Ages and Renaissance,* edited by C. Steel, G. Guldentops, and P. Beullens, pp. 355–396. Leuven, Belgium: Leuven University Press, 1999.

Carbourdin, G. *Terre et Hommes en Lorraine [1550–1635]: Toulouse et Comté de Vaudément.* Nancy, France: University of Nancy Press, 1977.

Cartmill, M. *A View to a Death in the Morning: Hunting and Nature through History.* Cambridge, MA: Harvard University Press, 1993.

[Casas, B. de las.] *The Log of Christopher Columbus.* Translated by R. H. Fuson. Camden, ME: International Marine Publishing, 1992.

Castiglione, B. *The Book of the Courtier.* Translated by G. Bull. Harmondsworth, UK: Penguin, 1967.

Castor, G. *Pléiade Poetics: A Study in Sixteenth-Century Thought and Terminology.* Cambridge, UK: Cambridge University Press, 1964.

Cave, T. *The Cornucopian Text: Problems of Writing in the French Renaissance.* Oxford, UK: Clarendon, 1979.

Cavendish, W. *A New Method and Extraordinary Invention to Dress Horses.* London, 1667.

Cerasano, S. P. "The Master of the Bears in Art and Enterprise." *Medieval and Renaissance Drama in England* 5 (1991): 195–209.

Cervantes, M. de. *Don Quixote.* Translated by P. Motteux. New York: Airmont, 1967.

Chambers, E. K. *The Elizabethan Stage.* 4 vols. Oxford, UK: Clarendon, 1923.

Chapman, G., J. Marston, and B. Jonson. *Eastward Ho!* London, 1605.

Charles, D. "Natural Kinds and Natural History." In *Biologie, logique et métaphysique chez Aristote,* edited by D. Devereux and P. Pellegrin, pp. 145–167. Paris: Editions du CNRS, 1990.

Chaucer, G. *The Riverside Chaucer.* General editor L. D. Benson. Boston: Houghton Mifflin, 1987.

Cheny, J. *A Historical List of All Horse-Matches Run.* London, 1739.

Le cheval dans le monde médiéval. Aix-en-Provence: Centre Universitaire d'Etudes at de Recherches Médiévales d'Aix, 1992.

Churchyard, T. *Churchyards Challenge.* London, 1593.

Cipolla, C. M. *Before the Industrial Revolution: European Society and Economy, 1000–1700.* London: Methuen, 1976.

Clark, W. B., and M. T. McMunn, eds. *Beasts and Birds of the Middle Ages: The Bestiary and Its Legacy.* Philadelphia: University of Pennsylvania Press, 1989.

Clutton-Brock, J. *A Natural History of Domesticated Mammals.* Cambridge, UK: Cambridge University Press, 1999.

Coczian-Szentpeteri, E. "L'évolution du coche ou l'histoire d'une invention hongroise." In *Voitures, chevaux et attelages du XVIe au XIXe Siècle,* edited by D. Reytier, pp. 85–87. Paris: Association pour Académie d'Art Equestre de Versailles, 2000.

Cogan, M. "Rodolphus Agricola and the Semantic Revolutions of the History of Invention." *Rhetorica* 2 (1984): 163–194.

Colliot, R. "Les chevaux symboliques *d'Amadas et Ydoine.*" In *Le cheval dans le monde médiéval,* pp. 93–113.

Coomes, O. "Cormorant Fishing in Southwestern China: A Traditional Fishery under Siege." *Geographical Review* 92 (2002): 597–603.

"Cormorantbusters." http://www.cormorantbusters.co.uk.

Cortés, H. *Fernando Cortés his five letters of Relation to the Emperor Charles V.* Translated by F. A. MacNutt. 2 vols. Cleveland: Arthur H. Clark Co., 1908.

Cottingham, J. *Descartes.* Oxford, UK: Oxford University Press, 1998.

Cranz, F. E. *A Bibliography of Aristotle's Editions, 1501–1600.* Revised by C. B. Schmitt. Baden Baden: Körner, 1984.

Cretensis, D. F. *In libros Aristotelis De partibus animalium commentarius primus.* Venice, 1574.

Crowley, R. *One and Thyrtye Epigrams.* London, 1550.

Cumbria R. O. (Kendal). *WQ/01 Order Book 1669–1696.*

Cummins, J. *The Hound and the Hawk: The Art of Medieval Hunting.* New York: St. Martin's Press, 1988.

Cuvier, G. *Histoire des sciences naturelles depuis leur origine jusqu'à nos jours, deuxième partie, comprenant les 16e et 17e siècles.* Tome deuxième. Paris: Fortin, Masson et Cie, 1841. Reprint, Brussels: Culture et Civilization, 1969.

Dando, J. *Maroccus Exstaticus, or Bankes Bay Horse in a Trance.* London, 1595.

Daniel, S. *The Queenes Arcadia.* In *Certaine Small Workes.* London, 1607.

Daston, L., and K. Park. *Wonders and the Order of Nature, 1150–1750.* New York: Zone, 1998.

Davenant, W. *The Works of Sir William Davenant.* London, 1673.

Davies, M. "Making Sense of Pliny in the Quattrocento." *Renaissance Studies* 9 (1995): 240–257.

Davis, R. H. C. "The Medieval Warhorse." In *Horses in European Economic History: A Preliminary Canter,* edited by F. L. M. Thompson, pp. 5–7. Reading, UK: The British Agricultural Society, 1983.

Davis, R. H. C. *The Medieval Warhorse.* London: Thames and Hudson, 1989.

Day, A. *The English Secretarie Wherein is Contayned a Perfect Method, for the Inditing of all Manner of Epistles and Familial Letters.* London, 1586.

De Maddalena, A. "Rural Europe 1500–1750." In *The Fontana Economic History of Europe, II, The Sixteenth and Seventeenth Centuries,* edited by C. Cipolla, pp. 273–353. Hassocks, UK: Harvester Press, 1977.

Demonet, M.-L. *Les voix du signe. Nature et origine du langage à la Renaissance (1480–1580).* Paris: Champion, 1992.

Desfayes, M. *A Thesaurus of Bird Names: Etymology of European Lexis through Paradigms.* 2 vols. Sion, Switzerland: Museum of Natural History, 1998.

Díaz, B. *The Conquest of New Spain.* Translated by J. M. Cohen. London: Penguin, 1963.

Dickenson, V. *Drawn from Life: Science and Art in the Portrayal of the New World.* Toronto: University of Toronto Press, 1998.

Doran, S., ed. *Elizabeth: The Exhibition at the National Maritime Museum.* London: Chatto and Windus, 2003.

Drummond, W. *Flowres of Sion.* London, 1623.

Dubos, R. *Beast or Angel? Choices That Make Us Human.* New York: Charles Scribner's Sons, 1974.

Dyer, C. *Standards of Living in the Later Middle Ages: Social Change in England c. 1200–1520.* Cambridge, UK: Cambridge University Press, 1989.

Dyer, D. "Alternative Agriculture: Goats in Medieval England." In *People, Landscape and Alternative Agriculture,* edited by R. W. Hoyle. Reading, UK: British Agricultural History Society, 2001.

Edward of Norwich. *The Master of Game*. Edited by W. A. Baillie-Grohman and F. Baillie-Grohman. 1909. Reprint, Philadelphia: University of Pennsylvania Press, 2005.

Edwards, P. R. "The Farming Economy of North-East Shropshire in the Seventeenth Century." PhD diss. Oxford University, 1976.

Edwards, P. R. *The Horse Trade of Tudor and Stuart England*. Cambridge, UK: Cambridge University Press, 1988.

Edwards, P. R. *Horse and Man in Early Modern England: A Special Relationship*. London: Hambledon, forthcoming.

Eisler, C. *Dürer's Animals*. Washington, DC: Smithsonian Institution, 1991.

Elphick, J. *Birds: The Art of Ornithology*. London: Scriptum Editions, 2004.

Elyot, Sir T. *The Boke named the Governour*. London, 1531.

Elyot, Sir T. *The Book named The Governor*. Edited by S. E. Lehmberg. New York: Dutton, 1962.

Estienne, C., and J. Liébault. *L'Agriculture et Maison Rustique*. Paris, 1598.

Evans, E. P. *The Criminal Prosecution and Capital Punishment of Animals: The Lost History of Europe's Animal Trials*. 1906. Reprint, London: Faber and Faber, 1987.

Everitt, A. M. "The Marketing of Agricultural Produce." In Thirsk, *Agrarian History*, pp. 466–592.

Ferber, M. *A Dictionary of Literary Symbols*. Cambridge, UK: Cambridge University Press, 1999.

F[idge]., G. *The Great Eater of Grayes Inne, or The Life of Mr. Marriot the Cormorant*. London, 1652.

Finberg, H. P. R., gen. ed. *The Agrarian History of England and Wales*. 8 vols. Cambridge, UK: Cambridge University Press, 1967–1991.

Findlen, P. "Jokes of Nature and Jokes of Knowledge: The Playfulness of Scientific Discourse in Early Modern Europe." *Renaissance Quarterly* 43 (1990): 292–331.

The First Part of the Nature of a Woman Fitly Described in a Florentine Historie. London, 1596.

Fitzherbert, J. *Boke of Husbandrye*. London, 1523.

Flores, N. C., ed. *Animals in the Middle Ages: A Book of Essays*. New York: Garland, 1996.

Flux, J. E. C. "World Distribution." In *The European Rabbit: History and Biology of a Successful Colonizer*, edited by H. V. Thompson and C. M. King, pp. 8–21. Oxford, UK: Oxford University Press, 2003.

Folkingham, W. *Feudigraphia*. London, 1610.

Foucault, M. *The Order of Things*. New York: Vintage, 1973.

Fouilloy, Hugh of. *The Medieval Book of Birds: Hugh of Fouilloy's Aviarum*. Edited and translated by Willene B. Clark. Binghamton, UK: Medieval and Renaissance Texts and Studies, 1992.

Freeman, G. E., and F. H. Salvin. *Falconry: Its Claims, History, and Practice*. London: Longman, Green, Longman, and Roberts, 1859.

Friedmann, H. *A Bestiary for Saint Jerome: Animal Symbolism in European Religious Art*. Washington, DC: Smithsonian Institution, 1980.

Fuchs, L. *De historia stirpium commentarii insignes. Adjectis earundem vivis, et ad naturae imitationem artificiose expressis imaginibus*. Lyon, 1549.

Fuchs, L. *Commentaires tres excellens de l'hystoire des plantes, composez premierement en latin par Leonarth Fousch, medecin tres renommé* [trans. E. de Maignan]. Lyon, 1549.

Fuchs, L. *L'Histoire des plantes* [trans. G. Gueroult]. Lyon, 1550.

Fudge, E. *Perceiving Animals: Humans and Beasts in Early Modern English Culture.* New York: St. Martin's Press, 2000.

Fudge, E., ed. *Renaissance Beasts: Of Animals, Humans, and Other Wonderful Creatures.* Champaign: University of Illinois Press, 2004.

Fussell, G. E. *The Classical Tradition in West European Farming.* Newton Abbot, UK: David and Charles, 1972.

Garin, E. *L'homme de la Renaissance.* Paris: Seuil, 1990.

[Gascoigne, G.] *The Noble Art of Venerie or Hunting.* 1575. Facs., Oxford, UK: Oxford University Press, 1908.

Gaza, T. *In libros Aristotelis de animalibus [...] praefatio.* In *Aristotelis Libri omnes ad animalium cognitionem spectantes.* Venetiis, 1562. Facs., Frankfurt: Minerva, 1962.

George, W. *Animals and Maps.* Berkeley: University of California Press, 1969.

George, W., and B. Yapp. *The Naming of the Beasts: Natural History in the Medieval Bestiary.* London: Duckworth, 1991.

Gerbi, A. *Nature in the New World, from Christopher Columbus to Gonzalo Fernandez de Oviedo.* Translated by Jeremy Moyle. Pittsburgh: University of Pittsburgh Press, 1985.

Gerhold, D. "Packhorses and Wheeled Vehicles in England, 1550–1800." *Journal of Transport History,* 3rd ser. 14 (1993): 1–26.

Gerhold, D. *Carriers and Coachmasters: Trade and Travel before the Turnpikes.* Chichester, UK: Phillimore, 2005.

Gesner, C. *Historiae animalium, liber I, de quadrupedibus viviparis.* Zurich, 1551.

Gesner, C. *De libris a se editis epistola ad Guilielmum Turnerum, theologum et medicum excellentissimum in Anglia.* Zurich, 1551.

Gesner, C. *Historiae animalium, liber II, de quadrupedibus viviparis.* Zurich, 1554.

Gesner, C. *Historiae animalium, liber III, de quadrupedibus viviparis.* Zurich, 1555.

Gesner, C. *Historiae animalium, liber IV, de quadrupedibus viviparis.* Zurich, 1558.

Gesner, C. *Nomenclator Aquatilium animalium animantium. Icones Animalium aquatilium in mari et dulcibus aquis degentium.* Zurich, 1560.

Gesner, C. *Historiae animalium liber V. Historiae insectorum libellus.* Zurich, 1587.

Gilles, P. *Ex Aeliani historia per P. Gyllium latini facti ... libri XVI. De vi & natura animalium.* Paris, 1533.

Glardon, P. *L'histoire naturelle au XVIe siècle: regards, lectures et discours sur la nature à travers l'exemple de La nature et diversité des poissons de Pierre Belon (1555).* Thesis defended at the University of Lausanne, Faculty of Letters, 2005.

Gontier, T. *De l'homme à l'animal. Montaigne et Descartes ou les paradoxes de la philosophie moderne sur la nature des animaux,* p. 41. Paris: Vrin, 1998.

Goodall, D. M. *A History of Horse Breeding.* London: Robert Hale, 1977.

Grant, T. "White Bears in *Mucedorus, The Winter's Tale,* and *Oberon, the Fairy Prince.*" *Notes and Queries,* n.s. 48, no. 3 (September 2001): 311–313.

Grant, T. "Drama Queen: Thomas Heywood's *If You Know Not Me.*" In *The Myth of Elizabeth,* edited by S. Doran and T. S. Freeman, pp. 120–142. Basingstoke, UK: Palgrave, 2003.

Grant, T. *The Uses of Animals in Early Modern English Drama, 1558–1642.* Ph.D. thesis. University of Cambridge, 2001.

Greenblatt, S. *Marvelous Possessions: The Wonder of the New World.* Oxford, UK: Clarendon, 1991.

Greenblatt, S. *Will in the World: How Shakespeare Became Shakespeare*. New York: W. W. Norton, 2004.

Gregory, S. *The Cormorant*. London: Heinemann, 1986.

Griffith, E. "Banks, William (*fl.* 1591–1637)." In *Oxford Dictionary of National Biography*, edited by H. C. G. Matthew and B. Harrison. Oxford, UK: Oxford University Press, 2004. http://www.oxforddnb.com/view/article/1292.

Gurr, A. *The Shakespearean Stage 1574–1642*. Cambridge, UK: Cambridge University Press, 1992. Reprint, 1997.

Hahn, D. *The Tower Menagerie*. New York: Jeremy P. Tarcher / Penguin, 2003.

Hakluyt, R. *The Principal Navigations Voyages Traffiques and Discoveries of the English Nation*. 12 vols. New York: Macmillan, 1904.

Hands, R. *English Hawking and Hunting in The Boke of St. Albans, A facsimile edition of The Boke of St. Albans*. Oxford, UK: Oxford University Press, 1975.

Hariot, T. *A Brief and True Report of the New Found Land of Virginia*. 1588. Facs., Ann Arbor: Edwards Brothers, 1931.

Harrison, W. *The Description of England*. Edited by Georges Edelin. Ithaca, NY: Cornell University Press, 1968 / Washington, DC, and New York: Folger Shakespeare Library and Dover Publications, 1994.

Harting, J. E. *The Ornithology of Shakespeare*. London: John Van Voorst, 1871.

Harting, J. E. *British Animals Extinct within Historic Times*. Boston, 1880.

Hassig, D. *Medieval Bestiaries: Text, Image, Ideology*. Cambridge, UK: Cambridge University Press, 1995.

Hassig, D., ed. *The Mark of the Beast: The Medieval Bestiary in Art, Life, and Literature*. New York: Garland, 1999.

Hay, D. *Europe in the Fourteenth and Fifteenth Centuries*. London: Longman, 1966.

Hearne, V. *Adam's Task: Calling Animals by Name*. New York: HarperCollins, 1994.

Heaton, H. C., ed. *The Discovery of the Amazon According to the Account of Friar Gaspar de Carvajal and Other Documents*. Translated by B. Lee. New York: American Geographical Society, 1934.

Hebel, J. W., and H. H. Hudson. *Poetry of the English Renaissance 1509–1660*. New York: Appleton-Century Crofts, 1957.

Heresbach, C. *Foure Bookes of Husbandry*. Translated by B. Googe. London, 1577.

Hernandez, F. *Rerum Medicarum Novae Hispaniae Thesaurus*. Rome, 1651.

Herr, M. *Gründtlicher underricht, warhaffte und eygentliche beschreibung [...] aller vierfüssigen thier ...* Edited by G. E. Sollbach. Würzburg, Germany: Königshausen and Neumann, 1994.

"History of PWSRCAC and the *Exxon Valdez* Oil Spill." Prince William Sound Regional Citizens' Advisory Council. http://www.pwsrcac.org/about/history.html.

Holinshed, R. *History of England*. London, 1587.

The Holy Bible [the "Bishops'" version]. London, 1585.

The Holy Bible [the "Authorized"]. London, 1625.

Hopcroft, R. L. *Regions, Institutions, and Agrarian Change in European History*. Ann Arbor: University of Michigan Press, 1999.

Hore, J. P. *The History of Newmarket and the Annals of the Turf, III*. London: Baily, 1886.

Howe, W. N. *Animal Life in Italian Painting*. London: George Allen and Company, 1912.

Hoy, C., Introductions, Notes, and Commentaries to Texts in *The Dramatic Works of Thomas Dekker*. Edited by F. Bowers. 4 vols. Cambridge, UK: Cambridge University Press, 1980.

Hudson, H. W. *British Birds*. London: J. M. Dent, 1923.

Humfrey, P. *Carpaccio*. London: Chaucer Press, 2005.

Hutchinson, R. *The Last Days of Henry VIII*. London: Weidenfeld and Nicolson, 2005.

Hyland, A. *The Medieval Warhorse from Byzantium to the Crusades*. Conshohoken, PA: Combined Books, 1994.

Inventory of King Henry VIII, 1547, Society of Antiquaries, MS 129.

Jackson, MacD. P. "Shakespeare's *Richard II* and the Anonymous *Thomas of Woodstock*." *Medieval and Renaissance Drama in England* 14 (2001): 17–65.

Jacquart, J. "French Agriculture in the Seventeenth Century." In *Essays in European Economic History 1500–1800*, edited by P. Earle, pp. 165–184. Oxford, UK: Clarendon Press, 1974.

James I, King of England. *The Kings Majesties Declaration to His Subjects, concerning Lawfull Sports to be Used*. London, 1618.

James I, King of England. *The Political Works of James I*. Edited by C. H. McIlwain. Cambridge, MA: Harvard University Press, 1918.

Jardine, L. *Worldly Goods: A New History of the Renaissance*. New York: W. W. Norton, 1996.

Jerdan, W., ed. *Rutland Papers*. London: Camden Society, 1842.

Joachimsen, P. *"Loci communes. Eine Untersuchung zur Geistesgeschichte des Humanismus und der Reformation." Luther-Jahrbuch* 8 (1926): 27–97.

Johnsgard, P. A. *Cormorants, Darters, and Pelicans of the World*. Washington, DC: Smithsonian Institution, 1993.

Jones, P. "Medieval Agrarian Society in Its Prime." In *The Cambridge Economic History of Europe, I, The Agrarian Life of the Middle Ages*, edited by M. M. Postan, pp. 341–431. Cambridge: Cambridge University Press, 1971.

Jones, V. "The Phoenix and the Resurrection." In Hassig, *Mark of the Beast*, pp. 99–115.

Jonson, B. *Ben Jonson*. Edited by C. H. Herford, P. Simpson, and E. Simpson. 11 vols. Oxford, UK: Clarendon, 1925–1952.

Jonson, B. *Bartholomew Fair*. Edited by G. R. Hibbard. London: Ernest Benn, 1977.

Jonson, B. *Every Man Out of His Humour*. Edited by H. Ostovich. Manchester, UK: Manchester University Press, 2001.

Jovius, P. *De Romanis Piscibus libellus ad Ludovicum Borbonium Cardinalem amplissimum*. Rome, 1524.

Jovius, P. *De Vita Leonis*. Florence, 1548.

Kamen, H. *European Society 1500–1700*. London: Unwin Hyman, 1984.

Keen, P. *Description of England*. London, 1599.

Kessler, E. *"Humanismus und Naturwissenschaft. Zur Legitimation neuzeitlicher Naturwissenschaft durch den Humanismus." Zeitschrift für Philosophische Forschung* 33 (1979): 23–40.

King Edward III. Edited by Giorgio Melchiori. Cambridge, UK: Cambridge University Press, 1998.

Klein, J. *The Mesta: A Study in Spanish Economic History, 1273–1836*. Cambridge, MA: Harvard University Press, 1920.

Klingender, F. *Animals in Art and Thought to the End of the Middle Ages*. Edited by E. Antal and J. Harthan. Cambridge, MA: MIT Press, 1971.

Kolb, A. F. *Jan Brueghel the Elder: The Entry of the Animals into Noah's Ark*. Los Angeles: The J. Paul Getty Museum, 2005.

Lambarde, W. *A Perambulation of Kent*. London, 1576.

Langdon, J. *Horses, Oxen and Technological Innovation: The Use of Draught Animals in English Farming from 1066–1500*. Cambridge, UK: Cambridge University Press, 1986.

Laroque, F. *Shakespeare's Festive World*. Translated by J. Lloyd. Cambridge, UK: Cambridge University Press, 1991.

Laufer, B. *The Domestication of the Cormorant in China and Japan*. Chicago: Field Museum of Natural History, 1931.

Lawrence, W. J. "Characteristics of Platform-Stage Spectacle." In *Pre-Restoration Stage Studies*, pp. 251–276. Cambridge, MA: Harvard University Press, 1927.

Lawrence, W. J. "Shakespeare's Use of Animals." *The Dublin Magazine* 7 (January–March, 1937): 16-25.

Lecercle, F. "Arts et littérature." In *Précis de littérature française du XVIe siècle. La Renaissance*, edited by R. Aulotte, pp. 333–369. Paris: Presses Universitaires de France, 1991.

Leff, M. C. "The Topics of Argumentative Invention in Latin Rhetorical Theory from Cicero to Boethius." *Rhetorica* 1 (1983): 23–44.

Leland, J. *Joannis Lelandi antiquarii. De rebus Britannicis collectanea*. 6 vols. London, 1770.

Léry, J. de. *Histoire d'un voyage fait en la terre de Bresil, autrement dit Amerique. Contenant la navigation et choses remarquables, veuës sur la mer par l'aucteur ...* Edited by J.-C. Morisot. Geneva: Droz, 1975.

Léry, J. de. *History of a Voyage to the Land of Brazil*. Translated by J. Whatley. Berkeley: University of California Press, 1990.

L'Escluse, C. de. *Exoticorum libri decem, quibus Animalium, Plantarum, Aromatum, aliorumque peregrinorum fructuum historiae describuntur. Item Petri Belonii Observationes, eodem Carolo Clusio interprete* [Antwerp], 1605.

A Letter to Mr. Marriot from a Friend of His: Wherein His Name Is Redeemed. London, 1652.

Letters & Papers of Henry VIII, 1, ii, 1513–1514.

Letters & Papers of Henry VIII, 3, ii, 1522–1523.

Letters & Papers of Henry VIII, 17, 1542.

Letters & Papers of Henry VIII, 19, 1544.

Levin, H. *Shakespeare and the Revolution of the Times*, pp. 121–130. New York: Oxford University Press, 1976.

Lloyd, G. E. R. "The Development of Aristotle's Theory of the Classification of Animals." *Phronesis* 1 (1961): 59–81.

Lloyd, G. E. R. *Aristotle: The Growth and Structure of His Thought*. Cambridge, UK: Cambridge University Press, 1986.

Lloyd, J. B. *African Animals in Renaissance Literature and Art*. Oxford, UK: Clarendon, 1971.

Loch, S. *The Royal Horse of Europe*. London: J. A. Allen, 1986.

Loisel, G. *Histoire des menageries de l'antiquite a nos jours*. 3 vols. Paris: Henri Laurens, 1912.

Lonitzer (Lonicerus), A. *Naturalis historiae opus novum in quo tractatur de natura et viribus arborum, fruticum, herbarum, Animantiumque terrestrium, volatilium et aquatilium ...* Frankfurt, 1551.

Look about You. London, 1600.

Louis, P. "Le mot ἱστορία chez Aristote." *Revue de philologie, de littérature et d'histoire anciennes* 29 (1955): 39–44.

Lovejoy, A. O., and G. Boas. *Primitivism and Related Ideas in Antiquity.* Baltimore: Johns Hopkins University Press, 1935. Reprint, 1997.

Lowry, M. *The World of Aldus Manutius: Business and Scholarship in Renaissance Venice.* Oxford, UK: Blackwell, 1979.

Lupton, T. *A Moral and Pitiefvl Comedie, Intituled, All for Money.* London, 1578.

Lyly, J. *Euphues and His England Containing His Voyage and His Aduentures.* London, 1580.

MacInnes, I. "Mastiffs and Spaniels: Gender and Nation in the English Dog." *Textual Practice* 17, no. 1 (2003): 21–40.

Mack. P. *Renaissance Argument. Valla and Agricola in the Traditions of Rhetoric and Dialectic.* Leiden, Belgium: E. J. Brill, 1993.

Mack. P. "*La fonction descriptive de* l'Histoire des animaux *d'Aristote.*" *Phronesis* 31 (1986): 148–166.

Maclean, H. "Time and Horsemanship in Shakespeare's Histories." *University of Toronto Quarterly* 35 (1965–1966): 229–245.

Maclean, I. *Logic, Signs and Nature in the Renaissance: The Case of Learned Medicine.* Cambridge, UK: Cambridge University Press, 2002.

Maclean, I. "White Crows, Graying Hair, and Eyelashes: Problems for Natural Historians in the Reception of Aristotelian Logic and Biology from Pomponazzi to Bacon." In *Historia: Empiricism and Erudition in Early Modern Europe,* edited by G. Pomata and N. G. Siraisi, pp. 147–179. Cambridge, MA: MIT Press, 2005.

Madden, D. H. *The Diary of Master William Silence: A Study of Shakespeare and of Elizabethan Sport.* New York: Longmans, Green, 1903.

Madden, D. H. *A Chapter of Mediaeval History: The Fathers of the Literature of Field Sport and Horses.* Port Washington, NY: Kennikat, 1924.

Malcolmson, R. W. *The English Pig: A History.* London: Hambledon, 1998.

Manning, R. B. *Hunters and Poachers: A Cultural and Social History of Unlawful Hunting in England, 1485–1640.* Oxford, UK: Clarendon, 1993.

Manwood, J. *A Treatise of the Lawes of the Forest.* 1598. Facs., Amsterdam: Theatrum Orbis Terrarum, 1976.

Marienstras, R. *New Perspectives on the Shakespearean World.* Translated by Janet Lloyd. Cambridge, UK: Cambridge University Press, 1985.

"Marine World." Marine Conservation Society. http://www.mcsuk.org/marine_world/marine_world.php?title = seabirds.

Markham, G. *Cavelarice.* London, 1607.

Markham, G. *Cheape and Good Husbandry.* London, 1614.

Markham, G. *Country Contentments.* 1615. Facs., Amsterdam: Da Capo, 1973.

Marston, J. *Histrio-mastix.* London, 1610.

Marston, J. *The Malcontent.* Edited by B. Harris. London: Ernest Benn, 1967.

Martyr, P. *De Orbe Novo: The Eight Decades of Peter Martyr D'Anghera.* Translated by F. A. MacNutt. 2 vols. 1912. Reprint, New York: Burt Franklin, 1970.

Mascall, L. *The Husbandrie Ordering and Gouernment of Poultrie.* London, 1581.

Mascall, L. *The First Booke of Cattell.* London, 1587.

Mascall, L. *The Second Booke, intreating the gouernment of Horses.* London, 1587.

Mascall, L. *The Third Booke intreating the Ordering of Sheep and Goates, Hogs and Dogs.* London, 1587.

Mate, M. "Pastoral Farming in South-East England in the Fifteenth Century." *Economic History Review,* 2nd ser. 40, no. 4 (1987): 523–36.

Mattioli, P. A. *Les Commentaires de M. P. André Matthiolus, medecin senois, sur les six livres de Pedacius Dioscoride Anazerbeen de la matiere Medicinale*. Translated by A. du Pinet. Lyon, 1605.

Mattioli, P. A. *Commentarii in sex libros Pedacii Dioscoridis Anazarbei de Medica materia* ... Venice, 1565.

Mattioli, P. A. *Commentaires de M. Pierre André Matthiole sur les six livres de Pedacius Dioscoride*. Translated by J. Desmoulins. Lyon, 1572.

Mauries, P. *Cabinets of Curiosities*. London: Thames and Hudson, 2002.

McMunn, M. T. "Bestiary Influences in Two Thirteenth-Century Romances." In Clark and McMunn, *Beasts and Birds*, pp. 134–150.

Mearns, B., and R. Mearns. *The Bird Collectors*. San Diego: Academic Press, 1998.

Meens, R. "Eating Animals in the Early Middle Ages: Classifying the Animal World and Building Group Identities." In *The Animal-Human Boundary*, edited by A. N. H. Creager and W. C. Jordan, pp. 3–28. Rochester, NY: University of Rochester Press, 2002.

Mellini, G. L., Ferrari, G. E., and Salmi, M. *The Grimani Breviary*. London: Thames and Hudson, 1972.

Merchant, W. M. *The Critical Idiom: Comedy*. London: Methuen, 1972.

Mezzalira, F. *Beasts and Bestiaries: The Representation of Animals from Prehistory to the Renaissance*. Turin: Umberto Allemandi and Co., 2001.

Middleton, T., and T. Dekker. *The Roaring Girl*. Edited by P. Mulholland. Manchester, UK: Manchester University Press, 1987.

Monfasani, J. "The Pseudo-Aristotelian *Problemata* and Aristotle's *De animalibus* in the Renaissance." In *Natural Particulars: Nature and the Disciplines in Renaissance Europe*, edited by A. Grafton and N. G. Siraisi, pp. 205–247. Cambridge MA: MIT Press, 1999.

Montaigne, M. de. *The Complete Essays of Montaigne*. Translated by D. M. Frame. Stanford, CA: Stanford University Press, 1943.

Montaigne, M. de. *Essais*. Paris: Éditions Garnier Frères, 1962.

Montaigne, M. de. *The Essayes of Montaigne*. Translated by John Florio. New York: Modern Library, n.d.

Mosley, C., ed. *Burke's Peerage*. 2 vols. Chicago: Fitzroy Dearborn, 1999.

Mullaney, S. "Shakespeare and the Liberties." *Encyclopaedia Britannica's Guide to Shakespeare*. 12 pars. April 23, 2006. http://www.britannia.com/shakespeare/article-9396031.

Munro, J. "Spanish Merino Wools and the *Nouvelles Draperies*: An Industrial Transformation in the Late Medieval Low Countries." *Economic History Review* 58, no. 3 (2005): 431–484.

Muratova, X. "Workshop Methods in English Late Twelfth-Century Illumination and the Production of Luxury Bestiaries." In Clark and McMunn, *Beasts and Birds*, pp. 53–68.

Naïs, H. *Les animaux dans la poésie française de la Renaissance*. Paris: n.p., 1961.

Nauert, C. G., Jr. "Humanists, Scientists, and Pliny: Changing Approaches to a Classical Author." *American Historical Review* 84 (1979): 72–85.

Nauert, C. G., Jr. "Caius Plinius Secundus." In *Catalogus translationum et commentariorum: Medieval and Renaissance Latin Translations and Commentaries*, edited by F. E. Cranz and P. O. Kristeller, vol. 4, pp. 297–422. Washington, DC: The Catholic University of America Press, 1980.

Neveux, H., et al. *Histoire de la France rurale, II, l'age classique 1340–1789.* Paris: Seuil, 1975.

Ní Dhuibne, E. *The Uncommon Cormorant.* Swords, Ireland: Poolbeg Press, 1990.

Nichols, J. *The Progresses and Public Processions of Queen Elizabeth.* 3 vols. 1823. Reprint, New York: Burt Franklin, n.d.

Nifo, A. *Expositiones in omnes Aristotelis libros: De historia animalium libri IX, De partibus animalium et earum causis libri IIII, ac De generatione animalium libri V.* Venice, 1546.

Norden, J. *Speculum Britanniae.* London, 1593.

Nutton, V. "The Rise of Medical Humanism: Ferrara, 1464–1555." *Renaissance Studies* 11 (1997): 2–19.

Odoni, C. *Aristotelis sparsae de animalibus sententiae in continuatam seriem ad propria capita revocatae nominaque secundum literarum ordinem disposita.* Bologna, 1651.

O'Flaherty, L. *The Short Stories of Liam O'Flaherty.* London: Jonathan Cape, 1948.

Ogilvie, B. "Natural History, Ethics, and Physico-Theology." In *Historia: Empiricism and Erudition in Early Modern Europe,* edited by G. Pomata and N. G. Siraisi, pp. 75–103. Cambridge, MA: MIT Press, 2005.

O'Malley, C. D. "John Caius." In *Dictionary of Scientific Biography,* vol. 3. New York: Charles Scribner's Sons, 1972.

Oppian. *Halieutica.* In *Oppian, Colluthus and Tryphiodorus.* Translated by A. W. Mair. London: William Heinemann, 1928.

Ortega y Gasset, J. *Meditations on Hunting.* Translated by H. B. Wescott. New York: Charles Scribner's Sons, 1972.

Oviedo, G. F. de. *Natural History of the West Indies [Sumario].* Translated by S. A. Stoudemire. Chapel Hill: University of North Carolina Press, 1959.

Pächt, O. *The Master of Mary of Burgundy.* London: Faber and Faber, 1948.

Patten, B. *The Sly Cormorant and the Fishes.* Harmondsworth, UK: Penguin, 1977.

Paynell, T. *The Moste Excellent and Pleasaunt Booke, Entituled: The Treasurie of Amadis of Fraunce.* London, 1572.

Pellegrin, P. *La classification des animaux chez Aristote. Statut de la biologie et unité de l'aristotélisme.* Paris: Les Belles Lettres, 1982.

Pellegrin, P. *Aristotle's Classification of Animals.* Berkeley: University of California Press, 1986.

Perfetti, S. "*Cultius atque integrius. Teodoro Gaza traduttore umanistico del* De partibus animalium." *Rinascimento,* 2nd ser. 35 (1995): 253–286.

Perfetti, S. "*Metamorfosi di una traduzione: Agostino Nifo revisore dei* De animalibus *gaziani.*" *Medioevo. Rivista di Storia della Filosofia Medievale* 22 (1996): 259–301.

Perfetti, S. "Three Different Ways of Interpreting Aristotle's *De Partibus Animalium:* Pietro Pomponazzi, Niccolo Leonio Tomeo and Agostino Nifo." In *Aristotle's Animals in the Middle Ages and Renaissance,* edited by C. Steel, G. Guldentops, and P. Beullens, pp. 297–316. Leuven, Belgium: Leuven University Press, 1999.

Perfetti, S. *Aristotle's Zoology and Its Renaissance Commentators (1521–1601).* Leuven, Belgium: Leuven University Press, 2000.

Perfetti, S. "*Giulio Cesare Scaligero commentatore e filosofo naturale tra Padova e Francia.*" In *La presenza dell'Aristotelismo padovano nella filosofia della prima modernità,* edited by G. Piaia, pp. 3–31. Rome / Padua: Antenore, 2002.

Perfetti, S. "How and When the Medieval Commentary Died Out: The Case of Aristotle's Zoological Writings." In *Il commento filosofico nell'Occidente latino (secoli*

XIII–XV), edited by G. Fioravanti, C. Leonardi, and S. Perfetti, pp. 429–443. Turnhout: Brepols, 2002.

Peterson, R. T., and G. Mountfort, and Hollom, P.A.D., *A Field Guide to the Birds of Britain and Europe.* London: Collins, 1974.

Phipson, E. *The Animal Lore of Shakespeare's Time.* London, 1883.

Pigafetta, A. "First Voyage around the World." In *Magellan's Voyage around the World: Three Contemporary Accounts,* edited and translated by C. E. Nowell. Evanston, IL: Northwestern University Press, 1962.

Pinon, L. *Livres de zoologie de la Renaissance: une anthologie.* Paris: Kincksieck, 1995.

Pinon, L. "Conrad Gesner and the Historical Depth of Renaissance Natural History." In *Historia: Empiricism and Erudition in Early Modern Europe,* edited by G. Pomata and N. G. Siraisi, pp. 241–267. Cambridge, MA: MIT Press, 2005.

A Pleasant Commedie called Look about you. London, 1600.

Pliny the Elder. *The Natural History.* Translated by J. Bostock. London: Taylor and Francis, 1855. Facs., http://www.perseus.tufts.edu/cgi-bin/ptext?lookup=Plin.+Nat.+toc.

Plutarch. *Regum et imperatorum apophtegmata.* Raphaele Regio interprete. *Laconica apophtegmata.* Raphaele Regio interprete. *Dialogus in quo animalia brura ratione uti monstrantur.* Ioanne Regio interprete. Venice, 1508.

Plutarch. *Opuscula LXXXXII.* Venice, 1509.

Plutarch. *The Philosophie, commonlie called, the Morals.* Translated by P. Holland. London, 1603.

Pollard, A. F., and M. Blatcher, eds. "Hayward Townshend's Journal." *Bulletin of the Institute of Historical Research* 12 (1934–1935): 1–31.

Pomata, G. "*Praxis Historialis:* The Uses of Historia in Early Modern Medicine." In *Historia: Empiricism and Erudition in Early Modern Europe,* edited by G. Pomata and N. G. Siraisi, pp. 105–146. Cambridge, MA: MIT Press, 2005.

Pomponazzi, P. *Expositio super primo et secundo De partibus animalium.* Edited by S. Perfetti. Florence: Olschki, 2004.

Pontano, G. *I trattati delle virtu sociali.* Edited by F. Tatteo. Rome: Edizioni dell'Ateneo, 1965.

Popham, A. E. "Elephantographia." *Life and Letters* 5, no. 27 (August 1930): 186–189.

Pratt, V. "Aristotle and the Essence of Natural History." *History and Philosophy of Life Sciences* 4 (1982): 203–223.

Prouty, C., and R. Prouty. "George Gascoigne, *The Noble Arte of Venerie,* and Queen Elizabeth at Kenilworth." In *Joseph Quincy Adams Memorial Studies,* edited by J. G. McManaway, G. E. Dawson, and E. E. Willoughby. Washington, DC: The Folger Shakespeare Library, 1948.

Pullan, B. *Crisis and Change in the Venetian Economy in the Sixteenth and Seventeenth Centuries.* London: Methuen, 1968.

Quinn, D. B., ed. *America from Concept to Discovery: Early Exploration of North America.* 6 vols. New York: Arno P. and Hector Bye Co., 1979.

Raber, K., and T. Tucker. "Introduction." In *The Culture of the Horse: Status, Discipline and Identity in the Early Modern World,* edited by K. Raber and T. Tucker, pp. 1–41. Basingstoke, UK: Palgrave Macmillan, 2005.

Ravelhofer, B. "'Beasts of Recreacion': Henslowe's White Bears." *English Literary Renaissance* 32, no. 2 (Spring 2002): 287–323.

Rede Me and Be Nott Wrothe for I Say No Thynge but Trothe. Strasbourg, 1528.

Repici, L. *"Teodoro Gaza traduttore e interprete di Teofrasto: la ricezione della botanica antica tra Quattro e Cinquecento."* *Rinascimento,* 2nd ser. 43 (2004): 417–505.

Reuterswärd, P. *The Visible and Invisible in Art: Essays in the History of Art.* Vienna: IRSA, 1991.

Roberts, J. *The Cormorant of Threadneedle Street.* London: Published by the author, 1875.

Robinson, C. "Seagulls Are Keeping Me a Prisoner." *Celebs on Sunday,* July 18, 2004, pp. 32–33.

Rondelet, G. *Libri de Piscibus Marinis in quibus verae Piscium effigies expressae sunt.* 2 vols. Lyon, 1554–1555.

Rondelet, G. *Universae aquatilium historiae pars altera, cum veris ipsorum imaginibus.* Lyon, 1555.

Rondelet, G. *La premiere et la seconde partie de l'histoire entiere des poissons.* 2 vols. Lyon, 1558.

Rondelet, G. *L'histoire entière des poissons.* Edited by F. Meunier and J.-L. d'Hondt, pp. 7–26. Paris: Éditions du CTHS, 2002.

Rooney, A. *Hunting in Middle English Literature.* Cambridge, UK: Boydell, 1993.

Rothfels, N. *Savages and Beasts: The Birth of the Modern Zoo.* Baltimore: Johns Hopkins University Press, 2002.

Rowley, W., T. Dekker, and J. Ford. *The Witch of Edmonton.* In *Three Jacobean Witchcraft Plays,* edited by P. Corbin and D. Sedge. Manchester, UK: Manchester University Press, 1986.

Ryder, M. L. "Medieval Sheep and Wool Types." *Agricultural History Review* 32, no. 1 (1984): 14–28.

Salisbury, J. *The Beast Within: Animals in the Middle Ages.* New York: Routledge, 1994.

Salviani, I. *Aquatilium animalium historiae, Liber primus, cum eorumdem formis, aere excusis.* Rome, 1554.

Sarton, G. *Appreciation of Ancient and Medieval Science during the Renaissance (1450–1600).* Philadelphia: University of Pennsylvania Press, 1955.

Scheibe, R. "The Major Professional Skills of the Dove in *The Buke of the Howlat.*" In *Animals and the Symbolic in Medieval Art and Literature,* edited by L. A. J. R. Houwen, pp. 107–138. Groningen, Netherlands: Egbert Forstein, 1997.

Scheve, D. A. "Jonson's *Volpone* and Traditional Fox Lore." *Review of English Studies* (1950): 242–244.

Schiesari, J. "'Bitches and Queens': Pets and Perversion at the Court of France's Henri III." In Fudge, *Renaissance Beasts,* pp. 37–49.

Schlueter, K. "Introduction." In *The Two Gentlemen of Verona* by W. Shakespeare. Edited by K. Schlueter. Cambridge, UK: Cambridge University Press, 1990.

Schmidt-Biggemann, W. *Topica universalis. Eine Modellgeschichte humanistischer und barocker Wissenschaft.* Hamburg: Felix Meiner, 1983.

Schmitt, C. B. "Science in the Italian Universities in the Sixteenth and Early Seventeenth Centuries." In *The Emergence of Science in Western Europe,* edited by M. P. Crosland, pp. 35–56. London: Macmillan, 1975.

Schmitt, C. B. "Philosophy and Science in Sixteenth-Century Italian Universities." In *The Renaissance: Essays in Interpretation to Eugenio Garin,* pp. 297–336. London: Methuen, 1982.

Schmitt, C. B. *The Aristotelian Tradition and Renaissance Universities.* London: Variorum Reprints, 1984.

Schorger, A. W. *The Wild Turkey: Its History and Domestication*. Norman: University of Oklahoma Press, 1966.

Sells, A. L. *Animal Poetry in French and English Literature and the Greek Tradition*. Bloomington: Indiana University Press, 1955.

Shakespeare, W. *The Tragicall Historie of Hamlet, Prince of Denmarke*. London, 1604.

Shakespeare, W. *Mr William Shakespeares Comedies, Histories, & Tragedies*. London, 1623.

Shakespeare, W. *The Riverside Shakespeare*. Edited by G. Blakemore Evans et al. Boston: Houghton Mifflin, 1997.

Shakespeare, W. *The Norton Shakespeare*. Edited by S. Greenblatt et al. 4 vols. New York: W. W. Norton, 1997.

Shapiro, J. *1599: A Year in the Life of William Shakespeare*. London: Faber and Faber, 2005.

Shell, M. "The Family Pet." *Representations* 15 (Summer 1986): 121–153.

Singer, C. *A Short History of Scientific Ideas to 1900*. New York: Oxford University Press, 1959.

Slicher van Bath, B. H. *The Agrarian History of Western Europe A.D. 500–1850*. London: Edward Arnold, 1963.

Slicher van Bath, B. H. "Agriculture in the Vital Revolution." In *The Cambridge Economic History of Europe, V, The Economic Organization of Early Modern Europe*, edited by E. E. Rich and C. H. Wilson, pp. 42–132. Cambridge, UK: Cambridge University Press, 1977.

"The St. James Park Pelicans." Royal Parks. http://www.royalparks.gov.uk/parks/st_james_park/flora_fauna/pelicans.cfm.

Stannard, J. *Herbs and Herbalism in the Middle Ages and Renaissance*. Edited by K. E. Stannard and R. Kay. Aldershot, UK: Ashgate, 1999.

Steel, C., G. Guldentops, and P. Beullens, eds. *Aristotle's Animals in the Middle Ages and Renaissance*. Leuven, Belgium: Leuven University Press, 1999.

Stewart, A. "Government by Beagle: The Impersonal Rule of James VI and I." In Fudge, *Renaissance Beasts*, pp. 101–115.

"Stop the Slaughter of Cormorants." Pisces. http://www.pisces.demon.co.uk/corm.html.

Stow, J. *The Survey of London*. London, 1598.

Stubbes, P. *The Anatomie of Abuses*. 1583. Facs., New York: Garland, 1973.

Syson, L., and D. Gordon. *Pisanello: Painter to the Renaissance Court*. London: National Gallery Company, 2001.

Taillevent. *Le cuisinier Taillevent*. Lyon, ca. 1495. Facs., Martin Harvard, http://visualiseur.bnf.fr/CadresFenetre?O = NUMM-106141&M = notice&Y = Image.

Taylor, J. *The Water-Cormorant His Complaint: Against a Brood of Land-Cormorants*. London: 1622.

Thévet, A. *Les Singularitez de la France Antarctique, autrement nommée Amerique: et de plusieurs Terres et Isles decouvertes de nostre temps*. Edited by P. Gasnault and J. Baudry. Paris: Le Temps, 1982.

Thévet, A. *The Newe Found World or Antarctike. [Les singularitez de la France Antarcticque]*. 1568. Facs., Amsterdam: Da Capo, 1971.

Thiébaux, M. *The Stag of Love: The Chase in Medieval Literature*. Ithaca: Cornell University Press, 1974.

Thirsk, J. "The Farming Regions of England." In *The Agrarian History of England and Wales, IV, 1500–1640*, edited by J. Thirsk, pp. 113–160. Cambridge, UK: Cambridge University Press, 1967.

Thirsk, J. "Farming Techniques." In Thirsk, *Agrarian History,* pp. 161–199.

Thirsk, J. "Enclosure and Engrossing." In Thirsk, *Agrarian History,* pp. 200–255.

Thirsk, J. *Economic Policy and Projects: The Development of a Consumer Society in Early Modern England.* Oxford, UK: Clarendon, 1978.

Thomas, K. *Man and the Natural World: Changing Attitudes in England 1500–1800.* London: Allen Lane / New York: Pantheon, 1983.

Thompson, F. L. M., ed. *Horses in European Economic History: A Preliminary Canter.* Reading, UK: The British Agricultural Society, 1983.

Thorndike, L. *A History of Magic and Experimental Science,* vol. 4. New York: Columbia University Press, 1941.

Tobey, E. "The Palio Horse in Renaissance and Early Modern Italy." In Raber and Tucker, *Culture of the Horse,* pp. 63–90.

Topsell, E. *The Historie of Foure-Footed Beastes.* London, 1607.

Topsell, E. *The Fowles of Heauen, or History of Birdes.* Edited by Thomas P. Harrison and F. David Hoeniger. Austin: University of Texas Press, 1972.

Topsell, E. *The Historie of Foure-Footed Beastes.* London, 1607. Facs., Amsterdam: Theatrum Orbis Terrarum, 1973.

Trochet, J-R. *"Les véhicules de transport utilitaires dans la France rurale traditionnelle."* In *Voitures, chevaux et attelages du XVIe au XIXe Siècle,* edited by D. Reytier. Paris: Association pour Académie d'Art Equestre de Versailles, 2000.

Turner, J. *Spice: The History of a Temptation.* London: HarperPerennial, 2004.

Turner, W. *Avium praecipuarum, quarum apud Plinium et Aristotelem mentio est, brevis et succincta historia …* Köln, 1544.

Uhlig, C. "'The Sobbing Deer': *As You Like It,* II.i.21–66 and the Historical Context." *Renaissance Drama* 3 (1970): 79–109.

Ure, P. "Introduction." In *King Richard II* by W. Shakespeare. Edited by P. Ure. London: Methuen, 1956.

Vale, M. *The Gentleman's Recreations: Accomplishments and Pastimes of the English Gentleman 1580–1630.* Cambridge, UK: D. S. Brewer, 1977.

Van Houtte, J. A. *An Economic History of the Low Countries 800–1800.* London: Weidenfeld and Nicolson, 1977.

Van Zanden, J. L. *The Rise and Decline of Holland's Economy: Merchant Capitalism and the Labour Market.* Manchester, UK: Manchester University Press, 1993.

Vasari, G. *Lives of the Artists.* Harmondsworth, UK: Penguin, 1965.

Vasoli, C. *"La retorica e la cultura del Rinascimento."* *Rhetorica* 2 (1984): 121–137.

Vasoli, C. *"L'humanisme rhétorique en Italie au XVe siècle."* In *Histoire de la rhétorique dans l'Europe moderne, 1450–1950,* edited by M. Fumaroli, pp. 45–129. Paris: Presses Universitaires de France, 1999.

Vegetti, M. *"Origini e metodi della zoologia aristotelica."* In *Opere biologiche* by Aristotle. Edited by D. Lanza and M. Vegetti, pp. 102–120. Turin: Utet, 1971.

Vespucci, A. *Letters from a New World: Amerigo Vespucci's Discovery of America.* Translated by David Jacobson. New York: Marsilio, 1992.

W., R. *A Necessary Family-Book … for Taking and Killing All Manner of Vermin.* London, 1688.

Watson, R. N. "Horsemanship in Shakespeare's Second Tetralogy." *English Literary Renaissance* 13, no. 3 (1983): 274–300.

Watts, S. *Epidemics and History: Disease, Power and Imperialism.* New Haven, CT: Yale University Press, 1999.

Weinstein, B. "Bye Bye Birdie." Socialist Viewpoint. http://www.socialistviewpoint.org/dec_02/dec_02_30.html.

Wendell, B. *William Shakespeare*. London, 1894.

Whatley, J. "Introduction." In *History of a Voyage to the Land of Brazil* by J. de Léry. Translated by J. Whatley. Berkeley: University of California Press, 1990.

White, L., Jr. "Natural Science and Naturalistic Art in the Middle Ages." *American Historical Review* 52, no. 3 (1947): 421–435.

Whitehead, G. K. *Hunting and Stalking Deer in Britain through the Ages*. London: B. T. Batsford, 1980.

Whitney, G. *A Choice of Emblemes and Other Devises*. Leiden, 1586.

Wiese, H., and J. Bölts. *Rinderhandel und Rinderhaltung in nordwest-europäischen Küstengebiet vom 15. bis zum 19. Jahrhundert*. Stuttgart: Gustav Fischer, 1966.

Wilkinson, D. *Early Horse Racing in Yorkshire and the Origins of the Thoroughbred*. York: Old Bald Peg Publications, 2003.

Wither, G. *Fidelia*. London, 1619.

The Wonder of All Nations!! Or the English Cormorants Anatomized. Norwich, 1831.

Woodstock. Edited by P. Corbin and D. Sedge. Manchester, UK: Manchester University Press, 2002.

Wotton, E. *De Differentiis animalium libri decem*. Paris, 1552.

Wright, L. B. "Animal Actors on the English Stage before 1642." *PMLA* 42 (1927): 656–669.

Yalden, D. *The History of British Mammals*. London: Academic Press, 1999.

Yamamoto, D. *The Boundaries of the Human in Medieval English Literature*. New York: Oxford University Press, 2000.

Yi-fu Tuan. *Dominance and Affection: The Making of Pets*. New Haven, CT: Yale University Press, 1984.

Young, A. *Tudor and Jacobean Tournaments*. London: Sheridan House, 1986.

Younge, R. *Philarguromastix; or, The Arraignment of Covetousnesse, and Ambition, in Our Great and Greedy Cormorants*. London, 1653.

Zanon, A. *Dell'agricoltura, dell'arti, e del commercio ... lettere*. Venice, 1763.

Ziolkowski, J. M. *Talking Animals: Medieval Latin Beast Poetry, 750–1150*. Philadelphia: University of Pennsylvania Press, 1993.

NOTES ON CONTRIBUTORS

Charles Bergman is professor of English at Pacific Lutheran University. He is the author of three books on environmental issues and wildlife conservation, including *Orion's Legacy: A Cultural History of Man as Hunter* (Dutton, 1997).

Bruce Boehrer is Bertram H. Davis Professor of Renaissance Literature at Florida State University. His two most recent books are *Shakespeare Among the Animals: Nature and Society in the Drama of Early Modern England* (Palgrave, 2002) and *Parrot Culture: Our 2500-Year-Long Fascination with the World's Most Talkative Bird* (University of Pennsylvania Press, 2004). He has served as editor of the *Journal for Early Modern Cultural Studies* since its inception in 2000.

Kevin De Ornellas is lecturer in English Renaissance literature at the University of Ulster. He has published articles and reviews in such publications as the *Times Literary Supplement, Shakespeare on Screen*, and *The Kingdom of the Horse* (Palgrave, 2005). His research interests are mainly in the fields of Renaissance drama, ecocriticism, animal studies, and twentieth-century drama.

Victoria Dickenson is executive director at the McCord Museum of Canadian History in Montreal, Canada. She obtained her Ph.D. in Canadian history from Carleton University in 1995. Her thesis on the role of visual imagery in early science, *Drawn from Life, Science and Art in the Portrayal of the New World,* was published by the University of Toronto Press in 1998 and was a nominee for the prestigious Klibansky Prize. She is Adjunct Research Professor of History at both Carleton and at McGill universities, and has taught history of science in early modern Europe and material culture at McGill University.

Peter Edwards is professor of early modern British social history at the University of Roehampton, London, and has written extensively on the history of animals, especially horses, in the early modern period. His notable publications include *The Horse Trade of Tudor and Stuart England* (Cambridge University Press, 1988/2004 reprint) and *Horse and Man in Early Modern England* (Hambledon/Continuum, 2007). His other research interests extend from rural society and the marketing of agricultural products 1500–1750 to the logistics of early modern warfare.

Philippe Glardon holds his doctorate from the Institut Universitaire d'Histoire de la Médecine at the Université de Lausanne. In addition to research interests that focus on the natural history of sixteenth-century Europe, he has edited a facsimile of the 1555 edition of Pierre Belon's *Histoire de la nature des oyseaux* (Geneva, 1997).

Teresa Grant is associate professor of Renaissance theatre at the University of Warwick, United Kingdom. She has published on various aspects of early modern drama and culture and is currently finishing a monograph on the uses of animals on the English stage between 1558 and 1642. She is general editor, with Eugene Giddens and Barbara Ravelhofer, of Oxford University Press's 10-volume *The Complete Works of James Shirley*, scheduled for publication between 2011 and 2015.

Stefano Perfetti is assistant professor (Ricercatore) of history of Medieval philosophy in the department of philosophy of the University of Pisa (where he also teaches philosophy of religions). He has published articles in late-Medieval and Renaissance Aristotelianism, focussing on the clash/encounter between scholastic commentary and humanistic philology, especially in the field of zoology. His books include *Aristotle's Zoology and its Renaissance Commentators (1521–1601)* (Leuven, 2000) and a critical edition of Pietro Pomponazzi, *Expositio super primo et secundo De partibus animalium* (Florence, 2004).

INDEX